My Kitchen
in Spain

My Kitchen in Spain

225 Authentic Regional Recipes

Janet Mendel

FRANCES LINCOLN

Frances Lincoln Limited
4 Torriano Mews
Torriano Avenue
London NW5 2RZ
www.franceslincoln.com

My Kitchen in Spain

British Library Cataloguing-in-Publication Data
A catalogue record for this book is available from the British Library.

Portions of this book have appeared in somewhat different form in *Lookout Magazine*
and *Foods from Spain News.*

First published in the United States of America by HarperCollins Publishers Inc.

First British edition published by Frances Lincoln Limited 2005.

ISBN 0 7112 2431 5

Printed in Singapore

9 8 7 6 5 4 3 2 1

To Daniel and Benjamin,
who were born in this olive grove
and grew up with this food

C O N T

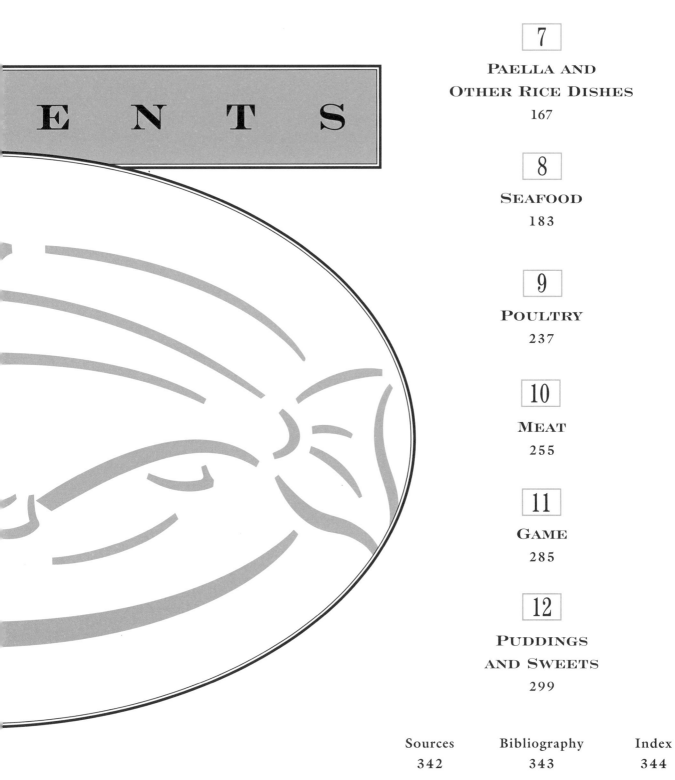

E N T S

Acknowledgments

I am forever grateful to my friend, cookery book author Paula Wolfert, for her enthusiasm, which got me going on this book, and for her deep knowledge of Mediterranean foods, which she so graciously shares.

I owe much to my first guides in the Spanish kitchen, Maria Pérez Garcia, who did the cooking in the tapa bar where I first sampled Spanish cooking, and to Antonia Tamayo Blanco, who helped me in my own kitchen. Over the years there have been many more Spanish cooks, both housewives and professionals, who have welcomed me into their kitchens and shared their favourite recipes.

Special thanks to Amanda Clark and Donna Ellefson, travel companions, research assistants and able readers.

Many, many more have helped me in the writing of this book, which really began more than thirty years ago. I want to thank the *gran dama* of Spanish gastronomy, Clara Maria de Amezua; cartographer Javier Belloso; wine writer Gerry Dawes; chef Tom Campbell (and his parents, David and Becky Campbell, tasters); Guy Hunter-Watts and Emma Baverstock, who introduced me to goatherds and sausage makers; Mark Little, a colleague sadly missed; wine maker Jesus Madrazo; fellow food writer Marlene Parrish; David Searl, background collaborator; chef Richard Stephens; Santos Ruiz Alvarez, who showed me the Valencia rice-growing region; Eva Ruiz of ASOLIVA; cheesemaker Maria Carmen Ugartetxea; Ariane van den Eden, who made sure my faxes arrived; and photographer John James Wood.

I wish to acknowledge the tourism departments of Valencia, Galicia and the Basque Country, which assisted me with research in those regions, and the International Olive Oil Council, which kept me up to date on olive oil research.

Many thanks to Susan Friedland, my editor at HarperCollins (New York), who helped me shape this book, and to Fred Hill and Mary Clemmey, my agents. Thanks to Jo Christian, editor of the present edition, and Delora Jones, who translated the measurements for British cooks.

Finally, I want to thank my good friends Luella Ramsay, Sheila Gormely and Charlotte and Harry Gordon, and my sons, Daniel and Benjamin, for sharing the food and good times in my kitchen in Spain.

1

INTO THE SPANISH KITCHEN

How I Came to Live in Spain

I came to live in Spain in 1966. I was recently graduated from journalism school, newly married and working in my first job as a reporter. My husband and I decided to quit our newspaper jobs in Chicago and spend a year abroad to explore and do some writing.

Why Spain? I had studied Spanish and visited Spain as a student. And, in 1966, the US dollar went a long way in the Spanish economy. A loaf of bread or a glass of wine cost about five cents. We hoped to be able to stretch our savings through a year abroad. And we did. When our funds finally ran out, we weren't ready to return to the United States, so we started scraping by, supporting ourselves with freelance writing and teaching. I even sold marmalade made from the bitter oranges that grew in my back garden.

It was an interesting time, for Spain was in transition. Although the end of the Franco dictatorship and the advent of modern democratic government did not come until 1975, the times were changing rapidly. Tourism and investment in industry were bringing prosperity to a country devastated by poverty since the Civil War at the end of the 1930s.

Notebook in hand, I started asking questions. My reporter's instinct led me, however, not to the big issues of politics and economics, but to the small and local stories about village life. These were the stories I heard at the market, in the kitchens, over the bar, on the street. Most of this was chitchat and gossip. Huge segments of conversation consisted of food talk – *'hoy voy a poner un emblanco'* (I'm making white fish soup today) or *'A mi gente, le gustan mucho las lentejas'* (My family really likes lentils). The price of potatoes, of eggs, of fish were important topics of discussion.

I found my way into kitchens everywhere. In search of recipes, I would be sent off to talk to someone's grandmother in the neighbourhood at the end of the village, or to a *tia* (aunt) way out in the country.

Travelling around Spain, whether in cities or villages, we would stop in local bars for a morning coffee, an afternoon beer, an evening *copita* of wine. I would ask the barman about the local specialities. He would usually send me to the kitchen, where the womenfolk would delightedly sit and talk about their favourite dishes. I scribbled notes wildly. Over the first few years, I filled many notebooks with recipes from the kitchens of Spain. Certainly, there was considerable repetition – I've lost count of how many versions of gazpacho I gathered! But I also found wonderful diversity from one region to another, even from one village to the next.

My collection of Spanish recipes led to a monthly cooking column in an English-language magazine and eventually to several cookery books about Spanish food. I became a culinary foreign correspondent.

THE VILLAGE, THEN AND NOW

The village where I live is in Andalusia, the southernmost region of continental Spain. It is the region that conjures up the romantic image of Spain – Moorish palaces, flamenco dancing, flower-bedecked patios, whitewashed villages, olive groves. It is a huge region, with an incredible variety of landscapes and countryside. There are wild regions where deer and boar roam freely, marshy river-bottom land that hosts some of Europe's largest wildlife reserves and undulating hills covered, as far as the eye can see, with olive trees. Barren, rocky mountain peaks, snow-covered in winter, descend to terraced hillsides planted in grapevines and lush, irrigated valleys, where citrus and other fruit orchards thrive. There are cork forests, wheat fields, scrub oak, strawberry fields. Even rice paddies.

How did we find our way to a small village on a hillside overlooking the Mediterranean? Well, months before we were to sail to Spain, we met a guy in a bar in Chicago who had lived in this village. He described it as paradise, so that's where we headed when the freighter docked. Laden with a trunk filled with books, typewriter and cameras, we wended our way along the coast, changing buses several times, until finally alighting in the village plaza. We stayed in a small guest house while we searched for a place to live. The place we found – my first kitchen in Spain – was magical.

On the outside the house looked like every other one on the narrow, cobbled street. It had a door opening directly on to the street and two small windows punched into 1-metre-thick whitewashed walls. But inside, the house had been beautifully remodelled by our landlady, a zany countess of mixed Russian and Swedish descent.

The kitchen-dining room was a big airy space. It had French doors opening on to the upper reaches of a huge old olive tree and balconies with pots of herbs and geraniums. From there, the views were due south, down across rolling hills to the blue, blue Mediterranean Sea. It was a gorgeous place in which to cook and a delicious location for summer supper, with the scent of jasmine wafting from the garden and the lights of the fishing boats sparkling out on the sea.

The village then was still fairly primitive. While I had a refrigerator and a huge American stove (with an electric rotisserie that blew all the fuses on the street every time I tried to use it), the woman across the street from me cooked in a pot set in a tripod on the hearth. Another neighbour, who had cooked on a charcoal brazier fitted into the tiled kitchen counter, proudly showed me her brand-new two-ring hob attached to a small butane gas cylinder.

The first woman on the street to purchase an electric blender soon found neighbours coming round at midday to zip a quick mayonnaise, which otherwise had to be slowly stirred by hand, the oil incorporated drop by drop. And when the first television set arrived in the neighbourhood, the family set it out on the balcony, tuned to the only channel, so that all the neighbours could pull up their chairs right in the street and watch.

Few cars and lorries came through the village streets. At that time there was one road up from the coast, but no road through to the next inland town. It was connected by a path only wide enough for goats and donkeys. Country people trekked to town by donkey, bringing produce from their country *fincas* (smallholdings) and returning with staples such as coffee, sugar and dry salt cod.

Many village houses had iron rings set into the outer walls, for tethering the *burro*, and an entryway paved with stone cobbles, so that hooves wouldn't crack terracotta floor tiles. The donkey was led through the wide double doors, across the cobbles of the front room and into its stable on the back patio.

Today, my village is very prosperous. Situated overlooking the Costa del Sol, a popular resort area, it attracts tourists who pour in by busloads to shop for souvenirs and ride the *burro taxis*. Wealthy expatriates have built retirement villas in the surrounding hills, and tourism and the construction and service industries that accompany it have brought prosperity. I am happy to see old friends driving nice cars, taking holidays and sending their kids to university.

In spite of enormous changes in life, it is surprising how little the cooking in village homes has changed. The same fish dishes, gazpachos, stews and soups are served at home. With occasional innovative additions, the salads and tapas in the local bars are the ones I loved many years ago. But now at the supermarket, I might hear a housewife rejecting fatty pork in favour of turkey for her *puchero* (boiled dinner) – too much *colesterol*, she says. Television teaches nutrition.

Over the years I have visited almost every region of Spain. I continue to be astonished at the variety and richness of Spanish cooking. Spain has fabulous cheeses, hams, sausages, breads, pastries, rice dishes beyond paella, wonderful seafood and great artistry in its preparation, superb fruits and vegetables and the world's best olive oil. There are dishes to suit every taste – light and fresh fare, hearty and soul-satisfying.

Why is Spanish cooking so little known in Britain and North America? The cuisines of Italy, France, India, Lebanon, China and Thailand are better known there than that of Spain because immigrants from those nations carried their food customs with them to Britain and North America, while Spaniards took theirs to Mexico City, Havana, Caracas, Quito and Buenos Aires. When Spaniards emigrated (and they did, in search of employment and a better life), they tended to go where they already had

connections, to South and Central America, where the language, after all, was their own. Ever since 1492, they have contributed hugely to the popular cookery of Hispanic America.

The exchange worked both ways. Spanish explorers returned home bringing New World products, such as beans, maize, potatoes, tomatoes and chocolate, which greatly enriched the cooking of the old country.

Nevertheless, Spanish is not Hispanic. The food of Spain is very different from Mexican food. Spanish food hardly ever contains hot, hot chillies, and corn tortillas are not used at all, so there are no tacos, enchiladas or chilaquiles.

Spain's cooking is profoundly Mediterranean, based on olive oil, seafood, fresh fruits and vegetables, pulses, bread, rice, potatoes and pasta. While it is akin to the cooking of Italy, Greece and Morocco, Spanish cuisine has its own flavour, its specialities that derive from a rich history that reaches from the spice routes of the East to the golden world of the conquistadores in the West.

For me, Spain is home. Here is my kitchen. I invite you to join me in my kitchen in Spain. I'll tell you about villagers, fishermen, bullfighters, olive pickers, shepherds and Sherry barons. About the fiestas and customs of this fascinating country, and all the food that goes with them.

INGREDIENTS AND PROCEDURES

It is possible to cook authentic Spanish food with no special tools or ingredients. Nevertheless, preparing the recipes in this book will be easier with a little knowledge about basic how-to and possible substitutions. For a list of sources of more esoteric ingredients, see page 342.

Almonds (*almendras*). Almonds grow widely in Spain and are much used in savoury dishes. Ground to a paste, they add flavour and serve as a light thickener in sauces. Almonds are usually blanched and skinned before use. To blanch almonds: Add the almonds to boiling water for 1 minute. Drain them. When cool enough to handle, slip off and discard the brown skins, leaving the white almond meats.

Bread (*pan*). In Spanish cooking, bread is used to thicken many sauces and gazpachos. Use bread from a dense country loaf of Spanish-, French- or Italian-style bread. Sometimes the bread is fried crisp, then ground in a mortar or blender. Otherwise it is usually soaked until soft, then mashed. When used for thickening, the bread can be several days old and slightly dry.

Capsicum: Sweet peppers and chillies (*pimiento*). The main types of pepper used in Spain are as follows:

1. *Pimiento gordo.* Sweet peppers, usually red or green. These fleshy peppers, also called bell peppers, are usually roasted and peeled.

2. *Pimiento para freir.* 'Frying' peppers. These are long, skinny, usually twisted or corrugated green peppers, thin-skinned and crisp. They are sweet to bittersweet, but not hot. They are chopped and added raw to salads and are fried, whole, in oil. The closest American peppers are green Anaheim, California long green chilli or

---

To Measure Bread as an Ingredient

In this book, 'one slice of bread' means a 12-mm (½-inch) slice of country loaf, measuring approximately 13 × 8 cm (5 × 3 inches).

One slice weighs about 30 g (1 oz). Four slices = 115 g (4 oz).

If using baguette instead of a country loaf, an 18-cm (7-inch) chunk weighs about 115g (4 oz).

It is not necessary to slice or cube bread when it is to be soaked in water, as for gazpacho. Just cut into chunks.

How to Roast Sweet Peppers

Preheat the grill. Place peppers (red and/or green) in a single layer in a grill pan. Place the pan about 10 cm (4 inches) from the heat source and roast them, turning 3 or 4 times, until they are charred on all sides, about 25 to 30 minutes.

Remove peppers to a bowl and cover them with a lid. Allow them to sit for 1 hour. Then remove stems and seeds. Slip off and discard skins. The peppers are then ready to be used in any recipe that calls for roasted peppers.

The peppers can also be roasted over a gas flame on the hob, over charcoal or on a gas barbecue.

green pepperoncini, all of which are somewhat hotter than the Spanish pepper. In recipes in this book, green sweet peppers have been substituted for the hard-to-find frying peppers.

3. *Pimiento de Padrón.* Padrón is a town in Galicia (not far from Santiago de Compostela), famous for its peppers. Usually marketed green, they are small and conical. Very flavourful, they are sweet peppers with the allure that one or two in every batch are inexplicably hot! Padrón peppers are cooked in sauces and fried whole, to be heaped next to grilled meat.

4. *Pimiento de piquillo.* Piquillo peppers, which come from La Rioja and Navárre, are small (8 cm/3 inches), triangular red peppers that end in a *pico* or 'beak'. They are rich in flavour, sweet with a mild piquancy. Piquillo peppers are sold roasted, peeled and tinned. They can be found in shops specializing in Spanish products.

5. *Guindilla.* The Spanish word for hot chilli. Mild green ones are pickled in vinegar. Pickled Italian pepperoncini are the nearest substitute. Hotter varieties are strung, *en ristra*, and dried. They turn from green-yellow-orange to red and are medium hot. They are closest to dried cayenne peppers or *chilli de arbol*, available from speciality food shops and by mail order. The easiest substitute is red chilli flakes.

6. *Choricero.* A bittersweet, dried pepper, brick-red in colour. Choriceros are soaked to rehydrate them, then ground and added to sauces. Pimentón (Spanish paprika) is the best substitute.

7. *Ñora.* A plum-sized dry sweet pepper, wrinkly, black-red in colour. Ground, this is the source of pimentón or sweet Spanish paprika. To use *ñoras*, first rehydrate by soaking in hot water, then scrape the flesh from the inside of the skin. If *ñoras* are not available, pimentón is the best substitute.

Cazuela. This traditional earthenware casserole, glazed on the inside, unglazed on the outside, can be used both in the oven and on the hob. Recipes that call for food to be cooked in a cazuela may require slightly different timing if cooked in a metal pan.

Chilli. See Capsicum.

Chorizo. Spain's most distinctive sausage, made with pork, flavoured with garlic and pimentón (Spanish paprika) or the pulp of sweet dried red pepper. It is not spicy-hot like Mexican chorizo. If it is not available, substitute any fresh pork sausage, preferably garlic sausage, and add extra pimentón, garlic and oregano to the pot.

DO (*denominación de origen*). DO is 'designation of origin', a term originally used with wines as a guarantee of origin, production, method and grape varietals. It is the Spanish equivalent of the French *appellation d'origine contrôlée*. DO applies to many categories of food as well as wine. Cheese, ham and olive oil are some foods that may carry DO labels. DO foods and wines are monitored by regulatory boards as a guarantee of quality.

Garlic (*ajo*). Garlic is used in many ways:

1. Raw, it is finely chopped and added to some salads and dressings, usually with lots of parsley, or crushed to a paste for gazpacho.

2. Whole cloves are lightly smashed to split the skins, sautéed without peeling, then braised.

To Roast a Whole Head of Garlic

Spear the head of garlic on a fork or grasp it with tongs and hold over a gas flame (or put under the grill), turning, until it is charred. Peel the garlic cloves, rinse in running water and add them to the stew to continue cooking.

---

3. Peeled, chopped or sliced and fried until golden, it is used with the oil in which it's fried as a topping for cooked foods such as grilled fish.

4. Peeled whole cloves, fried golden, are then mashed in a mortar or blender with a clove of raw garlic and some liquid. Usually spices such as peppercorns, clove and saffron are added with the garlic to the mortar mixture. It may also include fried bread and almonds as thickeners.

5. 'Roasted' garlic, in which the whole head of garlic is seared over a flame or under a grill until blackened. The cloves are peeled, then added to a stew to continue cooking.

Ham, serrano ham (*jamón, jamón serrano*). In cooking, substitute unsmoked pancetta, lean bacon or Parma ham for serrano ham. (More about serrano ham on pages 20–21.)

Hazelnuts (*avellanas*). Grown extensively in Catalonia, hazelnuts are an ingredient in the region's famous *romesco* sauce. To skin hazelnuts prior to grinding them for sauce, spread them in an oven pan and toast them in a medium (180°C/350°F/gas mark 4) oven for 12 minutes. Remove them and wrap in a towel until cooled. Rub the nuts in the towel to remove the skins.

Paprika. See Pimentón.

Peppers. See Capsicum.

Pimentón. Pimentón is Spanish paprika. It is produced by grinding dried peppers to a fine powder. Pimentón comes in varying intensities – sweet, bittersweet and hot – depending on the variety of pepper from which it is made. Paprika can be substituted if pimentón is not available. Pimentón de la Vera, produced in Extremadura, is smoke-dried, which adds a dusky, oak aroma to the spice. It is available in some supermarkets, from speciality food shops and by mail order.

Saffron (*azafrán*). This spice derives from the stigmas of a mauve-coloured autumn blooming crocus, which is grown in the central region of La Mancha. It takes 75,000 flowers to make 450 g (1 lb) of the spice. Saffron threads are deep-orange coloured. Pulverize them in a mortar, then dissolve in a small quantity of liquid before stirring into rice or sauce. If saffron is not available, substitute pimentón or yellow food colouring.

Salt cod (*bacalao*). Look for salt cod in Spanish and Portuguese markets or ask your fishmonger to get some (if he doesn't already have it in). Fresh cod can be used in recipes calling for salt cod. To prepare salt cod: A day before you plan to use the salt cod, scrape surface salt off the fish and wash it in running water. Put it in a bowl and cover with water. Soak the *bacalao*, covered and refrigerated, 24 hours, changing the water three times. Each time you change the water, wash the fish under running water, squeeze it gently and wash out the container.

After soaking, place the pieces of *bacalao* on a clean towel and cover with another to soak up excess water. Remove any scales and bones.

Some recipes call for the cod to be precooked. To precook salt cod, after the soaking step, place it in enough water to cover and bring it just barely to a simmer. Hold it at a simmer for five minutes, then remove. The *bacalao* is now ready to use in any of the recipes that call for precooked fish.

Squid, squid ink (*calamar, tinta de calamar*). Squid can be purchased already cleaned. However, if you need the squid ink for a recipe, you will need to buy fresh (not frozen), uncleaned squid and reserve the ink sac. To prepare squid: The squid's body is a slender pouch from which protrudes a head with short tentacles. Grasp the head and pull gently. It will come away from the body pouch bringing the innards with it. The ink is enclosed in a tiny silver sac, like a dot of mercury, on the innards. If the ink is required for your recipe, cut the ink sac free without breaking and reserve it in a small bowl. Still inside the body pouch is the quill or cartilage, which looks like a strip of transparent plastic. Grasp the top of it and pull; it should come out in one piece. Discard it.

Cut off the tentacles just above the eyes. Save the tentacles. Discard the remaining head with innards still attached.

Rinse out the pouch and pull off the purplish outer skin. The wing flaps will come off too. Save them. The cleaned squid consists of tentacles, two wing flaps and a body pouch. Use kitchen scissors to cut the pouch crosswise into rings or slit it lengthwise and cut into squares.

TWO BASIC TOMATO SAUCES
Sofrito y Salsa de Tomate Frito

Use this recipe to prepare both a *sofrito* that will be cooked further with other foods as well as a smooth tomato sauce that can be added to cooked foods or served as an accompanying sauce.

The sauce is best made with solid-fleshed, ripe tomatoes, but tinned chopped tomatoes can be used as well. If using tinned tomatoes, drain them and reserve the juice. Sauce made with tinned tomatoes, which contain citric acid, may need a pinch of sugar to balance the sharpness.

If using fresh tomatoes, skin them and remove seeds. To peel tomatoes, bring a large pan of water to the boil and plunge the tomatoes in. Return to the boil and boil about 30 seconds. Drain. When cool enough to handle, slit skins and slip them off. To de-seed tomatoes, cut them in half crosswise and squeeze them to expel seeds.

2 tablespoons olive oil

140 g (5 oz) chopped onion (½ large onion)

2 cloves garlic, chopped

450 g (1 lb) peeled, de-seeded and chopped tomatoes

½ teaspoon salt

120 ml (4 fl oz) white wine, Sherry, reserved tomato liquid or water

pinch of crumbled oregano (optional)

pinch of pimentón (optional)

Heat the oil in a frying pan and add the onion and garlic. Sauté on a medium heat until onion begins to brown, about 5 minutes.

Add tomatoes and continue frying on a high heat for 5 minutes. Add the salt and the wine or other liquid. Cook, uncovered, on a medium heat for 15 minutes, stirring frequently.

If necessary, add a spoonful of additional liquid to prevent the sauce from sticking.

The *sofrito* is now ready to be incorporated with other foods and continue cooking.

To turn the *sofrito* into a smooth tomato sauce (*salsa de tomate frito*), purée it in a blender. Return it to the frying pan and add the oregano and pimentón, if desired. Cook another 5 minutes until very thick. The smooth tomato sauce can be served hot or room temperature to accompany cooked foods or it can be used in recipes where a smooth tomato sauce is required.

Makes approximately 280 ml (½ pint) of *sofrito* or smooth tomato sauce.

2

TAPAS

CLASSIC TAPAS

Spiced Fried Almonds (*Almendras Fritas*)

Olives (*Aceitunas*)

Spanish Potato Omelette (*Tortilla Española*)

FRIED TAPAS

Batter-Fried Tapas (*Rebozados*)

Tangy Fried Fish (*Cazón en Adobo*)

Fried Stuffed Mussels (*Mejillónes Rellenos*)

Crispy Shrimp Fritters
(*Tortillitas de Camarones*)

Little Gypsy Pork Rolls
(*Flamenquines de Cerdo*)

Crispy Potatoes with Hot Sauce
(*Patatas Bravas*)

SALADS AND COLD DISHES

Orange and Cod Salad (*Salmorejo*)

Fresh Tomato and Pepper Salad (*Pipirrana*)

Flamenco Potato Salad with Lemon Dressing
(*Papas Aliñadas*)

Roasted Red Pepper Salad
(*Ensalada de Pimientos Asados*)

Devilled Eggs with Prawns and Olives
(*Huevos Rellenos con Gambas y Aceitunas*)

Marinated Fresh Anchovies
(*Boquerones en Vinagre*)

Mussels Vinaigrette (*Mejillónes a la Vinagreta*)

Shellfish Cocktail with Tomatoes and Peppers
(*Ensaladilla de Mariscos*)

TAPAS SERVED HOT

Sizzling Prawns with Garlic (*Gambas al Ajillo*)

Moorish Kebabs (*Pinchitos Morunos*)

Clams, Fishermen's Style
(*Almejas a la Marinera*)

Galician-Style Octopus (*Pulpo con Cachelos*)

Pork Braised in Fresh Tomato Sauce
(*Magro con Tomate*)

Chicken Sauté with Garlic and Sherry
(*Pollo al Ajillo*)

Spiced Meatballs in Almond Sauce
(*Albóndigas en Salsa de Almendras*)

Tripe Stew, Madrid Style
(*Callos a la Madrileña*)

Snails in Piquant Sauce
(*Caracoles en Salsa Picante*)

First Forays
into Village Kitchens

I learned to speak and cook Spanish in village kitchens. It began in the Bar Estéban, a bar in the town plaza run by two brothers, Estéban and Paco. Back in 1966, Spanish women didn't frequent local bars, except on holidays, when the whole family would go out together for a *paseo* (walk). Rather than stay at home, I often went along with my then-husband to Bar Estéban, the village bar best liked by a small band of resident *extranjeros* (foreigners).

The tables in the dim back room, where the old codgers sat playing dominoes, were sewing machine trestles topped with a slab of local marble. Above the bar hung whole serrano hams, each dangling a conical tin cup to catch drippings of fat. A fine espresso coffee machine produced excellent brew, which was served in short glasses with foamy, heated goats' milk. Behind the bar were bottles of wine, brandy and anise brandy. Anise came in wonderful serrated glass bottles, which, when scraped up and down with a blunt knife, laid down a background rhythm for vocalists.

The men leaned on the bar, drank their wine or brandy, spouted poetry or flamenco and, occasionally, politics. Politics in those days were secretive because, officially, there was only one party, one line. If you scratched too deeply below the surface, you might hear horrific stories about shootings during the Civil War, still in living memory. The weather, the tomato crop, new jobs on the coast were safer topics of conversation. The locals mainly complained about how boring life was. *¡Que aburrimiento!*

Every *copita* (small glass) of wine came with a *tapa*, a few bites of food served free. In the bar's kitchen, Paco's wife, Maria, her mother and a young helper did all the cooking. Every single day of the year these women put out an assortment of tapas. Every day there were ten or more different dishes, both hot and cold: olives, sausages and ham, plus potato omelette, two or three salads, prawns, kebabs grilled over a gas hob, meat stews, whole fish and fried fish.

I sampled everything, from superb fish, stews and salads to far-out dishes, such as chunks of congealed blood, fried up with garlic, and a stew that included spongy bits of lung. What an education it was! Back in the mid-sixties, straight out of midwestern America, I had never tasted squid nor seen a real artichoke. Even a head of garlic seemed fairly exotic! For me, the Spanish kitchen was an adventure, and I plunged into it with enthusiasm.

I gravitated two steps down from the bar to the kitchen. In the centre of Maria's kitchen was a small round table where her family would sit down to eat and which served as the staging centre for dishes going on to the bar. Here the baby was lulled to sleep by the *abuela* (granny), seated in a straight-backed chair on which she lurched back and forth, rhythmically singing, '*Eh-ah, eh-ah, eh-ah*'. It seemed to work, though some years later, when my first baby was born, I bought a regular rocking chair.

I began to sit at this table several evenings a week. In the beginning, I just watched and chatted, my vocabulary growing by leaps and bounds. Soon, I was asking questions and taking notes. Next, I was helping to peel and chop and even lend a hand at the cooker, if needed.

Maria set green and red peppers over the gas hob to char. Then we peeled them and added olive oil and vinegar for a popular salad. To prepare the marinated anchovies, we cut off the heads and pulled free the spines of the tiny, fresh fish and left them in vinegar until the following day, when they were dressed with olive oil, chopped garlic and parsley. Stuffed eggs were topped with hand-made mayonnaise.

The eggs for the mayonnaise came from hens that Maria kept in the back patio. The olive oil from the local mill was virgin oil, the plain 'olive juice' that has been used here for many, many centuries. It was kept in big jugs in a larder at the back of the patio. The tomatoes, peppers and other vegetables for salads and gazpacho came from the family's own *huertas* (gardens). Estéban, Paco or Vega, their aged godfather, walked down to the fields before dawn twice a week to open the irrigation ditches to water the terraced fields.

Maria often served two or even three different seafood tapas – fried fish, sauced fish, fresh boiled prawns, mussel salad. The fish came up to the village from the coast by the early bus, in six huge rubber buckets, which sloshed about at the back of the bus. Before my time, fish was delivered daily by runners, who made the uphill trek in an hour and who were known for their bulging calf muscles. They carried the fish in baskets woven of esparto grass, strapped across their heads.

The sausages, served as cold cuts or added to the stew pot, were made by the women at the butcher's shop just a few doors away from the bar. I would see a farmer driving his pig through the streets and in through the big double doors of the butcher's. A day later was a good time to buy pork chops.

The wine served at the bar, poured from a huge *garrafa* (demijohn), came from Montilla and was similar to dry Sherry. In those days, the local bars did not serve white table wine and only the better ones offered bottled red wine, which came from much further afield. Wine was always local and, as I travelled around the country, tasting the local wines was part of savouring the culture.

Tapas originated in Andalusia, in the wine-growing regions of Jerez, Montilla and Málaga.

The word *tapa* means a cover or lid. You would suppose that a custom such as the partaking of tapas, now so basic to Spanish life, could be easily explained but no. Nobody quite knows how the custom started, but here's what I think.

On one of my visits to the *bodegas* (wineries) in Jerez, where Sherry is made, a distinguished Sherry-maker had set out five *copas* (glasses) of wine to show us the different incarnations of this famous wine (see pages 16–17 for more about Sherry). We were late and he had lidded each *copa* with a little saucer to keep out the tiny fruit flies that proliferated in the damp spring weather. To me, this seemed to explain the whole evolution of tapas: once the little saucer is set on the *copa*, how shrewd for a bartender to place on it a few olives, a slice of ham or the home-made sausage. And, competition being what it is, the tavern that had the best selection of tapas would certainly draw more customers. Also, because Sherry is a wine with a higher degree of alcohol than ordinary table wines, the accompanying foods make it possible to keep sipping.

Tapas evolved in Andalusia's Sherry culture – but then each region individualized them. Life in Madrid would not be the same without the convivial rituals of the *tapeo*, the meeting and greeting, eating and imbibing. In Catalonia they sip *cava* (bubbly wine, made like Champagne) and nibble canapés, while in the Basque Country, tapas are called *pinchos* and are served buffet style. In Galicia, the northwest corner of Spain, wine bars display tapas in gargantuan portions – a huge wheel of a savoury pie, a whole leg of roast pork. In Madrid and northern provinces, red wine is favoured over Sherry to accompany tapas. In Asturias, cider houses serve up rustic foods to accompany the fizzy apple brew.

So, what are tapas? Way more than finger food – most tapas require at least a cocktail stick, maybe a tiny spoon and, for sure, a chunk of bread. My Spanish friends insist that tapas are foods served only in wine bars, where you consume them standing at the bar. If you serve the same foods at a party, they are *aperitivos*, not tapas. Whatever you call them, a spread of tapas is a fine excuse for a party. Serve tapas with chunks or slices of bread or breadsticks.

For a tapa party at home, you might offer Sherry fino or the somewhat similar wines of Montilla-Moriles, as well as red and white table wine and beer. Sparkling water is a nonalcoholic alternative. In Spain, mixed drinks, such as whisky and water, gin and tonic, rum and Coke, are for late-night imbibing when you go out dancing or to a club to listen to music, not what you drink with tapas.

Here are some of my very favourite tapa dishes. Many of them could also be served in larger portions as starters or main dishes. In addition, throughout this book you will find other recipes marked with a big 🅣 for tapas. Even though they appear in fish or meat sections, they could be served in tiny portions as tapas.

About Sherry

Sherry is a wine produced only in a small area of southwestern Spain, in a magic triangle comprising the towns of Jerez de la Frontera, El Puerto de Santa Maria and Sanlúcar de Barrameda. Sherry wines have official *denominación de origen*, or designation of origin (DO). Any wine without the DO mark is not a true Sherry. Sherry has been made in this region of Andalusia for hundreds of years. Shakespeare mentions it. The English traditionally have been fond of it, explaining why quite a few of the *bodegas* (wineries) have English names.

Once the great Sherry *bodegas* were family enterprises. Now almost all of them have been bought out by multinational companies. The Sherry barons – cultured, multilingual gentlemen, some with titles – are still there, but now they serve primarily in public relations functions.

Sherry acquires its aroma and bouquet by long ageing in oak barrels. The barrels, or butts, are stacked in tiers, typically three deep. The bottom row of barrels is called the *solera*, from *suelo* (floor) and thus the method of ageing Sherry is usually referred to as the *solera* system.

Newly fermented wine is introduced to barrels on the top tier. As some of the fully matured wine is drawn off from the bottom barrels for bottling, the butts are topped off with wine from the tier above, and those filled from the ones above them. Theoretically, the bottom barrel still has molecules of wine from whenever the *solera* was laid down – sometimes several centuries ago. Because Sherry is blended in the *solera*, it does not have vintage years.

Sherry is a fortified wine. It requires a minimum strength of 15.5 per cent alcohol for its proper development, so it is fortified with wine spirit. This makes Sherry, with between 15.5 and 20 per cent alcohol, higher in alcohol than table wines, which have between 11 and 13 per cent alcohol.

Although Sherry is not the sort of wine you usually drink with a meal, it goes beautifully with food, as an aperitif wine or, in certain cases, a dessert wine.

The wines of Montilla-Moriles in the province of Córdoba are also made by the *solera* process. Though they are made from a different grape variety, the wines are similar to those from Jerez. They are not called Sherry but are designated Montilla-Moriles.

Here are the main types of Sherry. Except as noted, all are made from the palomino grape.

Fino. A pale, straw-coloured wine, very dry, smooth, delicate and fresh. Fino is aged in wooden barrels for three years or more and matures beneath a layer of *flor*, a white yeast, which protects the wine from oxidation. The word *fino* means fine and delicate. It also refers to 'fining', the process by which wine is clarified. Fino, which has an alcoholic level of about 15.5 per cent, does not continue to improve once bottled, so drink it, slightly chilled, when it is fresh. It's the very best wine with tapas, especially good with cured ham, sausages, almonds, olives, cheese, cod and other fish dishes, marinated foods, fried foods, chicken, kidneys and meatballs.

Manzanilla. Also a fino, but made only in the town of Sanlúcar de Barrameda, a seaside town in the Sherry wine district. It's said the salt sea breezes cause the wine to mature differently than in Jerez and, if you take a fino from Jerez to Sanlúcar, it will turn into manzanilla. Manzanilla is subtly salty, lighter, paler and more bitter than fino from Jerez. It goes especially well with shellfish tapas. It is also the favoured tipple for Andalusia's great fiestas, such as the April *feria* in Seville.

Amontillado. This Sherry starts out as a fino. The addition of grape alcohol at a later stage causes the disappearance of the *flor*, which allows a mellowing of the wine by oxidation in the wooden casks. Amontillado is amber coloured, rich, warm and nutty, but quite dry. Sometimes aged for 12 years or more, it is always more expensive than fino. Serve it cool, with ham, smoked meats and cheese.

Oloroso. Mahogany in colour, with a walnut taste, the oloroso Sherries range from dry to those with a vestige of sweetness. They are mellowed by oxidation and have an alcohol content of 18–20 per cent. These are also aperitif wines. They are especially delicious with sausage, nuts and dried fruits, and with not-too-sweet cakes and biscuits. A touch of oloroso is a marvellous addition to consommé, soups and sauces. *Palo cortado* is a type of oloroso.

Pedro Ximenez. This is made from Pedro Ximenez grapes, which, after harvesting, are sun-dried for 10 to 15 days, then pressed. The wine is dark and tastes like liquid raisins, superb with dessert.

Cream Sherry. A dessert wine, which is often a combination of oloroso and Pedro Ximenez. Serve these sweet wines with puddings, pastries and other sweets.

Classic Tapas

While any tapa bar worth its salt has its specialities, most of them offer the classic tapas. Olives – of course. Ham and sausage. Chunks of potato omelette. Fresh unshelled prawns (*gambas*) are served absolutely plain – boiled in salt water for 2 to 3 minutes. You peel them yourself. They are so good that they need no lemon or sauce for dipping.

Spiced Fried Almonds
Almendras Fritas

Almond trees grow on the hillside near my home, so I have plenty of the delicious nuts to gather. Cracked, shelled and toasted in olive oil with just a touch of spice, they are perfect served with drinks.

2 tablespoons olive oil

230g (8 oz) unskinned almonds

1 teaspoon salt

Pinch of ground cumin

¼ teaspoon pimentón

Heat the oil in a large frying pan over medium heat and add the almonds. Fry them, stirring constantly, until they are toasted and very lightly browned, about 1 minute. Remove from heat and immediately sprinkle with salt, cumin and pimentón. Cool before serving.

Makes 570 ml (¾ pint)

Olives
Aceitunas

I built my present house in a small olive grove. Most of the olives are picked to be crushed for oil, but three or four trees produce varieties suitable for table olives, which I cure myself. When I serve tapas to my guests on the terrace, I like to tell them, 'These olives came from the tree you're sitting under.' They are cured in the local style in a brine and flavoured with garlic, thyme and fennel. If you cannot come by freshly picked olives, try marinating bottled green olives, drained and rinsed, in brine with the herbs for 48 hours.

Pick green olives. Discard any bruised or blemished ones. Using a stone or mallet, crack the olives lightly, just to split open the fruit. Wash them and place in a nonreactive container. Cover completely with water. Change the water every few days for several weeks, or until the olives, when tasted, are no longer bitter. This will take about a month.

Then prepare a brine, using 1 part salt to 8 parts water and make up enough brine to cover the olives. Place the drained olives in the brine along with cloves of garlic, quartered lemons and sprigs of thyme and fennel. Use 3 to 4 cloves of garlic and half a lemon for every 900 ml (1½ pints) of brine. Some people like to add strips of red pepper, too. Place a dish directly on to the olives to keep them submerged. Cover the container and let the olives rest for at least 1 week. They are then ready to eat. Store them in a cool, dark place, replenishing the brine as necessary. They keep for 2 or 3 months.

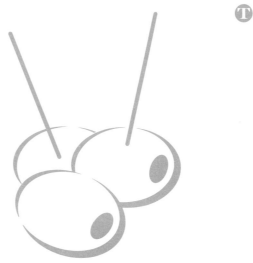

Cured Serrano Ham
Jamón Serrano

Jamón serrano means mountain ham, so-called because traditionally it was cured in upland regions where temperatures and humidity enhanced the curing process. Once every small farm produced its own ham in the cold winter months. Nowadays ham is also produced in well-regulated industrial plants. These are the serrano hams that are exported from Spain to the United Kingdom.

Good ham starts with prime raw material. Spanish serrano ham is made from pigs of Landrace, Duroc and large white crossbreeds, fattened on natural feed. One particular serrano ham, labelled *Ibérico,* comes from a native Iberian breed of pigs, which roam semi-wild and feed on acorns. This extraordinary ham should be tasted when visiting Spain, as it is not produced in sufficient quantity to allow for export.

Serrano ham is made by packing fresh ham – usually the hog's entire back leg, including hoof – in coarse sea salt for 10 to 20 days, depending on weight. It is then washed and brushed free of salt and hung in high-humidity rooms to 'sweat' for several weeks. Once dependent on natural weather conditions, the curing sheds now have temperature and humidity controls.

The hams are then transferred to maturing cellars where they hang for 6 months to 2 years, becoming covered with a protective layer of mould. Each ham is tested by inserting a fine bone skewer into the flesh. Ham experts can tell by sniffing the skewer whether the ham is properly cured. Good ones have a sweet, rounded aroma with no stale or rancid odour.

Serrano hams that carry the certification of the Spanish Serrano Ham Consortium must be cured for a minimum of 9 months and must meet certain specifications for weight and fat and salt content. A loss of at least 32 per cent of original weight, by slow dehydration, is proof that the ham is adequately aged. However, *de bodega* hams, matured for 14 to 16 months, reduce by 40 per cent.

Serrano ham is ready to eat at this point. It receives no smoking, no soaking, no cooking. Until it is cut, the ham keeps very well if it is hung in a cool, well-ventilated place, protected from the light.

The flavour of serrano ham varies, depending on the breed of pig and the length of curing. It should be somewhat sweet, slightly nutty and never excessively salty. Fine ham is succulent. The colour of the meat ranges from brick-red to violet-red to rosy pink and the colour of the fat is creamy white to pale gold.

In Spain, the slicing of fine ham is considered an art. There are even ham-slicing competitions, where the experts are judged for speed, presentation and yield. If you are buying serrano ham at the deli counter, where it is sliced to order, purchase only enough for immediate use. Sliced ham should be kept tightly wrapped in the refrigerator, but allowed to come to room temperature before serving. Chilling dampens the ham's mellow aroma. Presliced, vacuum-packed ham, which needs to be kept refrigerated, should also be served at room temperature.

Serve serrano ham raw, at room temperature, as an aperitif with baguette slices to accompany it. You eat the ribbon of fat too – it is lower in saturated fat than other animal fats. Serve serrano ham in any way you would serve Parma ham – paired with sweet melon or fresh figs, or wrapped round spears of asparagus.

Serrano ham loses its delicacy of flavour and texture with long cooking. However, used as 'seasoning', it lends character to sautéed vegetables, omelettes, prawns and dishes with lentils and beans. Just sauté the chopped ham very briefly in a little olive oil and combine it with the other ingredients at the end of cooking. If serrano ham is not available, substitute bacon or pancetta,

preferably unsmoked, in recipes. Small pieces of ham bone (*añejo*) are cooked in some stews and soups to add flavour.

In tapa bars, serrano ham is served in paper-thin slices, accompanied by nothing more than bread, often as part of a mixed selection of sliced ham and sausages.

Spanish Potato Omelette

Tortilla Española

Tortilla means a round, flat cake. Thus, the Mexican corn tortilla is one sort of round, flat cake. In Spain, where corn tortillas are not used at all, tortilla is a round, flat cake made of eggs and potatoes or other vegetables, rather like a thick omelette. Tortilla is made incorporating all sorts of ingredients – aubergine, tuna, green beans, brains – and is served for lunch or supper. (For more tortilla recipes, see chapter 5.) But it is the one with potatoes that is the most popular dish on tapa bars from one end of the country to the other.

It looks, at first glance, like a simple preparation, but a good tortilla takes practice.

It was Don José, a Madrid intellectual, who taught me to make a perfect tortilla. A former member of the Republican government, he had been exiled from the capital after the Civil War to our out-of-the-way village in Andalusia. I got to know Don José the first winter we spent in Spain. He lived in a tiny room overlooking the plaza and spent his days, a scarf wrapped around his neck, sitting in the sunshine, hoping someone would come along to play a chess match with him. He liked us because we were fellow journalists and could speak enough Spanish to make communication possible. We were as close as he got to an intellectual life.

Conversation ranged over literature, cinema, music, philosophy. (About politics he was very cagey.) And food. For a cultured man, he could get quite vicious about the standards of table in Andalusia. How could they take perfectly good eggs, olive oil and potatoes and turn out something they called *tortilla* which was totally inedible? 'A real tortilla', he told me, his eyes a little misty, 'is golden like sunshine, very thick and still juicy in the middle.'

So I invited Don José over to show me how to make a proper *tortilla española*. In spite of his directions, it was a disaster. The tortilla completely disintegrated, turning into chunks of fried potatoes scrambled with eggs. Challenged, I persisted until I had conquered the art. And invited him back another day. There it was, golden as sunshine, thick and still juicy in the centre. Don José proclaimed me an *ángel*.

Some tapa bars serve up tortillas almost 60 cm (2 feet) in diameter and more than 8 cm (3 inches) thick. For tapas, it is cut into squares. Cut into wedges, the tortilla makes an admirable brunch, lunch, supper or picnic dish. Before the era of high-speed rail travel, when a train trip meant long hours of starts and stops, a hamper packed with several tortillas was essential to the journey.

My son Benjamin, who makes a better tortilla than I, insists that the potatoes must be chopped, not sliced. You can try it both ways.

120 ml (4 fl oz) olive oil

900 g (2 lb) potatoes (7 to 8 medium), peeled and thinly sliced

2 tablespoons chopped onion

1 teaspoon salt

6 eggs

Heat the oil in a 24-cm (9-inch) nonstick or well-seasoned frying pan over medium heat. Don't use a cast-iron pan, because it's too heavy for the flipping operation. Add the sliced potatoes and turn them in the oil. Let them cook very slowly in the oil, without browning, turning frequently. When they are partially cooked after 10 to 15 minutes, add the chopped onion and sprinkle with ½ teaspoon of the salt. Continue cooking until the potatoes are tender, 20 to 30 minutes total.

Beat the eggs in a bowl with the remaining ½ teaspoon salt. When the potatoes are tender, put a plate over the pan and drain off any excess oil into a small bowl. Add the potatoes to the beaten eggs and combine well.

Return a little of the reserved oil to the pan and pour in the potato-egg mixture. Cook over medium heat until set, without letting the omelette get too brown on the bottom, about 5 minutes. Shake the pan to keep the tortilla from sticking.

Place a flat lid or plate on top, hold it tightly and invert the tortilla on to the plate. Add a little more of the reserved oil to the pan, if necessary, and slide the tortilla back in to cook on the reverse side, about 3 minutes more. Slide out on to a serving plate.

In tapa bars, tortilla is served at room temperature, cut into squares and speared with cocktail sticks.

SERVES 15 TO 20 AS A TAPA; SERVES 4 FOR LUNCH OR SUPPER

FRIED TAPAS

What I especially like to eat in tapa bars are the fried foods. Croquettes, fritters, fish and more emerge from the bubbling oil golden, crispy and perfectly cooked. If I am preparing a tapa party at home, I always include at least one of the *fritos*. Though they require last-minute attention, they are real crowd-pleasers.

Olive oil is absolutely the best for deep-frying or shallow-frying. It imparts flavour and crispness, yet never produces greasy food. However, as olive oil is expensive, you may choose to use other vegetable oils for deep-frying.

Don't mix olive oil with other oils for frying, because they all have different smoking temperatures. Cool the oil after use, strain it and store in a dark place. Olive oil can be used for frying four or five times before discarding. Any other oil should never be used more than twice. If you are using a thermometer to check the temperature, heat the olive oil to 182°C (360°F). It will be shimmering, but not smoking. At this temperature a crust forms around the food – though it doesn't brown – so the oil doesn't penetrate. If you are substituting other vegetable oils for deep-frying, heat them to 190°C (375°).

Foods to batter-fry:

- Cauliflower florets, precooked until crisp-tender

- Chard stalks, cut in 5-cm (2-inch) segments, precooked until crisp-tender

- Whole small mushrooms, or quartered large ones

- Aubergine cut in 2.5-cm (1-inch) cubes

- Courgettes cut in 4-cm (1½-inch) cubes or sticks

- Frozen artichoke hearts or precooked fresh ones

- Stuffed olives

- Fresh fish cut in 2.5-cm (1-inch) cubes

- Salt cod, soaked in water (see page 9), cut in pieces

- Raw prawns, peeled, tails intact

- Raw scallops or mussels

- Chorizo sausage, 2.5-cm (1-inch) diameter, cut in 12-mm (½-inch) slices

BATTER-FRIED TAPAS
REBOZADOS

Rebozados are Spain's version of tempura – vegetables, seafood, meat – dipped in a batter and deep-fried in bubbling olive oil. Select seasonal vegetables, such as cauliflower, chard and aubergine, as well as titbits of fish and meat, including salt cod, fresh prawns and sliced sausage. While these fritters are usually served as tapas, those made with vegetables make a nice side dish with meat or fish.

When prawns are batter-dipped and fried, they are widely known as *gambas en gabardinas* – prawns in overcoats. The puffy coating is actually more like a down-filled ski parka than an ovecoat! Here's a trick I picked up in a Málaga tapa bar many years ago: spear the prawn (or other food) on a cocktail stick, making it easier to dip in the batter and drop into the oil, stick and all, without getting your fingers sticky. Otherwise, drop food, such as florets of cauliflower into the batter, then use a slotted spoon to fish them out and drop into the boiling oil.

You can prepare the fritter batter up to 3 hours in advance, but be sure to serve the finished fritters immediately after frying.

3 large eggs

½ teaspoon olive oil

1 tablespoon finely chopped fresh flat-leaf parsley

1 garlic clove, finely chopped

Pinch saffron threads, crushed, or yellow food colouring (optional)

¼ teaspoon bicarbonate of soda

¼ teaspoon salt

140 g (5 oz) plain flour

3 dozen small pieces vegetables, prawns, sausage, etc. (see box, opposite)

Oil, for deep-frying

Beat the eggs for 1 minute with 3 tablespoons water and the olive oil. Add the parsley, garlic, saffron, if using, bicarbonate of soda and salt. Stir in the flour to make a smooth batter. Set aside to rest for at least 30 minutes.

Pour oil into a deep-fat fryer or a deep frying pan to a depth of at least 5 cm (2 inches). Heat until the oil is shimmering but not smoking (182°C/360°F). Fold pieces of food into the batter. Scoop them out with a spoon and drop into the hot oil. Fry until golden-brown and slightly puffed. If you are shallow-frying in a pan, turn the pieces to brown the second side. Drain them briefly on kitchen towels and serve hot.

MAKES 36 PIECES; SERVES 18

TANGY FRIED FISH

CAZÓN EN ADOBO

Cazón is dogfish, a kind of shark, which is perked up nicely with a tangy adobo marinade. Any solid-fleshed fish, such as monkfish or striped bass, could be substituted.

900 g (2 lb) shark or monkfish fillets

3 tablespoons olive oil

5 tablespoons white wine vinegar

3 garlic cloves, chopped

¼ teaspoon pimentón

1 teaspoon crumbled dried oregano

¼ teaspoon freshly ground black pepper

½ teaspoon salt

Plain flour

Olive oil, for deep-frying

Cut the fish into 4-cm (1½-inch) cubes, discarding any skin and bone. Put the cubes in a nonreactive container.

Mix together the oil, vinegar, 1 tablespoon water, garlic, pimentón, oregano, pepper and salt. Pour over the fish and mix well. Marinate for at least 6 hours, or as long as 24 hours.

Pour oil into a deep-fat fryer or deep frying pan to a depth of at least 5 cm (2 inches) and heat the oil until shimmering but not smoking (182°C/360°F).

Drain the fish well, dredge it in flour, shake off the excess and fry the pieces a few at a time in the hot oil until golden and crisp. Drain on kitchen towels and serve hot.

MAKES ABOUT 45 PIECES; SERVES 15

FRIED STUFFED MUSSELS

MEJILLÓNES RELLENOS

These tasty mussels can be prepared well ahead of a tapa party, then fried immediately before serving.

18 mussels, scrubbed and beards removed

2 tablespoons olive oil

1 tablespoon finely chopped onion

2 tablespoons plain flour

4 tablespoons white wine

1 egg, beaten with 1 tablespoon water

5 tablespoons fine dry breadcrumbs

120 ml (4 fl oz) olive oil, for frying

Combine the mussels with 140 ml (¼ pint) water in a deep pan. Cover and cook over high heat, shaking the pan, until mussels open, 3 to 4 minutes. Remove from the heat and discard any mussels that do not open.

When the mussels are cool enough to handle, remove and discard the empty half shells. Loosen the mussel meat from the bottom shell and arrange the mussels in their shells on a tray in a single layer. Strain the mussel liquid and reserve it.

Heat the oil in a saucepan over low heat and sauté the onion until softened, without letting it brown, about 3 minutes. Stir in the flour, cook for 1 minute, stirring, then whisk in the wine

and 120 ml (4 fl oz) of the reserved mussel liquid. Cook, stirring, until the mixture is thickened and smooth, 3 to 4 minutes. Put a spoonful of this white sauce on to each mussel and smooth it level with the top of the shell. Refrigerate until the sauce is firmly set, 2 to 3 hours.

Place the beaten egg in one dish and the breadcrumbs in another. Dip the mussels, open face down, first into egg, then breadcrumbs. Arrange them on the tray in a single layer and refrigerate until immediately before frying. (The mussels can be prepared up to this point, then frozen. Freeze them in one layer on the tray, then pack them carefully in a freezer bag or plastic container. Let them thaw for 1 hour at room temperature before continuing with the preparation.)

To fry the mussels, heat enough oil to cover the bottom of a frying pan. Fry them on medium-high heat in two or three batches, breaded side down, until golden brown, 30 to 60 seconds. Drain briefly on kitchen towels and serve hot.

MAKES 14 TO 18 PIECES; SERVES 6 TO 9

CRISPY SHRIMP FRITTERS

TORTILLITAS DE CAMARONES

In the market at Cádiz, an ancient seaport on the Atlantic coast that is said be the oldest town in Europe, I spotted vendors with baskets of small creatures hopping around like grasshoppers. They turned out to be tiny live shrimp. The vendors cooked the shrimp for an instant in boiling salt water and sold them wrapped in paper cones. You eat the shrimp whole, shells and all. They are also folded into this fritter batter and crisply fried in oil. If you can't find the tiny shrimp, use small shelled prawns.

140 g (5 oz) plain flour

3 tablespoons finely chopped spring onion with some of the green

1 tablespoon chopped fresh flat-leaf parsley

¼ teaspoon salt

Pinch ground cayenne pepper

170 g (6 oz) peeled, chopped raw shrimp

Olive oil, for frying

In a bowl combine the flour, onion, parsley, salt, cayenne and 170 ml (6 fl oz) of water. Stir to blend thoroughly and refrigerate the batter for at least 1 hour and no more than 3 hours.

Fold in the shrimp and enough additional water (1–2 tablespoons) to make a loose pancake batter.

Heat a frying pan over medium heat with enough oil to cover the bottom. Use a soupspoon to drop the batter into the pan. Spread the batter into an 8-cm (3-inch) round with the back of the spoon. Fry until browned on the bottom, then turn and brown the reverse side (about 1 minute on each side). The fritters should be thin and crisp. Continue frying the fritters in batches, adding oil as needed. Drain on kitchen towels. Serve immediately.

MAKES ABOUT 18 FRITTERS; SERVES 8 TO 10

LITTLE GYPSY PORK ROLLS

FLAMENQUINES DE CERDO

A *brazo de gitano*, or 'gypsy's arm', is a popular dessert, a thick cake roll filled with pastry cream. This pork roll, named for a little gypsy, is diminutive only in comparison. As a tapa it is fried to order, a whole one per person.

570 g (1¼ lb) thinly sliced boneless pork or veal escalopes

8 slices lean bacon, trimmed of rind

4 thin slices serrano or cooked ham, fat trimmed

60 g (2 oz) firm, flavourful cheese, such as Manchego, cut into eight 10-cm (4-inch) long fingers

4 tablespoons plain flour

½ teaspoon salt

⅛ teaspoon freshly ground black pepper

Pinch dried thyme, crumbled

¼ teaspoon pimentón

1 egg, beaten with 1 tablespoon water

5 tablespoons fine dry breadcrumbs

Oil, for frying

Lemon wedges, to serve

Trim the escalopes to make rectangles more or less 18 × 13 cm (7 × 5 inches). Place them between layers of cling film and pound them to a thickness of 6 mm (¼ inch).

Across each escalope lay two slices of bacon, a slice of ham and two fingers of cheese. Starting with the wide edge, roll up the escalopes, Swiss-roll style, and secure them with one or two cocktail sticks. (They should be at least 2.5 cm/1 inch thick.)

Combine the flour, salt, pepper, thyme and pimentón and place in a dish. Place the beaten egg in a dish long enough to hold the pork rolls. Place the breadcrumbs in another dish.

First dredge the rolls in the flour mixture, patting off excess. Then put them in the dish of beaten egg and rock the dish back and forth to coat the rolls with egg. Remove and roll them in the breadcrumbs, taking special care to seal the ends with egg an d crumbs. Let the rolls dry for at least 30 minutes. They can be prepared up to 4 hours in advance at this point and refrigerated, but bring them to room temperature before frying.

Pour oil into a frying pan to a depth of 2.5 cm (1 inch). Heat the oil until it is shimmering but not smoking (182°C/360°F). Fry the rolls until they are very browned and crisp on all sides, about 8 minutes. The meat should be cooked through and the cheese melted. Drain briefly on kitchen towels and serve hot with a wedge of lemon.

SERVES 4

CRISPY POTATOES WITH HOT SAUCE
PATATAS BRAVAS

This tapa bar favourite is usually prepared to order. A plate heaped with the crisp potato cubes topped with the piquant sauce is placed in the middle of the table for several friends to share. Spear the cubes with cocktail sticks.

120 ml (4 fl oz) smooth tomato sauce, home-made (see page 10) or bottled passata

1 garlic clove, crushed

1 tablespoon olive oil

¼ teaspoon ground cumin

1 teaspoon hot pimentón or, if unavailable, ¾ teaspoon paprika and ¼ teaspoon cayenne

½ teaspoon dried oregano, crumbled

2 teaspoons white wine vinegar

900 g (2 lb) baking potatoes

Olive oil, for frying

Salt

Garlic Mayonnaise I (page 177), optional

In a small bowl, combine the tomato sauce, garlic, oil, cumin, pimentón, oregano and vinegar. Set aside.

Peel the potatoes and cut them into 4-cm (1½-inch) cubes.

Pour oil into a deep frying pan to a depth of 2.5 cm (1 inch). Heat the oil until it is shimmering but not smoking (182°C/360°F). Fry the potato cubes for 2 minutes. Reduce the heat so the oil is just bubbling. Fry the potatoes for 10 minutes, or until they are cooked all the way through. Then raise the heat again and fry until they are golden and crisp, about 3 minutes more.

Drain the potatoes on kitchen towels. Sprinkle with salt. Heap them in a bowl. Dribble the sauce over them. If desired, garlic mayonnaise can also be dribbled over the potatoes. Serve them with cocktail sticks or cocktail forks.

SERVES 6

Salads and Cold Dishes

Tapa bars in Spain may feature six or more salads and cold dishes every single day. They make great party food.

Orange and Cod Salad
Salmorejo

In my village this exotic salad is called *salmorejo*. But in Córdoba and Seville, *salmorejo* is something else altogether, a thick gazpacho (see page 75).

I like to make this salad with black olives and red onions, a stunning contrast with the sliced oranges. The cod is scattered on top almost like a seasoning. In this case, the salt cod isn't soaked for many hours: it is toasted to soften it and soaked briefly so that it can be flaked. Chunks of tinned tuna, drained, or well-rinsed tinned anchovies can be substituted for the dry salt cod.

115–170 g (4–6 oz) dry salt cod (*bacalao*)

4 oranges, peeled and pith removed

1 small red onion or 6 spring onions (white and green parts), thinly sliced

10 green or black stoned olives

1 garlic clove, finely chopped

2 tablespoons olive oil

1 tablespoon Sherry wine vinegar

Pinch crushed red chilli flakes (optional)

Turn on the grill or preheat a griddle. Brush excess salt from the cod. Place it on a sheet of heavy-duty aluminium foil with the edges turned up. Toast the salt cod under the grill or on the griddle, 8–10 cm (3–4 inches) from heat, until it is lightly browned and softened, about 5 minutes on each side. Put it in a bowl of water to soak for 1 hour.

Slice the oranges or separate them into segments and cut the segments in half to make bite-sized pieces. Arrange on a serving plate. Scatter the onions on top. Arrange the olives on the oranges.

In a small bowl, combine the garlic, oil, vinegar and red chilli flakes. Rinse the cod in fresh water. Remove and discard all skin and bones and shred the flesh.

Scatter the bits of cod over the salad and drizzle with the dressing.

Serves 12

FRESH TOMATO AND PEPPER SALAD
PIPIRRANA

From my kitchen window I look down a long *arroyo* (a deep ravine), across low hills to the Mediterranean. Sometimes after a strong north wind blows away the haze on the horizon, the air turns crystal-clear, and a line of mountains appears across the blue sea, like a mirror-image of the low coastal range in southern Spain. They are the Rif mountains in Morocco in North Africa; another continent and yet close. So close that in 711 AD Arab invaders crossed over at the Straits of Gibraltar and succeeded in capturing much of Spain, thus establishing the kingdom of Al-Andaluz. They ruled for eight centuries, leaving their indelible traces on the cuisine, art, architecture and folk customs.

This salad, served in tapa bars, is nearly identical to one I've enjoyed in North Africa. The main difference is that the Andalusians use chopped parsley and the Moroccans use chopped fresh coriander leaves. Ham, prawns or sliced fish roe can be substituted for the tuna.

6 medium fresh ripe tomatoes, chopped

3 spring onions or 1 small onion, chopped

2 green sweet peppers, finely chopped

1 small cucumber, peeled and diced (optional)

1 garlic clove, finely chopped

1 teaspoon salt

2 tablespoons chopped fresh flat-leaf parsley

¼ teaspoon ground cumin

3 tablespoons white wine vinegar

6 tablespoons olive oil

85 g (3 oz) tinned tuna, drained

1 egg, hard-boiled and chopped

Combine the tomatoes, onions, peppers, cucumber and garlic in a bowl. Sprinkle with the salt, parsley and cumin. Drizzle with the vinegar and oil and toss the salad gently. Arrange it on a platter. Garnish the top with chunks of tuna and chopped egg and serve.

SERVES 6 AS A STARTER; SERVES 18 TO 20 AS A TAPA

FLAMENCO POTATO SALAD WITH LEMON DRESSING
PAPAS ALIÑADAS

The most exciting *juerga* (flamenco performance) I ever experienced was at a *venta* (country bar) in the province of Cádiz. Wine flowed, spirits rose and tapas appeared. It was nearly midnight before the music and dancing began. There was no stage. Guitarists, singers and dancers simply sat on chairs at one end of the room. A few strums, the sound of staccato clapping, a voice rising over the guitar, then a dancer stood and began moving to the complicated flamenco rhythms. The *juerga* went on until the early hours of the morning, building in intensity until the whole place seemed to throb with electricity.

This potato salad with its tangy lemon dressing was one of the tapas served at that night of flamenco. While mayonnaise is never mixed into this salad, some bars serve it with an 'icing' of mayonnaise.

900 g (2 lb) baking potatoes (5 to 6 medium potatoes)

1 teaspoon salt

4 spring onions or 1 small onion, finely chopped

2 medium tomatoes, chopped

4 tablespoons olive oil

5 tablespoons fresh lemon juice

2 tablespoons chopped fresh flat-leaf parsley

2 eggs, hard-boiled and sliced, to garnish

85 g (3 oz) tinned tuna, drained, to garnish

Strips bottled red pimiento, to garnish

12 green olives, stoned to garnish

Lettuce, to serve

In a large saucepan, bring 1.4 litres (2½ pints) water to the boil. Add potatoes and boil in their skins until just tender, 20 to 25 minutes. Drain, then peel and slice the potatoes.

In a large bowl, combine the salt, onions, tomatoes, oil, lemon juice and parsley. Add the potatoes and combine gently so the potatoes are evenly covered with the dressing. Allow the salad to marinate for at least 2 hours at room temperature before serving. (The potatoes can be prepared up to 1 day in advance and kept, covered and refrigerated, until serving time.)

Spread the potatoes on a platter. Garnish the top with the sliced egg, chunks of tuna, strips of pimiento and olives. Place a few lettuce leaves around the potatoes.

SERVES 10 TO 12 AS A TAPA; SERVES 6 AS A SIDE DISH

ROASTED RED PEPPER SALAD
ENSALADA DE PIMIENTOS ASADOS

This simple and versatile salad is a favourite at tapa bars, where it is sometimes layered on toasted triangles of bread brushed with olive oil and topped with an anchovy fillet. I also like roasted peppers as a starter or an accompaniment to grilled foods such as tuna, chicken or pork, and as a filling or condiment for sandwiches. This dish can be made well in advance and refrigerated, but serve it at room temperature.

6 medium red sweet peppers (or a combination of red and green)

1 garlic clove, finely chopped

3 tablespoons olive oil

3 tablespoons white wine vinegar

Salt and freshly ground black pepper

Roast the peppers over a gas flame, over charcoal or under the grill, turning them until charred on all sides, 25 to 30 minutes. Remove them to a bowl and cover. Let stand 1 hour.

Peel off the skin from the peppers and cut out the stems and seeds and discard. Tear or cut the peppers into strips and put on a serving plate. Add the garlic, oil, vinegar, salt and pepper. Toss gently.

SERVES 8 TO 10 AS A TAPA OR A SIDE DISH

DEVILLED EGGS WITH PRAWNS AND OLIVES
HUEVOS RELLENOS CON GAMBAS Y ACEITUNAS

Growing up in the American Midwest, I remember devilled eggs as special for picnics and parties. This Spanish version makes an unusual alternative, with prawns and olives in the stuffing. Tinned tuna can be substituted for the prawns to make this an economical dish, and, if desired, the egg yolks can be eliminated, to make a low-cholesterol version.

8 eggs, hard-boiled

Lettuce leaves, to serve

85 g (3 oz) cooked, peeled and chopped prawns

3 tablespoons chopped pimiento-stuffed olives

2 teaspoons finely chopped onion

1 tablespoon chopped fresh flat-leaf parsley

1 tablespoon plus 2 teaspoons fresh lemon juice

¼ teaspoon salt

1 tablespoon olive oil

120 ml (4 fl oz) mayonnaise

1 red sweet pepper, roasted, skinned and cut into strips (see page 34) (or bottled pimiento)

Cherry tomatoes, to garnish (optional)

Peel the eggs and cut in half lengthwise. Remove the yolks and set them aside. Remove a sliver from the bottom of the whites so they will sit flat. Place the lettuce on a serving platter and set the whites on it.

In a bowl, mash four of the yolks. Add the prawns, olives, onion, parsley, 2 teaspoons lemon juice, salt and olive oil and combine well. Scoop this mixture into the egg whites so each white is just filled.

Stir the mayonnaise with the remaining 1 tablespoon lemon juice until it reaches spreading consistency. (If necessary, thin with a little water.) Top each egg with a cap of mayonnaise. Grate the reserved yolks over the stuffed eggs. Lay a strip of red pepper on top of each. (The eggs can be prepared and kept chilled for up to 3 hours before serving.) Garnish the platter with cherry tomatoes.

SERVES 16

MARINATED FRESH ANCHOVIES
BOQUERONES EN VINAGRE

Fresh anchovies, which measure 13–14 cm (5–5½ inches) long, are abundant on the Mediterranean and Bay of Biscay coasts. Lightly floured and fried in olive oil, they are among my favourite foods. I eat them bones and all.

But one of the most popular tapas in the whole country is fresh marinated anchovies. For these, the centre spine is removed, leaving two tiny fillets attached by the tail. These are marinated, raw, in vinegar, which firms and whitens them, then dressed with oil and garlic. They are redolent of the briny taste of the sea without being unpleasantly salty, like tinned anchovies. I've tried substituting strips of mackerel, which taste fine but just aren't the same as delectable fresh anchovies.

Serve the anchovies accompanied by fingers of bread. Some people like to lay an anchovy on the bread; others use the bread to dip into the garlicky dressing in the dish.

450 g (1 lb) fresh whole anchovies (or two 340-g/12-oz mackerel)

240 ml (8 fl oz) white wine vinegar

1 teaspoon salt

2 tablespoons olive oil

3 garlic cloves, coarsely chopped

2 tablespoons chopped fresh flat-leaf parsley

Shredded lettuce, to garnish

Lemon half, to garnish

Chopped spring onion, to garnish

Fresh anchovies are simple to fillet. Using a sharp knife, first cut off the heads and pull out the innards of the fish. Then grasp the top of the spine with thumb and knife edge and pull the spine down across the belly of the fish. Cut off the spine, leaving the fillets attached at the tail.

Place the anchovies, skin side down, in a single layer in a nonreactive container. Pour over the vinegar, 2 tablespoons water and ½ teaspoon of the salt. Cover and refrigerate for 24 hours. The fillets will turn white and opaque. (They can be kept, refrigerated, for several days.)

Before serving, drain off all the vinegar marinade and rinse the anchovies in ice-cold water. Drain well. Arrange them skin-side down, like spokes of a wheel, on a serving dish. Sprinkle with remaining ½ teaspoon salt, oil, garlic and parsley. Garnish the dish with lettuce, a lemon half in the centre, and a little chopped spring onion.

SERVES 12

VARIATION: Substitute two 340-g (12-oz) mackerel instead of the anchovies. Have the fish filleted and skinned. Cut the two fillets into four segments, removing all pin bones. Cut these into strips about 9 cm (3½ inches) long and 4 cm (1½ inches) wide. Marinate the strips as for the fresh anchovies.

MUSSELS VINAIGRETTE
MEJILLÓNES A LA VINAGRETA

This popular tapa is a good hors d'oeuvre to pass at a party. You eat the mussel with the dressing right off the shell. The mussels can be cooked as much as a day in advance. Strain some of the liquid from the pan in which the mussels steamed and pour it over them to keep them juicy. Refrigerate, covered. The vinaigrette can also be prepared in advance.

30 mussels, scrubbed and beards removed

Shredded lettuce, to serve

2 tablespoons finely chopped spring onion

2 tablespoons finely chopped green sweet pepper

2 tablespoons finely chopped red sweet pepper

1 tablespoon chopped fresh flat-leaf parsley

4 tablespoons olive oil

2 tablespoons wine vinegar or fresh lemon juice

Dash of hot pepper sauce

Salt

Combine the cleaned mussels in a deep pan with about 2.5 cm (1 inch) of water, cover and place over high heat, shaking the pan until mussels open, 3 to 4 minutes. Remove from the heat and discard any that do not open. When the mussels are cool enough to handle, remove and discard the empty half-shells.

Shortly before serving, arrange the mussels on a bed of shredded lettuce on a serving platter.

In a bowl, combine the onion, green and red peppers, parsley, oil and vinegar. Season with hot sauce and salt to taste. Spoon the mixture over the mussels in their shells.

SERVES 24

SHELLFISH COCKTAIL WITH TOMATOES AND PEPPERS
ENSALADILLA DE MARISCOS

This salad, sometimes called *salpicón*, can be made with any combination of prawns, mussels, diced octopus or other cooked shellfish. I like it as a fresh alternative to prawn cocktail.

255 g (9 oz) cooked and chopped shellfish

340 g (12 oz) chopped fresh tomatoes

85 g (3 oz) chopped green sweet pepper

60 g (2 oz) chopped spring onion

2 garlic cloves, finely chopped

3 tablespoons chopped fresh flat-leaf parsley

½ teaspoon salt

3 tablespoons olive oil

2 tablespoons fresh lemon juice

Combine the shellfish in a bowl with the tomatoes, pepper, onion, garlic, parsley, salt, oil and lemon juice. Stir to combine. Serve at once.

SERVES 8 AS A TAPA; SERVES 4 AS A STARTER

NOTE: The salad can be prepared up to 3 hours in advance, omitting the tomatoes, and refrigerated until serving time. Add the chopped tomatoes at the last minute, as refrigeration dulls the taste of fresh tomatoes.

Tapas Served Hot

Sizzling Prawns with Garlic
Gambas al Ajillo

This is one of the all-time favourites at Spanish tapa bars. It should be made with absolutely fresh prawns (preferably not frozen), peeled and cooked on the spot. Garlic and a touch of hot chilli flavour the oil in which the prawns sizzle. This is traditionally prepared to order in individual ramekins and served, still sputtering, with chunks of bread for soaking up the flavourful sauce. Just multiply the ingredients listed by the number of guests you wish to serve. You can cook the prawns in one pan (frying pan or cazuela), but they lose their sizzle when transferred to individual servings. I make 4 servings at once, placing four individual cazuelitas, or ramekins, each measuring 13–15 cm (5–6 inches), on four burners and divide the ingredients between them. By the way, you peel the prawn tails, too. And, though Spanish cooks don't bother with deveining (veins are perfectly edible), this does add a refining touch.

2 tablespoons olive oil

1 garlic clove, sliced

1 slice dried chilli, such as cayenne

10–12 peeled small prawns (45 g/1½ oz)

Bread, to serve

Combine the oil, garlic and chilli in a flameproof ramekin. Place over high heat and heat until the garlic starts to sizzle, about 1 minute.

Add the prawns and cook just until they turn pink and curl, about 1 minute. Remove from the heat, add 2 teaspoons water and serve sizzling. Accompany with chunks of bread for soaking up the flavourful sauce.

Serves 1

MOORISH KEBABS
PINCHITOS MORUNOS

These spicy tapas are called Moorish kebabs because they are seasoned with the same blend of spices used in Morocco, on the other side of the Mediterranean. However, they are Moorish only in their seasonings, for now they are almost always made with pork, which Muslims do not eat.

The blend of spices, called *ras-el-hanout* in Morocco and *especia para pinchitos* (kebab spice) in Spain, contains a lot of cumin plus coriander seed, turmeric, ginger, cardamom, cayenne and pepper. An easy substitute is to combine curry powder, which contains most of the same spices, with ground cumin.

For these miniature kebabs, the meat is cut into 2.5-cm (1-inch) cubes and threaded four cubes per skewer on to short metal skewers. They make a good hors d'oeuvre to pass around at a party or barbecue. (Figure on one skewer per person.) A hibachi-size barbecue is perfect, because the skewers fit crosswise without needing a rack. However, I find it easiest to grill them on a *plancha*, an unridged cast-iron griddle.

Serve them with chunks of bread stuck on to the ends of the skewers.

1 tablespoon ground cumin

1 tablespoon Madras-style curry powder

½ teaspoon hot pimentón or, if unavailable, ½ teaspoon paprika and a pinch of cayenne

900 g (2 lb) pork fillet, cut into 2.5-cm (1-inch) cubes

5 tablespoons chopped fresh flat-leaf parsley

10 garlic cloves, chopped

2 teaspoons salt

120 ml (4 fl oz) fresh lemon juice

Combine the cumin, curry powder and pimentón in a small bowl.

Layer the cubes of pork in a nonreactive bowl with the parsley, garlic, salt, spice mixture and lemon juice. Marinate, covered and refrigerated, for 24 hours. Turn the meat 2 or 3 times.

Thread four or five pieces of meat on to sixteen thin metal skewers. Prepare a hot fire in a charcoal barbecue or preheat an oven grill or griddle. Brush the grill or griddle with oil. Grill the skewers over charcoal, under the oven grill or on a hot griddle, turning 2 or 3 times, until browned on all sides, 7 to 8 minutes.

SERVES 16

CLAMS, FISHERMEN'S STYLE
ALMEJAS A LA MARINERA

While most tapas are served in individual portions, some are particularly good presented in a larger portion to share with friends. This clam dish is one. Everybody helps himself from the communal platter and dunks pieces of bread into the garlicky juice. Use hard-shell clams or mussels.

900 g (2 lb) clams

3 tablespoons olive oil

2 tablespoons chopped onion

2 garlic cloves, chopped

1 tablespoon plain flour

120 ml (4 fl oz) dry white wine

Piece dried chilli (optional)

1 bay leaf

2 tablespoons chopped fresh flat-leaf parsley

Soak the clams in a bowl filled with salted water for 10 to 15 minutes, then carefully remove them with a large spoon or with your hands, leaving the sand at the bottom of the bowl. Wash the clams under running water. (If you are using mussels, scrub them and remove beards.) Discard any shells that are opened or cracked.

In a deep frying pan, heat the oil over medium heat. Add the onion and garlic and sauté until the onion is softened, 3 to 4 minutes. Stir in the flour, then add the clams. Raise the heat to high, add the wine, 120 ml (4 fl oz) water, chilli, if using, and bay leaf. Cover the pan and shake it until the clam shells open, 3 to 4 minutes.

Remove the pan from the heat when most of the shells have opened. Pour into a serving dish and top with chopped parsley.

SERVES 8 AS A TAPA; SERVES 3 TO 4 AS A STARTER

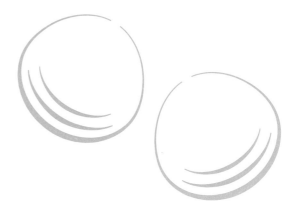

Galician-Style Octopus
Pulpo con Cachelos

This tapa dish originates in Galicia, where it is typically served in taverns, at town fairs and in street markets. Traditionally, the octopus vendor cooks the tentacled creature in cauldrons of boiling water and serves it cut into bite-sized pieces on wooden plates. I love the chewy octopus with its ever-so-simple dressing of oil, garlic and pimentón. If you like, add just a pinch of hot pimentón or cayenne as well. Freezing octopus tenderizes it, so it cooks more rapidly than fresh octopus. Frozen cooked octopus can be found in Oriental food shops.

Cachelos are boiled potatoes.

1 whole octopus (about 1 kg/2¼ lb), fresh or frozen (or about 450 g/1 lb frozen cooked and cleaned octopus, thawed)

1 onion slice

2 bay leaves

900 g (2 lb) baking potatoes, peeled

1 teaspoon coarse salt

1½ tablespoons pimentón

2 garlic cloves, chopped

5 tablespoons olive oil

Bring a large pan of water to the boil and blanch the whole octopus for 1 minute. Drain. Bring another large pan of water to the boil with the onion and bay leaves. Add the blanched octopus and let it simmer for about 1 hour. It should be tender, just a little chewy.

Transfer the octopus to a platter or bowl and allow to cool while you prepare the potatoes.

Cut the potatoes in half and add them to the same water in which the octopus cooked and cook them at a slow boil, over medium heat, until tender, about 20 minutes.

When the octopus is cool enough to handle, slide off the pinkish skin and discard, if desired. This is optional; many prefer to leave the skin. With kitchen scissors, cut the octopus into bite-sized pieces. Arrange them on individual plates with the potatoes. Sprinkle with salt, pimentón and garlic and drizzle with the oil.

SERVES 8

PORK BRAISED IN FRESH TOMATO SAUCE
MAGRO CON TOMATE

At the end of summer, Antonio, who farms the *huertas* (fields) adjoining my land, rips out all the tomato vines – still loaded with fruit – so he can plant his tiny new cabbages. I used to haul a wheelbarrow full of his tomatoes home, then wonder what to do with them. I found a delightful solution in this tapa dish, one traditionally prepared by village women when tomatoes are at their ripest.

Though the intense tomato flavour requires no additional seasoning, I like to add just a pinch of fennel seeds. As it so happens, wild fennel goes to seed just as the last glut of tomatoes ripens.

Magro means 'lean', so this is pork from a lean cut, such as the leg. As a tapa, it is served with bread chunks to mop up the sauce. I find it makes a wonderful sandwich, spooned hot on to a split baguette. You can also turn it into a main dish by serving over pasta or rice. If fresh tomatoes aren't available, use tinned ones.

4 tablespoons olive oil

450 g (1 lb) lean pork, cut into 2.5-cm (1-inch) cubes

1 garlic clove, finely chopped

120 ml (4 fl oz) white wine

1 bay leaf

Pinch fennel seeds (optional)

900 g (2 lb) peeled, de-seeded and chopped tomatoes

1 teaspoon salt

Heat the oil in a deep frying pan over moderately high heat and brown the pieces of pork. Keep turning them in the oil until they start to brown, about 5 minutes.

Add the garlic, then the wine, bay leaf and fennel seeds, if using. Cover and simmer until the pork is tender, about 45 minutes.

Turn up the heat until the remaining liquid evaporates, about 5 minutes, and the meat is sizzling. Add the tomatoes and salt. When tomatoes are bubbling, about 5 minutes, turn down to a simmer and cook, stirring frequently, until tomatoes are almost syrupy, 25 to 35 minutes, depending on how juicy the tomatoes are. Stir constantly during the last few minutes, so the sauce doesn't scorch. Serve hot.

SERVES 8 FOR TAPAS; SERVES 4 AS A SANDWICH FILLING; OR SERVES 6 AS A TOPPING FOR PASTA

CHICKEN SAUTÉ WITH GARLIC AND SHERRY
POLLO AL AJILLO

In 1966, Maria's kitchen at the Bar Estéban had no running water. To wash the dishes, she fetched water from the well at the back of the patio. For drinking, water had to be carried from a spring outside the village and kept in a *botijo* (an unglazed earthenware jug), which sweated and kept the water cool by evaporation. Wine was readily to hand, so Maria often used it as a cooking liquid. The wine not only saved trips to the spring, but also imparted its rich, full flavours to many of her dishes, including this chicken sauté. Although dry Sherry (*fino*) is excellent, I especially like to prepare this chicken dish using a medium Sherry, called *oloroso seco*.

Maria prepared this tapa dish with a whole chicken hacked into bite-sized pieces. I don't like the splintery bones that result, so I prefer to substitute whole wing joints and split thighs when preparing the chicken for tapas. For a main course, chicken parts – legs, thighs and breasts – can be used, but allow a longer cooking time.

Don't be shy about the garlic! The whole garlic cloves are left unpeeled so the skins prevent them from burning. Real aficionados of this dish eat the whole, sweet cloves of garlic along with the chicken.

This recipe is also delicious with rabbit.

The chicken is usually served with Spanish Chips (page 162) added right to the sauce. Chunks of bread are essential for dipping into the garlicky juices.

900 g (2 lb) small chicken wings and thighs
Salt and freshly ground black pepper
1 whole head garlic (12 to 16 cloves)
5 tablespoons olive oil
1 bay leaf
2 tablespoons Spanish brandy (optional)
120 ml (4 fl oz) dry or medium-dry Sherry
Chopped fresh flat-leaf parsley

Cut off the wing tips and discard (or save for stock). Divide each wing into two joints. Cut the thighs lengthwise along the bone. Pat dry the pieces of chicken and dust them with salt and pepper.

Lightly smash the garlic cloves to split the skins. Set aside eight of them, unpeeled. Peel the remaining cloves and slice them.

Heat the oil in a deep frying pan over medium heat. Add the sliced garlic and sauté just until golden, 1 to 2 minutes, then skim them out and reserve.

Add the chicken pieces to the oil and fry over medium-high heat, until the chicken is browned on all sides, 12 to 15 minutes. Add the unpeeled cloves of garlic, the bay leaf, brandy, if using, and Sherry. Continue cooking over high heat until the liquid is almost cooked away and the chicken begins to sizzle again, 8 to 10 minutes.

Serve immediately, garnished with the reserved fried garlic bits and chopped parsley.

Serves 6 to 8

SPICED MEATBALLS IN ALMOND SAUCE
ALBÓNDIGAS EN SALSA DE ALMENDRAS

Most Spanish words that start with 'al', as in *albóndigas* and *almendras*, derive from the Arabic. The Moors – Arabs who invaded Spain in 711 AD and ruled parts of the country for nearly eight centuries – contributed much besides language. Many spices, such as the saffron, cloves and nutmeg in this recipe, as well as almonds were introduced into Spanish cooking by the Moors. This meatball dish, popular in tapa bars today, comes from a recipe I found in a twelfth-century Moorish cookbook – with a few changes, of course, as the Muslims did not use pork or wine.

I make a 'light' version of this dish, using minced turkey instead of beef and pork, then poaching the meatballs in salt-free stock. I use the stock in the sauce.

If served as a main course, the meatballs typically would be accompanied by Spanish Chips (page 162). I like them served with noodles.

MEATBALLS

340 g (12 oz) minced beef

340 g (12 oz) minced pork

2 slices stale bread, crusts removed

1 garlic clove, finely chopped

3 tablespoons finely chopped onion

2 tablespoons chopped fresh flat-leaf parsley

½ teaspoon salt

⅛ teaspoon freshly grated nutmeg

2 eggs, beaten

Plain flour, for dredging (about 4 tablespoons)

4 tablespoons olive oil

SAUCE

2 tablespoons olive oil

115 g (4 oz) almonds, blanched and skinned (page 6)

1 slice bread, crusts removed

3 garlic cloves

10 peppercorns

½ teaspoon saffron threads

1 clove

½ teaspoon salt

140 ml (¼ pint) white wine

240 ml (8 fl oz) chicken or meat stock

Chopped fresh flat-leaf parsley

To make the meatballs, combine the minced beef and pork in a bowl. Soak the bread in water to cover until soft. Squeeze it out and add to the meat with the garlic, onion, parsley, salt, nutmeg and eggs. Knead well to make a smooth mixture.

Form the meat mixture into 2.5-cm (1-inch) balls and roll them in flour. Heat the oil in a large frying pan over medium heat and fry the meatballs in batches slowly until browned on all sides, about 6 minutes. Remove and drain.

To make the sauce, pour the oil into a deep frying pan or other deep pan over medium heat and fry the almonds, bread and 2 garlic cloves in the oil until golden, about 2 minutes. Remove, reserving the oil in the pan. Set aside a few almonds for garnish.

In a mortar, crush the peppercorns, saffron, clove and salt. In a blender or food processor, grind together the fried almonds, bread, fried garlic and remaining garlic clove with the wine to make a smooth paste. Add the spices to this mixture.

Stir the almond mixture into the oil remaining in the pan and add the stock. Bring to the boil, then add the fried meatballs. Simmer the meatballs, covered, for 20 to 30 minutes, adding a little additional liquid if needed.

Serve the meatballs garnished with the reserved toasted almonds and chopped parsley.

SERVES 10 TO 12

TRIPE STEW, MADRID STYLE
CALLOS A LA MADRILEÑA

I first visited Spain in 1962, when I was a summer school student at the University of Madrid. I lived in a university residence and, for about two weeks, I actually attended classes. Classes began in the mornings at about 9 AM, just as they would on an American campus. However, I quickly realized that much of Madrid life, intellectual, social and otherwise, didn't begin until late in the night.

Once I gave up trying to get to classes, I met lots of interesting people – intense intellectuals who had no money, covert socialists who could have been jailed for their politics, and well-to-do students who lived in big villas with swimming pools in the suburbs.

I thought the Spanish schedule was brilliant. I could go out with one guy early in the evening – a stroll in the Retiro Park with stops at a few tapa bars – then go back to my residence for the evening meal at 9.30 PM, then go out dancing with another crowd at 11 PM until the wee hours of the morning.

This hearty stewed tripe is one of the dishes I tried on those thrilling forays into Madrid nightlife. I found it so exotic on my first visit, and it is still a favourite. It was once made only in huge quantities, when a butcher sold off all of the tripe (lining of the stomach) from a calf, the calf's foot (which is more than a foot long), and sometimes the fleshy parts of the muzzle, in one big package. Many tapa bars still prepare it in big batches, then freeze small servings to be microwaved to order.

If you can buy already cooked tripe, this is an easy dish to prepare – just make the sauce (use beef or chicken stock in place of the cooking liquid) and add to the tripe to simmer a while longer. The directions given are for tripe that is clean and ready to cook.

T

TRIPE

900 g (2 lb) calves' tripe, cleaned and ready
to cook

120 ml (4 fl oz) white wine vinegar

½ calf's foot or 1 pig's trotter

1 small onion, peeled

4 cloves

8 peppercorns

1 teaspoon salt

3 bay leaves

SAUCE

4 *ñoras* (dried red sweet peppers) or
additional pimentón

1 small, dried, medium-hot chilli

3 tablespoons olive oil

1 onion, chopped

1 carrot, sliced

4 garlic cloves

1½ tablespoons plain flour

2 teaspoons pimentón

4 tablespoons dry Sherry

230 g (8 oz) chopped tomato

½ teaspoon salt

⅛ teaspoon freshly ground black pepper

¼ teaspoon ground cumin

⅛ teaspoon ground cinnamon

Cooking liquid or stock

TO FINISH THE COOKING

2 tablespoons olive oil

4 thick slices bacon (about 115 g/4 oz),
chopped

85 g (3 oz) soft chorizo or longaniza
sausage, sliced

2 tablespoons brandy

Cut the tripe into 4-cm (1½-inch) squares.
Combine them in a large pan with the vinegar
and water to cover. Bring to a full boil and cook
for 5 minutes. Drain and return the tripe to the
pan with fresh water to cover. Bring again to the
boil and drain.

Blanch the split calf's foot or pig's trotter in
boiling water for 5 minutes and drain. Combine
the tripe and calf's foot in a large, clean pan.
Stud the onion with cloves and add to the pan
with 2.25 litres (4 pints) water, peppercorns, salt
and bay leaves. Bring to the boil, then turn
down to a simmer, cover the pan and cook
gently until the tripe is very tender, about 2½
hours. Drain, saving the liquid, but discarding
the onion and bay leaves.

Remove and discard the skin and bone from
the calf's foot. Set aside the tripe and reserved
meat from the calf's foot. Cool the stock and
skim off any fat. (Tripe can be cooked in
advance and kept refrigerated or frozen.)

To make the sauce, remove the seeds and stems from the dried *ñoras* and chilli and put them to soak in hot water to cover for 1 hour.

Heat the oil in a frying pan over medium heat and add the onion and carrot. Sauté until the onion is browned, about 5 minutes. Add the garlic and fry for another minute, then stir in the flour and pimentón. Add the Sherry and tomato to the pan, with the salt, pepper, cumin and cinnamon.

Scrape the pulp from the *ñoras* and chilli, discarding the skins, and add to the pan. (The soaking liquid can be saved to use later in the recipe.) Add about 340 ml (12 fl oz) of the reserved liquid in which the tripe cooked. Simmer the sauce for 40 minutes. Purée it in a blender or food processor and, if desired, sieve the sauce.

To finish the cooking, heat the oil in a cazuela over high heat and fry the bacon for 1 minute. Add the cooked tripe and calf's foot meat to the oil and let it just begin to brown, about 3 minutes. Add the sauce, the sliced sausage, the brandy and a little additional liquid (such as the soaking liquid from the peppers).

Simmer the tripe for 40 minutes, adding additional liquid if needed to prevent the sauce from sticking. Refrigerate (or freeze) the tripe stew. To serve, reheat on the hob or in the microwave.

SERVES 8

SNAILS IN PIQUANT SAUCE

CARACOLES EN SALSA PICANTE

Some tapa bars specialize in snails served in a spicy sauce. You use a straight pin to extract the snails from the shells, then mop up the sauce with bread. Finish off with finger licking.

Markets in Spain sell three or four different varieties of live snail. I realize you probably won't have this selection available in Britain. But the sauce is so good that perhaps you would like to try this dish using tinned snails, which require no previous fasting or cooking. They are sometimes sold with the shells in a separate packet. These can be used over and over again.

If you should be able to buy or collect live snails, keep them fasting in a box for a week, with only a little wheat flour or maize meal (polenta). Then wash them and put in a basin with water to cover and 4 tablespoons of vinegar and 1 tablespoon salt. Let them soak for 1 hour. Drain, then rinse in running water until they no longer froth. Put the snails in a pan of warm water and bring very slowly to the boil. Cook for 10 minutes at a slow boil. Drain and discard the water.

6 dozen cooked or tinned snails

4 tablespoons olive oil

115 g (4 oz) bacon, diced

1 onion, chopped

1 leek (white part only), chopped

1 carrot, chopped

4 garlic cloves, chopped

450 g (1 lb) chopped tomatoes, fresh or tinned

2 teaspoons pimentón

Crushed red chilli flakes

½ teaspoon ground cumin

¼ teaspoon fennel seeds

Salt and freshly ground black pepper

240 ml (8 fl oz) white wine

1 tablespoon chopped fresh flat-leaf parsley

Bread, to serve

If you are using tinned snails, rinse them. Stick one cooked or tinned snail into each shell.

Heat the oil in a cazuela or casserole over medium heat. Sauté the bacon, onion, leek, carrot and garlic until softened, about 15 minutes. Add the tomatoes, pimentón and red chilli flakes. Use enough red chilli to give the sauce a little jolt. Season with cumin, fennel seeds, salt and pepper. Simmer for 15 minutes, until the tomatoes are somewhat reduced.

Add the wine, parsley and the snails. Bring to the boil, then simmer slowly, covered, for 45 minutes.

Serve the snails and sauce in bowls with bread to accompany.

SERVES 6

3

BREAD

Country Bread (*Pan Campesino*)

Catalan Toasts (*Pan Catalán*)

Olive Oil Breakfast Buns (*Tortas de Aceite*)

Breadsticks (*Piquitos*)

Farm-Style Bread Crumbs (*Migas a la Cortijera*)

OUR DAILY BREAD

After several years of living in the village, I moved to a mill house a few miles outside town. It was no longer a working mill, because the mill stream that once drove the wheels that ground the wheat had disappeared into the earth. The water now emerged in a roaring torrent, well below the house. I did my laundry in the stream – hanging on to every sock so that it not be carried away by the strong sweep of water. I paid a man to carry water up to the house, filling huge clay jars which served for household purposes. The granite mill wheel was my patio table.

Pedro and Isabel were our nearest neighbours. Pedro farmed the big field below the mill house, growing wheat, maize and beans in succession. He ploughed the field with a pair of oxen. They were massive creatures, cows with horns, named Clavellina and Sevillana ('little carnation' and 'little one from Seville'). If I had to cross the field to visit a friend on the far side, I made sure these beasts were nowhere around.

After harvesting his wheat, Pedro threshed it on a cobbled threshing floor, driving a wooden sledge pulled by a mule through the wheat. Once threshed, the wheat was tossed into the wind, to separate the grain from the chaff, then carried to a mill to be ground into flour.

Today, hardly any wheat is grown locally and the threshing floors, usually located on promontories with spectacular views, are desirable building sites. The wheat comes from industrial mills. But village bakeries still bake bread fresh every day.

I learned to make country bread with Antonia, who grew up on a smallholding about five miles from the village on a rough dirt path. Before country folk had Land-Rovers, they seldom shopped in the village. Bread-making was part of the self-sufficient life. Even after Antonia's family moved to town, her mother, Ana, frequently returned to the country house on weekends, to tend a garden and bake bread the old-fashioned way in a wood-fired oven. Antonia invited me to come along.

To make the bread, Ana poured about 5.5 kg (12 lb) of flour into a wide earthenware bowl, called a *lebrillo*, which measured about 75 cm (30 inches) across. When they lived in the country, Ana told me, she made 20 kg (45 lb) at a time, enough bread to last the family an entire week.

Ana knelt on the floor in front of the hearth, where a big saucepan of soup was bubbling over a fire. On her knees she got better leverage for kneading. To the flour she added about 1 kg (roughly 2 lb) of starter dough, *masa de levadura*, which she purchased at a bakery in town. This is, like sourdough, simply some of the dough from the previous day that is left to ferment.

Some salt was added, a *puñado* (a little handful), and nothing else. No sugar, no fat, no milk, no egg. Ana made a well in the centre of the heap of flour and Antonia poured in water heated in a blackened kettle near the coals. Ana plunged her arms elbow-deep into the sticky dough and began kneading. Antonia stayed close at hand and seemed always to know when to add more water. The dough was worked for more than 30 minutes, a strenuous job.

When the dough was finished, the two women began shaping the loaves. Ana would pull free a double handful of dough, knead it briefly, and hand it to her daughter, who patted and shaped it quickly into a flattened circle, the typical *hogaza* (round loaf). They made eight of these big loaves and another dozen smaller ones.

The loaves were placed on top of a doubled cloth on a wooden table and covered so as not to 'catch a cold'. Bread dough must never touch cold surfaces such as marble, cautioned Ana. When all the loaves were shaped, they were 'put to sleep', tucked snugly in a folded blanket. The bread was to be left sleeping for about two hours.

During this time Ana and her son started the fire in the domed bread oven. Typically, it was situated at a little distance from the house. Made of brick, the inside of the oven is vaulted to provide the best circulation of heat. The floor surface, measuring about 1.5 metres (5 feet) in diameter, can hold several loaves in a single layer. A mortar of clay and whitewash holds the bricks of the oven together. The outside is usually 'plastered' with a similar mixture and kept whitewashed. It has a small arched door and, at the back, a small hole to provide an inlet for fresh air.

Earlier, the family had gathered heaps of small branches pruned from the olive trees the previous winter and wild shrubs, such as gorse, furze, broom and a few twigs of rosemary. These were added to the oven as fuel.

The brittle twigs of the brush burst quickly into flame, slowly igniting the thicker roots and wood stalks. They continued feeding in fuel, adding more as the previous layer burned down. Ana explained that the oven had to be heated till the bricks inside the oven door turned white.

Once the oven was hot enough, the table with the loaves was moved outside. Unwrapped from their blanket, they were not quite doubled in bulk, but would continue to rise in the oven.

Antonia pushed the coals and ashes to one side of the oven and swabbed the bottom of the oven with a rag mop soaked in water to clean it of ash. Ana made the *bendición* (a blessing with the sign of the Cross) on each loaf before placing it on a baker's peel, a long-handled wooden paddle. Antonia slid each loaf on to the oven floor. When all were placed, she closed the oven door and the air inlet with metal sheets.

The large round loaves took almost an hour to bake. Using the paddle, Antonia pulled them out one by one. Ana caught them in her apron, brushing off the ash, and placed them again on the table. The bread was kept wrapped until partially cooled to sweat out excess humidity. Properly baked and cooled, the bread could be stored in a big wicker basket or a *talega* (a cloth bag) for an entire week. By the end of the week, although the crust was hard as rock, the bread would still be good.

Knowing Ana was baking bread, various neighbours had gathered on the patio, shaded by fronds of wild cane. Ana laid out a shallow dish of olive oil and brought a knife. She picked up a still-warm loaf and with the tip of the knife made the sign of the Cross on the bread and kissed it. She cut it into thick slabs and handed them around.

This bread was a deep gold colour with a thick, hard crust. Inside, the crumb was a little moist, very dense and fine-textured. And the fragrance – faintly smoky, with a subtle, sour, yeasty aroma and the soul-satisfying smell of toasted grain.

El pan nuestro de cada día. Our daily bread. As it has been made since time immemorial.

It is hard to overestimate the importance of bread in Spanish cooking and Spanish life. There is an expression that says *sin pan no se puede comer* (you can't eat without bread). Without bread, there is no food. Another old proverb says that every child comes into the world with a loaf of bread tucked under his arm. Bread accompanies every meal, or becomes the meal itself. Spoon in the right hand, chunk of bread in the left, it is used as a tool, a sop.

For breakfast at home, bread is dipped into a dish of olive oil. In simple working men's cafés, it is drizzled with oil from a cruet placed on every table. I once watched an old farmer pour olive oil on a slab of bread, then break it into small bits and add it to a big cup of sweetened barley coffee with hot milk, thus making instant porridge.

No crumb is wasted. Even when several days old, this bread makes great toast (see Catalan Toasts, page 58). Stale bread can be wrapped and frozen for use in thickening sauces (for example, see Chicken in Almond-Saffron Sauce, page 247), soups (see Castilian Garlic Soup, page 81), gazpachos, stuffing and even desserts. You can use shop-bought bread for all of these recipes, but I think that you'll find them even better with home-baked bread.

COUNTRY BREAD

PAN CAMPESINO

This is the essential, basic bread recipe, adapted for a home kitchen. I have used yeast in place of the 'mother' dough. However, should you have a sourdough starter, do try it in this recipe. If you have a brick pizza oven or other wood-fired oven, by all means use it for baking bread. If you have a stone for baking pizza, place the loaves on it for baking. Or slide the loaves into wide earthenware cazuelas that have been preheated in the oven. The preheated stone or cazuela helps to give the loaves a good crust. If one is not available, just bake the loaves on baking sheets.

Note that you must start this recipe the day before you plan to bake the bread.

670 ml (1¼ pints) warm (46°C/115°F)
    water

2 packets active dried yeast

1 teaspoon sugar

1.4 kg (3 lb) strong flour

4 teaspoons salt

DAY BEFORE BAKING

Pour 240 ml (8 fl oz) of warm water in a medium bowl and sprinkle on the yeast. Stir to dissolve it. Add the sugar and stir in 280g (10 oz) of the flour until combined. Cover the bowl with a damp cloth and set it in a draught-free place to ferment overnight.

BAKING DAY

Rinse a large, wide china mixing bowl in very hot water to warm it and wipe it dry. Combine the remaining flour and salt in the warmed bowl. Make a well in the centre. Add the soft dough that fermented overnight to the flour, then gently pour in 240 ml (8 fl oz) warm water. With a wooden spoon, begin stirring the flour into the liquid in the centre, incorporating the yeast dough. When the dough is too stiff to work with the spoon, add the remaining 240 ml (8 fl oz) warm water.

Begin kneading the dough. Work it in the bowl or turn it out on to a board. Don't work the dough on marble, tile or other cold surfaces. The dough will be dry and crumbly at first, but becomes smooth with kneading. Knead the dough for at least 15 minutes, until it is smooth, stretchy and almost glossy looking.

Divide the dough in half. Cover one half with a clean tea towel and set aside. Knead the other half for 1 minute, then shape it into a smooth ball. Pat it out into a 20-cm (8-inch) round. Sprinkle a clean cloth with a little flour and place the loaf of dough on top. Cover the loaf with a clean, dry cloth and set it in a warm place to rise. (A Spanish housewife would cover the loaves with a folded blanket.)

Repeat with the second piece of dough. Or, alternatively, divide the remaining dough in half and shape each piece into a 30-cm (12-inch) oblong loaf. Place them on a floured cloth and cover with a dry cloth.

Let the dough rise for 1½ to 2 hours. The dough will not double in bulk.

Preheat the oven to 230°C/450°F/gas mark 8. If you are using a baker's stone or earthenware cazuelas, place them in lower third of oven and preheat them also.

When loaves have risen, use a baker's peel or a thin baking sheet to slide under the risen loaves, and then ease them on to the preheated stone.

Bake for 15 minutes.

Lower the oven temperature to 180°C/350°F/gas mark 4. Spray or brush loaves with water to encourage a thicker crust. Bake for 15 minutes more. Small loaves should be done, and can be removed at this point.

Spray the larger loaves again with water and bake for 20 to 25 minutes more. The loaves should be golden-brown and, if tapped, have a hollow resonance.

Remove from the oven and let them cool completely.

MAKES TWO 1-KG (2-LB) ROUND LOAVES

CATALAN TOASTS
PAN CATALÁN

In Catalonia, this dish is called 'bread with tomato', but elsewhere in the country it's usually known as 'Catalan toast'. It is served for breakfast, as a snack or as a tapa. Use day-old country bread or baguette to make the toasts.

1 ripe tomato

6 diagonal slices baguette, about 4 cm (1½ inches) thick

1 garlic clove, cut in half

2 tablespoons extra virgin olive oil

6 thin slices serrano ham (60 g/2 oz)

Cut the tomato in half crosswise and grate it coarsely, discarding the skin. Arrange the bread slices on a grill pan and place under the grill until lightly toasted on both sides.

Rub each toast with a cut clove of garlic and spread the tomato pulp on top. Drizzle each with a teaspoon of oil. Arrange the sliced ham on top. Serve immediately.

SERVES 6

OLIVE OIL BREAKFAST BUNS
TORTAS DE ACEITE

I go into the village several mornings a week to shop, to check the post and buy a newspaper and, most importantly, to sit in a café in the plaza and have a *café con leche* (espresso coffee with milk), served in a small glass. Sometimes I order one of these slightly sweet, cinnamony buns to go with the coffee. *Torta* just means a round, flat cake, so quite a few different foods receive the name. (A different sort of *torta de aceite* appears in chapter 12.)

½ recipe for Country Bread dough
    (page 56)

240 ml (8 fl oz) olive oil

1 strip orange zest

1 tablespoon aniseed

115 g (4 oz) plus 1 tablespoon sugar,
    for sprinkling tops

1 teaspoon bicarbonate of soda

1 teaspoon ground cinnamon

140 g (5 oz) plain flour

4 tablespoons almond halves

Oil a large bowl. Place the kneaded bread dough in the bowl, turn it to oil both sides and cover with a damp cloth. Put in a warm place to rise until doubled in bulk, 1 to 2 hours.

Combine the oil in a small pan with the orange zest and heat over medium heat until the zest begins to turn brown, 2 to 3 minutes. Remove from the heat and stir in the aniseed. Let the oil cool completely, then remove and discard the orange zest.

Stir 115 g (4 oz) of sugar, the bicarbonate of soda and cinnamon into the cooled oil.

Knock back the dough. Pour the oil mixture into the depression in the dough and begin kneading it in. Sprinkle with some of the flour and continue working the oil into the dough, gradually adding the remainder of the flour. When most of the oil has been absorbed, turn the dough out on to a floured board and knead it for a few minutes.

Cover with a cloth and allow to rise for 30 minutes.

Lightly dust 2 or 3 baking sheets with flour. Break off pieces of dough about the size of an egg. Pat them out into 10-cm (4-inch) circles. Place them on the prepared baking sheets. Sprinkle the tops with the remaining tablespoon of sugar and place an almond half in the centre of each. Let rise in a warm place for 30 minutes.

Preheat the oven to 180°C/350°F/gas mark 4.

Bake the buns in upper and lower oven shelves, switching position and rotating pans halfway through baking until they are lightly golden, about 20 minutes total.

Cool the buns on a rack. They may be stored in an airtight container for up to 1 week.

MAKES 24 BUNS

BREADSTICKS

PIQUITOS

Breadsticks are often served with tapas. These crisp and crunchy whole-grain breadsticks are so good you can eat them without the tapa.

1 packet active dried yeast

1 teaspoon sugar

170 ml (6 fl oz) warm water (46°C/115°F)

4 tablespoons olive oil

1 teaspoon salt

340 g (12 oz) wholemeal flour

Combine the yeast and sugar in a mixing bowl and add the warm water. Let stand for 5 minutes to activate the yeast.

Add the oil and salt to the yeast. Stir in the flour. Then turn out on a lightly floured board and knead until the dough is smooth and elastic, about 5 minutes.

Place the dough in an oiled bowl. Turn it to coat both sides. Cover with a dampened cloth and put it in a warm, draught-free place to rise until doubled in bulk, about 1 hour.

Preheat the oven to 200°C/400°F/gas mark 6.

Lightly dust baking sheets with flour. Knock the dough back. Divide it into 15 or 16 balls. Roll them out into long, thin ropes (3 mm/⅛ inch thick). Cut them into 13-cm (5-inch) lengths. Place them on the baking sheets.

Bake for 15 minutes. Shake the breadsticks on the baking sheets to turn them, rotate the sheets and return them to the oven for 5 to 10 minutes more, until golden and crisp. (The baking time depends on how thickly you have rolled the sticks.)

Cool the breadsticks on a rack and store in an airtight container.

MAKES 36 BREADSTICKS

FARM-STYLE BREADCRUMBS
MIGAS A LA CORTIJERA

This is breakfast food for country people everywhere. *Migas* means 'crumbs', and most versions are made with crumbled stale bread, fried up with bits of ham and garlic. Other versions may be made with semolina or with maize meal – much like polenta.

Migas are served with an eclectic selection of accompaniments, including fresh grapes or raisins, raw spring onions, thick chocolate sauce, tinned or fresh sardines, pomegranates, radishes and melon. *Migas* make a fine side dish with pork chops or fried eggs.

Ideally, the bread should be dense, fine-textured country bread, baked in a round loaf, two days old.

230 g (8 oz) stale bread (8 slices)

5 tablespoons olive oil

2 garlic cloves, quartered lengthwise

**3 thick slices lean bacon (85g/3 oz),
    cut crosswise in strips**

½ teaspoon salt

1 teaspoon pimentón

Pinch ground cumin

Pinch ground cloves

Pinch freshly ground black pepper

A few grapes or raisins

Cut the bread into 1-cm (½-inch) cubes. Place the cubed bread in a bowl and sprinkle with ½ cup water. Toss the bread bits until they are damp, but not soaked. Place them on a dampened tea towel and wrap them tightly. Leave to stand overnight (or for at least 6 hours).

Heat the oil in a deep frying pan or earthenware casserole over medium heat. Fry the pieces of garlic and strips of bacon until lightly browned, 3 to 4 minutes, then skim them out and reserve, keeping the bacon fat in the pan.

Add the bread bits to the pan. Fry the crumbs over medium heat, turning them constantly with a spatula. At first they will tend to stick to the pan. Keep stirring until they are loose and lightly toasted, about 20 minutes. Keep cutting the bread with the edge of the spatula to gradually reduce the cubes to crumbs.

Stir in the salt, pimentón, cumin, cloves and pepper. Return the fried garlic and bacon to the pan and give everything another few turns. The breadcrumbs should be slightly crunchy, not crisp. Garnish with grapes or raisins.

SERVES 4 AS A SIDE DISH; SERVES 2 FOR BREAKFAST

In the Olive Groves

It is February and I have just decanted 4 gallons of new, virgin olive oil from plastic jugs – which I distrust – into glass bottles. This golden treasure is the return on my olive crop for this year and will last me well into the next year. In my kitchen, it is virtually the only cooking fat used. I use butter in a few baked goods; I never use margarine, and I never use other vegetable oils. I even use olive oil for Chinese stir-fry. Lard enters in for some specific Spanish dishes.

To sample the new oil, I first dribble it over toasted bread. So good! But the real test is always chips ('French' fries, which, of course, are 'Spanish' fries). Sensational. The oil is fruity, with just a slight touch of bitterness, which I like. The new oil is golden, not green. It is cloudy, but will clear somewhat as it settles in the coming months.

I built my house in southern Spain in a small olive grove, on a steep hillside overlooking the Mediterranean. In excavating the footings for the house, we had to uproot one small olive tree. The workmen cut off all the top foliage and dug down only several feet and cut off the tap root. Moved to a new location, the tree has thrived.

Although I come from a place very different from Spain – the American Midwest, Illinois, maize and soya bean country – after so many years here, I feel I have put down roots as deep as the trees. My children were born right here in this very olive grove.

After I bought the land, I asked Bernabé, a ploughman with two mules who hired himself out to farmers in the area, to plough the terraces on which the olives were planted. The first year, with sunny winter days, my husband and I knocked olives and picked them, a handful at a time, filling hessian bags and lugging them to the mill. Our 'cash crop' earned us about 5p an hour.

The next year I arranged for a local family to pick the olives. *Muy formal*, they tallied the sacks and agreed to pay me a landowner's percentage. I just asked that they bring me some oil. That year, after the pickers had finished, a youth came to the door and asked if he could gather the *huesos al suelo*, the withered olive pits still on the ground, which he could sell for lesser-grade oil. I let him. Even the local goatherd came round and asked if he could prune the trees and use the olive prunings to feed his goats.

Then for many years, Antonia's mother, Ana, was in charge of the olive picking. She walked to and from the village, even on rainy days, scrambled up trees, knelt on the ground to strip the fruit from branches cut down by her son. On weekends in fine weather, her grandchildren spent the day with her. As she became more elderly, her children retired her from olive picking.

Since then, I cannot find anyone to pick my olives. Well-paying jobs are more plentiful and olive picking on such a small scale is not worth anyone's while. So, I am delighted when my grown sons come home for Christmas holidays and help me pick olives.

Olive Oil and Spain Olive oil is basic to Spanish cooking, and it has been for several millennia. The tree is native to the Mediterranean countries of the Middle East and has been cultivated in the countries around the Mediterranean for more than six thousand years.

The olive was first planted in Spain by the Greeks and the Phoenicians. Besides its use in cooking, the oil was valued for light, for medicinal purposes and for beauty treatments. When Spain became part of the Roman Empire, the olive plantations were extended in a wide swathe across what is now Andalusia, the provinces of Jaén, Córdoba and Seville. Hundreds of oil mills were situated on the banks of the Genil and Guadalquivir rivers, and from there the oil was easily transported to the sea to be shipped to Rome.

In 711 AD, the Moors – Muslim Arabs – swarmed across the Straits of Gibraltar, taking over most of Spain. They extended the cultivation of olive trees even further. In the Spanish language, the word for the tree is *olivo*, which derives from the Latin; but the names for the fruit and the oil, *aceituna* and *aceite*, come from the Arabic. The Arabic word for oil – *al-zait* – translates as 'olive juice'.

Spain's Production of Olive Oil
Spain produces a huge amount of olive oil. Production ranges from 600,000 to 800,000 metric tons yearly and represents between 35 and 47 per cent of the worldwide production. Olive groves extend over 5 million acres of Spain's landscape. There are 309,000,000 olive trees.

About 75 per cent of Spanish olive oil comes from Andalusia. The provinces of Jaén and Córdoba, where vast expanses, as far as the eye can see, are covered with olive trees, are Andalusia's largest producers.

However, if you take a look at the shelves in an American supermarket, you might decide that all olive oil comes from Italy. That's because Spain came late to marketing. Spanish olive oil is shipped in bulk to Italy, where it is bottled and exported to the United States and elsewhere. If the label says, 'Imported from Italy', it could well be Spanish oil, packaged in Italy for export.

How Olive Oil Is Produced
The olive is a drought-tolerant tree that typically has been dry-farmed in frost-free regions where few other crops would grow. The tree is not deciduous, and it is extremely long-lived. Trees that are hundreds of years old still produce olives.

However, modern agricultural research has shown that yield is heaviest with young trees. So there has been quite a revolution in olive growing in the past twenty years. New groves are being planted with all the trees equidistant, so they can easily be cultivated with tractors. In some regions, irrigation from underground aquifers is used. There are even mechanical vibrators that shake the olives off the trees. New varieties and clones are being developed.

In spite of some changes in the harvesting, olive picking is still labour-intensive. In just one province, Jaén, the olive crop generates 62,000 jobs.

Olives for oil are picked when they have ripened sufficiently. Most varieties – there are dozens in Spain – do not turn really black when ripe, but a greenish-purplish colour.

The harvest begins in late November and continues until around the first of February. (Table olives, which are a special variety, are usually picked green, much earlier than oil olives.)

The pickers spread nets or tarpaulins under the tree to catch the olives. Then they use long poles to thrash the branches, causing the fruit to drop. The olives are collected in baskets and hauled to the oil mill. The sooner they are pressed, the better will be the oil. Olives that are stored in huge bins for many days before pressing begin to ferment, producing bad oil. Nowadays this stronger oil is refined.

Olive oil is practically the only oil that can be consumed virgin and crude, without further refining. In the extraction of other oils, both heat and solvents are used, so the resulting oil must then be treated by chemicals to neutralize, decolourize, and deodorize it before it's fit for human consumption.

In small local olive mills, called *almazaras,* the olives are first washed, then crushed by stones or steel wheels to release the oil. The pulp is spread on mats woven of esparto grass or of polymer synthetics. These are stacked on a hydraulic press, which squeezes the pulp tighter and tighter, allowing the oil to flow out through channels at the bottom.

The oil is filtered into a series of settling tanks. The oil rises to the top and is drawn off. The sediment and water content settle to the bottom.

In more modern mills, a centrifugal process is used. The olives are crushed and mixed with warmed water, then spun at high speed to separate the oil from the water. Either way, the resulting product is virgin olive oil.

How good that oil tastes depends on several factors, such as the variety of olive, the soil, the climate, the ripeness, but, most important, how the olives are picked, transported, stored and milled. Its colour can vary from pale gold to amber to almost green, depending on the variety of olive.

Olive Oil and Health For centuries, olive oil has been the principal fat in the cuisine of Mediterranean peoples. Everything from glowing complexions to good digestive systems and strong hearts have been attributed to its beneficial qualities. Now, of course, modern nutritional science is verifying the folklore.

Olive oil is a mono-unsaturated fat. Mono-unsaturates lower the bad cholesterol levels (LDL) and raise the good cholesterol levels (HDL), the ones that help clear your arteries of plaque. Comparative dietary studies show that the mortality rate for cardiovascular disease is much lower among Mediterranean peoples who consume olive oil than it is among northern Europeans and North Americans who consume more fats of animal origin.

Virgin olive oil contains a natural balance of antioxidants, which prevent the oil from turning rancid without additives. It also has a good dose of natural vitamins – A, E, D and K. So digestible is olive oil that it is used in protective diets for ulcer patients and diabetics.

Selecting Olive Oil There's really no such thing as 'light' olive oil. All oils and fats have 9 kcal per gram. Olive oil contains no cholesterol. Some olive oils, however, may be paler in colour or blander in flavour.

Virgin olive oil is oil that has been extracted solely by mechanical means – crushing and pressing – without the use of high temperatures or chemicals that alter the oil's composition.

Virgin oil can be labelled virgin or extra virgin. Extra virgin oil has a maximum of 1 per cent acidity (oleic acid). This is the most expensive olive oil, though even among the extra virgins there are variations in quality and price. For example, those made by artisan methods might be better in flavour and much more expensive. Organic olive oil is also pricier, as are those oils which have *denominación de origen* (DO), a designated origin label.

Next are virgin oils that are not labelled extra. They are still 100 per cent natural but are allowed an acidity of between 1 and 2 per cent. They may be stronger in flavour than extra virgin oils, but are less expensive. However, this category is hard to find in Britain or North America.

The third category of oil is simply labelled 'olive oil' or 'pure olive oil'. This, in fact, is olive oil that has been refined. It comes from virgin oil that, after extraction, is deemed to be too strong or with off flavours or too high in oleic acid to be consumed virgin. It is refined – as other seed oils are refined – by a process of neutralization, decolouration and deodorization. A distillation process is involved, which changes the structure of the oil. Once purified, it is then mixed with a small portion of good virgin oil in order to restore some of the olive flavour. These oils are the least expensive.

How do you choose olive oil? You really have to experiment a little. If olive oil is a new flavour for you, start with a bland oil. Extra virgin oil is fairly expensive compared to other oil, so use it where you want its special flavour to stand out, especially in any dish where the oil is uncooked.

Extra virgin oil is also excellent for cooked dishes, including frying. But because it's expensive, this might be where you want to use a refined oil. Use olive oil to sauté, stir-fry, deep-fry and braise.

Olive Oil in Spanish Cooking Spanish cooking isn't Spanish without olive oil. There is no substitute for it. It is a basic food, a basic flavour. Some of the most famous Spanish dishes, such as gazpacho, paella and potato tortilla, depend on olive oil. In Spanish cuisine, sauces are almost all based on olive oil.

Frying in olive oil not only produces tasty food, but tests have shown that potatoes fried in olive oil absorb less fat than those fried in sunflower or soya oil. Additionally, the olive oil can be used many times, whereas the other oils begin to decompose and release toxic components.

Tips for Cooking with Olive Oil Virgin olive oil has natural protection against oxidation and rancidity but I still don't recommend keeping it longer than 12 to 18 months. Don't refrigerate olive oil, but do keep it in a cool place (not by the cooker), tightly capped and, most importantly, protected from the light. A dark cupboard is fine. Although some oils are marketed in plastic containers, fine virgin oils are best stored in glass.

For deep-frying, heat the oil to 182°C/ 360°F, just below the smoking point. At this temperature, a cube of bread will turn golden in 25 seconds. Whether you use a deep-fat fryer or a deep frying pan, don't crowd the pieces of food in the oil. After use, cool the oil and strain it and it can be used again.

Serve olive oil on breakfast toast. Use it in cake baking, in stir-fries and in sautés. Olive oil makes the best chips in the world. Fry eggs in it. Drizzle it on baked potatoes. Toss it with cooked vegetables. On popcorn. Sprinkle on sliced fresh tomatoes. Use it for browning meat, in marinades, for basting. It is wonderful stuff.

4

GAZPACHOS, SOUPS AND ONE-POT MEALS

GAZPACHOS

Country Gazpacho (*Gazpacho Campesino*)

Gazpacho Today (*El Gazpacho de Hoy*)

Gazpacho Cream, Córdoba Style
   (*Salmorejo Cordobés*)

Almond Gazpacho with Grapes (*Ajo Blanco con Uvas*)

White Gazpacho with Pine Kernels
   (*Gazpacho Blanco con Piñones*)

Winter Gazpacho (*Gazpacho de Invierno*)

Hot Gazpacho (*Gazpacho Caliente*)

SOUPS

Castilian Garlic Soup (*Sopa de Ajo Castellana*)

Simple Stock (*Caldo Sencillo*)

Almond Soup (*Sopa de Almendras*)

Garnished Stock (*Sopa de Picadillo*)

Majorcan 'Dry' Soup with Cabbage
   (*Sopas Mallorquinas*)

Fish Soup with Sour Orange (*Cachorreñas*)

Seafood Chowder (*Gazpachuelo*)

Simple Fish Stock (*Caldo de Pescado*)

Tomato Soup with Seafood and Figs
   (*Sopa de Tomate con Pescado e Higos*)

Seafood Soup (*Sopa de Pescados y Mariscos*)

ONE-POT MEALS WITH BEANS, LENTILS AND CHICKPEAS

Andalusian Vegetable Stew (*Berza Andaluza*)

Pumpkin and Chickpea Stew (*Boronia*)

Chickpeas with Spinach (*Garbanzos con Espinacas*)

Lentil Pot (*Potaje de Lentejas*)

Catalan Broad Beans (*Habas a la Catalana*)

Black-Eyed Beans (*Potaje de Chícharos*)

Asturian Bean Stew (*Fabada Asturiana*)

Galician Soup with Beans and Greens (*Caldo Gallego*)

Peasant Soup with Wheat Kernels (*Olla de Trigo*)

Red Beans, Basque Style (*Alubias Rojas a la Vasca*)

Chestnut and Bean Stew
   (*Potaje de Castañas y Alubias*)

Everyday Soup Pot (*El Puchero de Todos los Dias*)

Spanish Boiled Dinner (*El Cocido Español*)

THE GAZPACHO STORY

Gazpacho, although known the world over as a cold soup, is not really a soup at all. For one thing, it is not cooked. Moreover, it is sometimes not soupy, but a thick cream. Nor is it necessarily cold. Some versions are served hot or at room temperature. And by no means is gazpacho always tomato-based, for white ones are made with ground almonds, pine kernels or eggs. Common to all are olive oil, bread, salt, garlic and vinegar.

Gazpacho was born in the fields. It is peasant food in the most real sense. It consists of bread, olive oil and garlic, mashed to a paste, then combined with other ingredients, such as tomatoes. While there are many variations, they all begin with bread and olive oil.

The origins of gazpacho are lost in the mists of time. A form of gazpacho was probably known to the pre-Roman Celt-Iberians as a simple gruel of bread and oil. Certainly the Roman legions that maintained the empire consumed it. The later Moorish influence is evident too, especially in some of the variations on the basic theme, such as white gazpacho, made with ground almonds.

Of course, none of those forerunners of gazpacho contained tomatoes, which are considered fundamental today. That's because tomatoes were unknown in Spain until after the discovery of the New World. Suspected of being poisonous, tomatoes were hardly eaten at all until the seventeenth century.

Gazpacho belongs to Andalusia. There, day labourers working in vineyards, olive plantations, citrus groves, wheat fields or cork forests were given rations of bread and oil for their meals. Bread soaked in water with the addition of olive oil made a simple, uncooked soup, to which was added garlic and salt for flavour, plus whatever fresh vegetables were available – tomatoes, peppers and cucumbers in the summer, broad beans in the spring. Everything was pounded together in a mortar or *dornillo*, a large wooden bowl hollowed from olive wood. Gazpacho provided nourishment, quenched the thirst and sustained a body working in the hot sun.

From these humble beginnings, gazpacho has become quite cosmopolitan, appearing on the menus of sophisticated restaurants in many parts of the world. I am amazed at some of the ingredients that turn up in 'foreign' gazpachos – tomato juice, beef stock, ketchup, hot chilli salsa, grapefruit sections, prawns, lobster, meatballs, black beans and maize. Many of these versions don't even contain bread or olive oil. Unfortunately, something is lost in the translation – namely, the freshness of gazpacho made with raw ingredients and, especially, the flavour of olive oil. There is no such thing as a true gazpacho without olive oil.

I remain faithful to the country origins of gazpacho – it has to start with an emulsion of bread and olive oil. I also have a 'thing' about tomatoes. I refuse to buy those long-life varieties that look as if they are stamped out of a mould, all calibrated to a millimetre and of identical colour. If I can't get big, heavy, misshapen, vine-ripened tomatoes, then I don't make tomato gazpacho.

The bread for gazpacho should be from a country-style loaf, one or two days old. The bread is first softened by soaking in water, then mashed or blended. It isn't necessary to cube it. See page 6 for how to measure bread as an ingredient.

A Spanish refrain says, *De gazpacho no hay empacho*, or there's never too much gazpacho. It hits the spot any time of the day or night – a mid-morning snack, a starter at lunch, an afternoon refresher, an evening's supper. It's great on picnics and at the beach. Serve it in mugs at your next barbecue. Should there be any gazpacho left over, use it as a salad dressing or let it come to room temperature and toss with hot pasta.

COUNTRY GAZPACHO
GAZPACHO CAMPESINO

I was taught to make real country gazpacho by old man Vega, the godfather of the brothers who ran the bar where I learned Spanish cooking (see chapter 2). Vega had no family, but he did have a sizeable plot of land. The brothers provided him with room and board and helped him farm his plot. In exchange, they were to inherit the land.

'Why don't you come to the *campo* [country] with me some day and make gazpacho?' Vega asked one summer's day. 'Many tomatoes in the fields now.'

We arranged a day and organized a small party for the expedition. Our friend Irma, from Kentucky, contributed fried chicken and devilled eggs. Vega's donkey was enlisted to carry Irma and supplies. A case of beer, wine and soft drinks had been carried down to the *finca* (small farm) in the early morning, and were already cooling in the *alberca* (spring-fed reservoir).

We were quite a caravan on the dusty *camino real*, an ancient country thoroughfare travelled by people, donkeys and goats. It was a steep downhill trek.

At the *finca*, we cooled off in the chilly *alberca* and enjoyed a beer in the deep shade of a huge carob tree.

Vega took a basket and went to pick tomatoes, peppers and cucumbers. Then he dipped them in the reservoir to rinse off the sun's heat. He set the basket at my feet with some bread, onions and garlic. He brought a giant earthenware bowl from the house, gave me a knife and stepped back.

I looked at him blankly. 'But I don't know how to make gazpacho,' I cried. I had never made it without a blender. 'We don't make gazpacho in America.'

He thought this was puzzling. 'You mean, you don't have tomatoes in America? What kind of country is that?'

He took the knife from me and proceeded to cut the bread into the bowl, moistening it with a little water. He crushed the garlic on a stone and added it to the bread. He cut up tomatoes into the bowl, mashing them as he went. Next came olive oil poured from a jug stored in a shed. We all helped chop up the cucumbers, peppers and some onion.

'Lazarito,' called Vega to the boy who helped in the bar and on the farm, 'bring us some lemons from the tree.' The fragrant tang of lemon juice was added to the gazpacho, then cool spring water to thin it slightly.

This was a thick, chunky gazpacho, absolutely satisfying. Should you find yourself without an electric blender, here is how it's made.

230 g (8 oz) bread (about 8 slices), crusts removed (see page 6 for measuring instructions)

2 garlic cloves, crushed

900 g (2 lb) tomatoes, peeled and de-seeded

120 ml (4 fl oz) olive oil

1 teaspoon salt

2 tablespoons fresh lemon juice or white wine vinegar

8 tablespoons chopped green sweet pepper

8 tablespoons peeled chopped cucumber

8 tablespoons chopped onion

Break the bread into big chunks and soak it in water to cover until it is softened, about 15 minutes. Squeeze out the water and put the bread in a large bowl. Add the crushed garlic and mash into the bread.

Chop the tomatoes and add them to the bread, mashing them as much as possible. (Country housewives would crush them in a mortar, discarding the skin once the pulp is crushed. Otherwise, to skin tomatoes for gazpacho, try running the edge of a knife blade against the skin to loosen it, then pulling it off.)

Slowly add the olive oil to the bowl, stirring so the oil is absorbed by the bread mixture before adding more oil. Add the salt and lemon juice.

Stir in 340 ml (12 fl oz) cold water to thin the gazpacho and add the chopped pepper, cucumber and onion.

SERVES 6

Gazpacho Today
El Gazpacho de Hoy

When, in 1972, I moved from the mill house, which had no electricity, to my new house, the first thing I bought was an electric blender, to make modern-day gazpacho in minutes. It was a hand-held blender, which came with a sieve that fitted inside the larger container. For gazpacho, I would put chunks of tomatoes into the sieve without skinning them or removing seeds. When I pureed the mixture, the juice and pulp were strained through, while seeds and skin stayed in the sieve. Brilliant design. Twenty-five years – and many gazpachos, baby-food purées and mayonnaises – later, my blender finally gave out. I made gazpacho in a food processor for a season, but decided it was just not as good as gazpacho made in that blender, so I bought another one just like it.

The main thing in choosing the right blender for gazpacho is watts – 150 watts is not enough; 300 is good. With 300 watts and a sharp blade, you don't even need to skin the tomatoes. The seeds, though, should be removed either before processing or else after, by passing the gazpacho through a sieve. To seed tomatoes, cut out the stem and core, then cut the tomatoes in half crosswise. Either spoon out the seeds or else squeeze the tomatoes into a sieve placed over a bowl. The seeds will squeeze out; the juice will collect in the bowl and you can add it to the gazpacho.

Green pepper, cucumber and onion are optional ingredients in the gazpacho purée. I make it without these vegetables, then add them afterwards as garnish.

In Andalusia, gazpacho is often much paler and 'creamier' than this version. If you would like to try it that way, use 6 slices of bread and 120 ml (4 fl oz) oil for the same amount of tomatoes.

115 g (4 oz) stale bread (about 4 slices), crusts removed (see page 6)

2 garlic cloves

900 g (2 lb) ripe tomatoes, de-seeded

5-cm (2-inch) square piece of green sweet pepper (optional)

5-cm (2-inch) chunk peeled cucumber (optional)

¼ teaspoon ground cumin

2 teaspoons salt

5 tablespoons olive oil, preferably extra virgin

2 tablespoons white wine vinegar

5 tablespoons chopped green pepper (optional)

5 tablespoons chopped onion (optional)

5 tablespoons peeled chopped cucumber (optional)

8 tablespoons croûtons or cubed bread, toasted crisp (optional)

Break bread into big chunks and soak it in water to cover until it is softened, about 15 minutes. Squeeze out the water and place the bread in a blender (or, if you are using a hand blender, into a mixing bowl) with the garlic. Blend until the bread and garlic are smooth.

Add the tomatoes (it may be necessary to process the tomatoes in two batches) and the pieces of pepper and cucumber, if using, and purée. Add the cumin and salt. With the motor running, add the olive oil in a slow stream. As the oil is incorporated, the gazpacho will turn from tomato-juice red to a paler, orange colour. Blend in the vinegar and 120 ml (4 fl oz) water.

Place the gazpacho into a tureen, bowl or jug and stir in 240 ml (8 fl oz) cold water. Chill until serving time.

Place each of the garnishes – chopped pepper, onion, cucumber and croûtons – in small bowls or on a relish dish and pass them around when the gazpacho is served. This gazpacho can also be served, thinned with additional water, in tall glasses for sipping, without the garnishes.

SERVES 6

Gazpacho Cream, Córdoba Style
Salmorejo Cordobés

Although this gazpacho shares the same name as an orange and cod salad in the tapas chapter (page 31), the two are actually nothing alike. This version is a thick cream, perfect for serving as a party dip, accompanied by breadsticks and vegetable dippers, or as a starter in individual ramekins.

340 g (12 oz) stale bread (12 slices), crusts removed (see page 6 for measuring instructions)

680 g (1½ lb) ripe tomatoes, peeled and de-seeded

3 garlic cloves

5 tablespoons olive oil

1 teaspoon salt

1 tablespoon white wine vinegar

60 g (2 oz) serrano ham, cut into thin strips

2 eggs, hard-boiled and sliced

Break the bread into big chunks and soak it in water to cover until it is softened, about 15 minutes.

Cut the tomatoes into chunks and combine in a food processor bowl with the garlic. Process until puréed.

Use your hands to squeeze out as much water as possible from the bread. Add the bread to the food processor bowl. (If necessary, process in two batches.) Process until smooth. With the motor running, slowly add the oil, salt and vinegar to make a thick cream. Chill until serving time.

Spread in a dish or in individual ramekins and garnish the top with strips of ham and sliced egg.

Serves 10 to 12 as a party dip; serves 6 as a starter

Almond Gazpacho with Grapes
Ajo Blanco con Uvas

I love this version of gazpacho, which is typical of Málaga, my adopted region. It is sometimes made with 'green' almonds, those still on the trees, which have not yet formed hard shells. In the springtime, ground broad beans (*habas*) or broad bean flour are substituted. In Málaga, golden muscatel grapes garnish the *ajo blanco*, though any sweet grape, or even chopped apples or melon balls, could be used. This gazpacho is best made with fresh almonds, shelled, blanched and skinned. Otherwise, use best-quality vacuum-packed almonds. It is traditionally made in a brass mortar, the almonds crushed to a paste. The processor leaves them grainy, so, if desired, the soup can be sieved.

170 g (6 oz) stale bread (6 slices), crusts removed (see page 6 for measuring instructions)

115 g (4 oz) almonds, blanched and skinned (see page 6)

3 garlic cloves

120 ml (4 fl oz) extra virgin olive oil

5 tablespoons white wine vinegar

2 teaspoons salt

12 muscatel grapes, halved and de-seeded

Soak the bread in water to cover until it is softened, about 15 minutes.

Combine the almonds and garlic in a food processor or blender and pulse until the almonds are finely ground.

Squeeze out the water from the bread and add the bread to the food processor. Blend to a smooth paste.

With the motor running, add the oil in a slow stream, then the vinegar and salt. Beat in 120 ml (4 fl oz) cold water, then pour the mixture into a tureen, wooden bowl or jug and add an extra 340 ml (12 fl oz) water (the full quantity will not fit in the processor). Taste for seasoning, adding more salt or vinegar if needed. The soup should be fairly tangy.

Serve immediately or chill the gazpacho. Stir before serving in bowls, garnished with grapes.

Serves 4

White Gazpacho with Pine Kernels

Gazpacho Blanco con Piñones

In parts of Spain where pine trees are abundant, such as in the *marismas* (marshlands) of the Guadalquivir River basin, pine kernels are often used instead of almonds in white gazpacho. The eggs in this recipe give the gazpacho a silky texture.

115 g (4 oz) day-old bread (4 slices), crusts removed (see page 6 for measuring instructions)

85 g (3 oz) pine kernels

2 garlic cloves

2 eggs

120 ml (4 fl oz) extra virgin olive oil

3 tablespoons wine vinegar

1 teaspoon salt

2 tablespoons peeled and chopped pear or apple

Tear the bread into large chunks and soak it in water to cover until it is softened, about 15 minutes.

Combine the pine kernels and garlic in a food processor and pulse until the pine kernels are finely ground.

Squeeze out the water from the bread and add the bread to the pine kernels with the eggs. Process until smooth.

With the motor running, slowly add the olive oil. Then add the vinegar, salt and 240 ml (8 fl oz) cold water. Pour the mixture into a bowl or jug and add another 240 ml (8 fl oz) of water.

Chill the gazpacho. Add a little chopped pear or apple to each serving.

SERVES 4

WINTER GAZPACHO
GAZPACHO DE INVIERNO

This winter gazpacho uses the juice of the bitter orange. (There's another soup with sour orange juice on page 86.) Where real sour orange is not available, use orange juice and lemon juice with a little vinegar. The dried peppers from which pimentón (Spanish paprika) is made, *ñoras*, are used in this recipe. If they are not available, use an extra teaspoon of pimentón.

8 slices baguette, toasted

4 *ñoras* (dried sweet red peppers), seeds and stems discarded

1 strip orange zest

1½ teaspoons salt

2 garlic cloves

1 teaspoon pimentón

120 ml (4 fl oz) juice from sour oranges (or 4 tablespoons fresh orange juice, 4 tablespoons fresh lemon juice and 1 tablespoon vinegar)

Crisp bacon bits, to garnish

Break the toasted bread into pieces and place in a tureen or large saucepan. In another saucepan, combine the *ñoras*, orange zest, salt and 1.4 litres (2½ pints) of water. Bring to the boil and cook for 10 minutes.

Skim out the *ñoras* and reserve. Discard the orange zest. Purée the *ñoras* in a blender with the garlic, pimentón and a little of the liquid from the pan. Return this paste to the liquid in the pan. Bring to the boil and pour over the bread. Cover and let stand for 15 minutes, until the bread is spongy.

With a hand blender, purée the gazpacho. (Or blend in batches in a regular blender.) Stir in the sour orange or orange and lemon juices and vinegar.

Serve warm or at room temperature topped with the bacon bits.

SERVES 4

HOT GAZPACHO

GAZPACHO CALIENTE

Although in America we think of gazpacho as a cool soup, it isn't always. Some versions are cooked and served hot. They still qualify as gazpacho because they are made with bread and olive oil, as in previous renditions. In this recipe I suggest using tinned tomatoes.

1 onion, chopped

1 green sweet pepper, chopped

1 (400 g) tin chopped tomatoes

2 garlic cloves, finely chopped

5 tablespoons olive oil

¼ teaspoon pimentón

¼ teaspoon ground cumin

¼ teaspoon freshly ground black pepper

1 dried chilli pepper (optional)

1 teaspoon salt

1.15 litres (2 pints) stock or water

4 slices bread, cubed

Mint sprigs, to garnish

Chopped spring onion, to garnish

In a large saucepan, combine the onion, pepper, tomatoes, garlic and 4 tablespoons of the oil over high heat. Simmer for 10 minutes. Add the pimentón, cumin, pepper, chilli, if using, salt and stock. Bring to the boil and cook for 10 minutes more. Heat remaining oil in a frying pan and toss the bread cubes over a medium-high heat until they are golden.

Immediately before serving, add the fried bread cubes. Garnish with mint. Sprinkle with chopped spring onion.

SERVES 4

SOUPS

From light and refreshing summertime gazpacho, which doesn't even require cooking, to heart-warming soups and lusty one-pot meals filled with pulses and vegetables, *la comida de cuchara* – spoon food – is favourite fare in Spain.

Spanish has several words for soup. *Sopa* is soup, whether made with vegetables, meat or fish. *Caldo* is stock, the liquid part of the soup, and *crema* is a cream or puréed soup. *Cocido*, which means 'cooked', is a boiled dinner, of which the first course is the boiling liquid, *caldo*. *Puchero* is a regional variation of *cocido*. *Potaje* means 'pottage', a very thick soup invariably containing pulses.

Some of my favourite soups are not so different from gazpacho – bread, olive oil, plus vegetables and garlic. But, instead of being combined raw, the ingredients are cooked together. These soups started out as simple peasant soups. Other wonderful soups, concocted with fish and shellfish, began as fishermen's fare, made on board a fishing boat or by a frugal fishwife, yet their flavourings and combinations are truly inspired.

In Spain, soup is usually served as a first course at the midday dinner or as a main course for a lighter supper.

Castilian Garlic Soup

Sopa de Ajo Castellana

While gazpacho is familiar everywhere, its cohort, garlic soup, is hardly known outside Spain. Like gazpacho, garlic soup and its variations are made with bread, olive oil and garlic, which are then embellished with vegetables and other seasonings.

Although every region has its rendition of garlic soup, the Castilian one is the best known. I first tasted it at a famous old Madrid restaurant where it was the first course of a gargantuan meal that included roast suckling pig. Huge in flavour and simple to prepare, this rustic recipe may become one of your favourites.

230 g (8 oz) baguette, sliced 12 mm (½ inch) thick (18 to 20 slices)

5 tablespoons olive oil

60 g (2 oz) ham or bacon, diced (optional)

6 garlic cloves, coarsely chopped

1 tablespoon pimentón

¼ teaspoon ground cumin

1.4 litres (2½ pints) Simple Stock (page 82) or water

Salt

4 eggs

Toast the bread and set aside.

In a large cazuela or saucepan, heat the olive oil over medium heat. Add the ham, if using, and garlic and sauté until the garlic begins to take on colour, about 4 minutes. Stir in the pimentón and cumin and immediately add the stock. Add salt to taste.

Add the toasted bread to the cazuela. Bring the soup to the boil, then reduce the heat and simmer for 5 minutes.

With the soup bubbling, break each egg into a saucer and slide it on to the top of the soup. Cover and let the eggs poach until the whites are set and yolks still liquid, about 4 minutes. Serve the soup from the same cazuela.

Alternative serving method: Divide the soup between four individual soup bowls. Break one egg into each, pierce the yolk with a needle, then microwave for 2 minutes on high, or until the whites are set and yolks still liquid.

Serves 4

SIMPLE STOCK
Caldo Sencillo

1 kg (2¼ lb) chicken backs, wings, carcasses

1 piece ham bone or 2 slices bacon

2 celery stalks

½ onion

Parsley stems and leaves

1 sprig fresh thyme, or ¼ teaspoon dried

2 bay leaves

1 carrot, quartered

Few peppercorns

1 tablespoon salt

Combine all the ingredients with 3 litres (5 pints) water in a large saucepan. Bring to the boil, then skim off any foam that rises to the top. Cover and simmer for 1 hour. Strain the stock, discarding solids. Cool, then refrigerate. Skim off and discard any fat from the stock. The stock can be kept up to 3 days in the refrigerator or 3 months in the freezer.

MAKES ABOUT 2 LITRES (3½ PINTS)

ALMOND SOUP

SOPA DE ALMENDRAS

This version of almond soup, typical of Granada, has Moorish nuances – saffron and cumin – whereas in Castile, almond soup contains cinnamon and sugar and is served on Christmas Eve.

3 tablespoons olive oil

115 g (4 oz) almonds, blanched and skinned (see page 6)

3 garlic cloves

100 g (3½ oz) cubed stale bread, crusts removed

¼ teaspoon saffron threads, crushed

⅛ teaspoon freshly ground black pepper

Salt

1 litre (about 2 pints) Simple Stock (page 82)

2 teaspoons white wine vinegar

Chopped fresh flat-leaf parsley, to garnish

Heat the oil in a large saucepan over medium heat and toast the almonds, garlic and cubed bread. Skim out when they are golden, 1 to 2 minutes.

Reserve a quarter of the bread. Combine the remaining bread, almonds and garlic in a food processor with the saffron, pepper, salt, 280 ml (½ pint) of the stock and the vinegar. Process to a smooth paste.

Add the remaining stock to the oil in the saucepan. Stir in the almond paste. Bring to the boil, then simmer the soup for 15 minutes.

Serve garnished with chopped parsley and the reserved bread cubes.

SERVES 6

GARNISHED STOCK
SOPA DE PICADILLO

Make this soup with leftover liquid from *puchero* or *cocido*, one of the boiled dinners (see pages 107 and 109). Or, if a full-fledged *cocido* is impossible, use a chicken stock enriched with a piece of ham or bacon, such as Simple Stock (page 82). If you have leftover chickpeas, they can be included, too.

In Spain this soup is served for a light supper, perhaps followed by one of the egg dishes in chapter 5. It is also thought to be restorative, so it is considered excellent food for a hangover.

3 tablespoons olive oil

2 slices bread, crusts removed and cubed

2 litres (3½ pints) stock

85 g (3 oz) serrano ham, chopped

2 eggs, hard-boiled and chopped

4 tablespoons dry Sherry

6 sprigs mint, to garnish

Heat the oil in a frying pan over medium heat and fry the bread until crisp, 1 to 2 minutes. Set aside.

Heat the stock to boiling. Immediately before serving, add the ham, eggs and Sherry.

Serve the soup garnished with the fried croûtons and sprigs of mint.

SERVES 6

MAJORCAN 'DRY' SOUP WITH CABBAGE
SOPAS MALLORQUINAS

The English word *soup* derives from the verb 'sop'. Likewise, the Spanish word *sopa* comes from the same root – pieces of bread soaked in stock. In this recipe, the bread absorbs all the liquid, making it a 'dry soup'. This is a peasant dish, not unlike gazpacho.

4 tablespoons olive oil

2 leeks, white and tender green parts, chopped

1 onion, chopped

1 green sweet pepper, chopped

2 tomatoes, peeled, de-seeded and chopped

3 garlic cloves, chopped

Crushed red chilli flakes

2 tablespoons chopped fresh flat-leaf parsley

1 bay leaf

1 small cabbage, chopped

1 tablespoon salt

450 g (1 lb) wholemeal bread, sliced (12 slices)

Boiling water

Heat the oil in a deep pan over medium heat and sauté the leeks, onion and green pepper until soft, about 5 minutes. Add the tomatoes and garlic and cook for a few minutes more, then add the red chilli flakes, parsley, bay leaf and cabbage. Season with salt, add 670 ml (1¼ pints) water, bring to the boil, then cover and simmer until the vegetables are soft, about 35 minutes.

In a large cazuela or casserole, layer the bread slices and vegetables and their liquid. Add just enough boiling water to barely cover the ingredients. Cover the cazuela and let stand for 15 minutes, until the liquid is absorbed. Serve hot or at room temperature.

SERVES 6

FISH SOUP WITH SOUR ORANGE
CACHORREÑAS

I love this soup, which is unusual and delicious, subtly flavoured with the sour juice of the Seville orange. The fruit, with its bitter peel, is the marmalade orange. The trees were brought to Spain by the Moors, long before the arrival of the sweet orange, and are widely planted in courtyards and plazas in Andalusian cities. Nothing is so enchanting as a stroll through the old Santa Cruz district of Seville in the springtime, when the heady scent of orange blossoms perfumes the narrow alleyways. Later, when the fruit ripens to glowing orange globes, tourists can't resist picking them. What a shock when they taste that sour juice!

Affectionately called *cachorreñas*, these oranges are used in quite a few Andalusian dishes. They are usually only available in Britain for a brief period in late January and early February. At other times of the year, use half orange juice and half lemon juice in this recipe.

I like to make this soup with a whole hake, using the head and trimmings to prepare the stock in which to poach the fillets. I serve it as a main course, possibly preceded by a vegetable dish. However, you can prepare the soup with a lesser quantity of fish and serve it as a first course. Cod, haddock or whiting could be used instead of hake. The soup is also concocted with *bacalao* (dry salt cod) which has been soaked to remove the salt.

900 g (2 lb) whole hake or cod, filleted, heads and trimmings reserved, or 680 g (1½ lb) fish fillets

5-cm (2-inch) strip orange zest

1 tablespoon salt

Sprig parsley

½ onion, chopped

1 tomato

1 small green sweet pepper, seeds removed and chopped

1 bay leaf

60 g (2 oz) torn pieces of bread

3 tablespoons olive oil

1 garlic clove

1 teaspoon pimentón

¼ teaspoon ground cumin

120 ml (4 fl oz) juice from sour oranges (or 4 tablespoons fresh orange juice, 4 tablespoons fresh lemon juice and 1 tablespoon vinegar)

Thinly sliced orange, to garnish

Chopped spring onion, to garnish

Combine the fish head, bones and trimmings in a large saucepan and cover with 1 litre (about 2 pints) of water. Add the orange zest, salt, parsley, onion, tomato, green pepper and bay leaf. Bring to the boil and simmer for 30 minutes. (If the head and trimmings are not available, cook the zest, parsley, onion, tomato, green pepper and bay leaf in water for 15 minutes.)

Strain the liquid into another pan. Discard the fish heads and bones, parsley, zest and bay leaf. Remove and discard the tomato core. Combine the rest of the tomato with the onion and green pepper in a blender, add 120 ml (4 fl oz) of the reserved liquid, the bread, oil, garlic, pimentón and cumin. Blend until smooth. (The mixture may be sieved, if desired.)

Add the tomato mixture to the soup. Bring to the boil and cook at a slow boil for 5 minutes.

Cut the fish fillets into four pieces. Add them to the soup and simmer for 5 minutes more. Hake is very delicate, so take care not to break it up. Stir in the orange juice and simmer for 1 minute more.

Serve the soup into four soup bowls, each with a piece of fish, garnished with a thin slice of orange and a sprinkling of chopped spring onion.

SERVES 4

SEAFOOD CHOWDER
GAZPACHUELO

At its most basic, this soup – with obvious roots in gazpacho – consists of olive oil, egg and water. The oil and egg are emulsified, then blended into the hot stock. In this version, typical of Málaga, it is embellished with seafood.

I start out with a whole fish weighing 340–450 g (12–16 oz). The head, bones and trimmings make the stock. Then I cook the sliced fish or fillets in the stock. Once cooked, it's easy to separate the chunks of fish, discarding any bones, but you could also use prepared fish stock and fish fillets for the soup.

1 egg, at room temperature

120 ml (4 fl oz) olive oil

4 tablespoons fresh lemon juice

2 litres (3½ pints) Simple Fish Stock
    (see below)

230 g (8 oz) peeled, diced potatoes

4 tablespoons peas, fresh or frozen

340 g (12 oz) chunks raw or cooked fish

4 tablespoons chopped serrano ham

85 g (3 oz) medium or small peeled prawns

4 tablespoons dry Sherry

Place the egg in the blender. With the motor running, add the oil in a slow stream until it is emulsified. Blend in the lemon juice. Set aside.

In a large saucepan, bring the fish stock to the boil. Add the potatoes and simmer, covered, for 10 minutes. Add the peas and simmer for 5 minutes more.

Then add the fish, ham, prawns and Sherry. Bring the soup to the boil, then reduce to a simmer.

With the motor of the blender running, ladle some of the hot soup into the emulsion in the blender. Remove the soup from the heat and whisk the emulsion into the soup. Serve immediately. The soup can be reheated, but do not boil.

SERVES 6

SIMPLE FISH STOCK
Caldo de Pescado

450 g (1 lb) small fish, fish heads, bones,
    trimmings plus any prawn shells

1 tablespoon salt

½ onion

Strip lemon zest

Strip orange zest

1 celery stalk

1 small carrot, split lengthwise

Several parsley stems

Pinch dried thyme

Combine all the ingredients in a large saucepan with 3 litres (about 5 pints) of water. Bring to the boil and skim off any foam. Partially cover and simmer for 1 hour. Strain the stock and discard solids.

MAKES ABOUT 2 LITRES (3½ PINTS)

TOMATO SOUP WITH SEAFOOD AND FIGS
SOPA DE TOMATE CON PESCADO E HIGOS

Village housewives prepare this simple soup with whatever fish is fresh in the daily market. If you can't get clams, you could substitute mussels. If fresh fish isn't available, *bacalao* (dry salt cod) would be used instead. Today, the soup is usually made with frozen fish fillets. Fresh figs or peeled prickly pears (*higos chumbos*) are added during the summer when they are in season.

340 g (12 oz) hard-shell clams, scrubbed

3 tablespoons olive oil

1 onion, chopped

1 green sweet pepper, chopped

2 garlic cloves, sliced

450 g (1 lb) fresh tomatoes (2 large), peeled, de-seeded and coarsely chopped

⅛ teaspoon ground cumin

Pinch crushed red chilli flakes

900 ml (1½ pints) Simple Fish Stock (page 88) or water

Salt

230 g (8 oz) white fish fillets, cut into 12-mm (½-inch) cubes

2 large ripe figs, peeled and sliced

8 slices baguette, toasted

4 sprigs mint, to garnish

Combine the clams in a large saucepan with 120 ml (4 fl oz) of water. Cover and cook over high heat just until the shells open, about 3 minutes. Sieve the liquid and reserve. When clams are cool enough to handle, remove the clam meat and reserve. Discard the shells.

In a large saucepan, heat the oil over medium heat and sauté the onion, pepper and garlic until softened, 3 to 5 minutes. Add the tomatoes and cook over high heat for 5 minutes more.

Add the cumin, red chilli flakes and 450 ml (¾ pint) of the stock. Cook for 15 minutes. Purée the mixture in a blender.

Return the vegetable mixture to the soup pan and add the reserved clam liquor and the remaining stock. Bring to the boil, reduce the heat to a simmer and add the fish. Simmer for 2 minutes. Add the clams.

Divide the figs between four shallow soup plates and ladle the soup over. Add two toasted baguette slices to each bowl. Garnish each plate with a sprig of mint.

SERVES 4

SEAFOOD SOUP

SOPA DE PESCADOS Y MARISCOS

While many of these seafood soups are simple and economical – the sort of dish a village housewife would serve her family or that fishermen aboard a trawler would eat – this one is impressive enough to serve to guests on special occasions, especially if it is made with luxurious ingredients, such as lobster.

Crustacean shells (prawns, lobster, crab or mussels) add depth of flavour to the soup, so, if possible, choose prawns with heads and shells intact. You can even leave clams in their shells, as long as your guests don't mind using their fingers to remove them. (Again, if you can't get clams you can substitute mussels.) Although this fish soup is usually served as a first course, it is substantial enough to make a whole meal for a light supper.

230 g (8 oz) whole small prawns

230 g (8 oz) hard-shell clams (or 4 tablespoons shucked clams)

2 litres (3½ pints) Simple Fish Stock (page 88)

4 tablespoons olive oil

2 leeks, white part only, chopped

1 onion, chopped

1 carrot, chopped

4 tablespoons brandy

120 ml (4 fl oz) white wine

230 g (8 oz) chopped tomatoes, fresh or tinned

Pinch ground cayenne pepper

Pinch crushed saffron threads

Salt

2 slices bread, toasted and broken into pieces

450 g (1 lb) boneless monkfish, cut into 2.5-cm(1-inch) pieces, and/or lobster

Peel the prawns and reserve them. Keep the heads and shells in a separate bowl.

Combine the clams in a small pan with 120 ml (4 fl oz) water. Cover and place the pan over high heat until shells open, about 3 minutes. When cool, remove the shells and discard them. Reserve the clams. Sieve the liquid and add to the fish stock.

In a large saucepan, heat the oil over medium heat and sauté the leeks, onion and carrot until softened, about 5 minutes. Add the prawn shells and continue sautéing over high heat until the vegetables just begin to brown, 5 minutes. Remove from the heat.

Add the brandy. (If you like, you can set it alight and flambé the mixture.) Then add the wine, 280 ml (½ pint) of the fish stock, the tomatoes, cayenne, saffron and salt to taste. Cook the mixture for 20 minutes at a slow boil.

Add the toasted bread, and simmer for another 10 minutes.

Transfer the soup to a food processor or blender and process until as smooth as possible. Press the pulp through a sieve, discarding the remains of the prawn shells.

Return the pulp to the pan and add the remaining fish stock. Bring to the boil, then simmer for 45 minutes. (The soup can be prepared in advance up to this point.)

Shortly before serving time, add the chunks of monkfish or lobster to the soup and simmer for 3 minutes. Then add the reserved prawns and cook for 2 minutes. Then add the clams and cook for 2 minutes. Taste again and add a bit more salt if needed. Serve immediately.

Serves 6

ONE-POT MEALS WITH BEANS, LENTILS AND CHICKPEAS

The *olla* is a tall, pot-bellied cooking pot, also called *puchero*, shaped to fit into a tripod on the hearth. In days past, it was made of iron, copper or earthenware.

My first *olla* was of thin rolled steel with an enamel finish of brick-red colour on the outside, blue speckles on the inside. This was the sort used by most housewives – although a few, those with gas cookers, had the very modern *olla exprés* (pressure cooker).

In the *olla* is cooked the main meal of the day. This is the source of soul food, Spanish style. Nourishing, slow-cooked meals, usually containing pulses, which can be stretched to serve whole families for little money, or embellished with quantities of good poultry, beef and sausages for holiday meals.

In today's high-powered world, even well-heeled businessmen and politicos have a weakness for the comforting food from the *olla*: lentils like mama used to make, or Grandma's *puchero*.

Food cooked in the *olla* includes hearty soups; sturdy stews with pulses, vegetables and meat; and, especially, the important meals, *cocido* and *puchero*. These are one-pot dinners served as two or three separate courses – first a soup, then meat and vegetables. In a Spanish home, *potaje*, thick soup with vegetables and pulses, is served as a first course, to be followed by meat or fish. But many *potajes* are substantial enough to provide a main course, with perhaps a salad to start. Bread accompanies all of these soups and stews.

In Spain, a meal with pulses is served at the midday dinner, at 2 PM, never for supper, which comes very late.

Quite a few of these stews contain sausages and other cured meats, which lend flavour (and calories). Chorizo and morcilla (blood) sausage are the two most common. (See chapter 10 for more about chorizo.) Because morcilla is not widely available, I suggest alternative flavourings in the recipes.

Any large saucepan or casserole can be used in place of the traditional *olla*.

Andalusian Vegetable Stew

Berza Andaluza

This is my favourite dish cooked in the *olla*. I like the combination of pulses, meat, sausages and vegetables. Loaded with rich meat, the *pringá*, it is a stick-to-the-ribs meal that is perfect for cold weather. In summer, it's made with olive oil and without meat, pork fat and sausage. The usual vegetables are chard stems and/or green beans plus pumpkin, carrots and potatoes. If chard stems are used, the leaves are traditionally saved for another use, though I often shred them and add to the pot, too.

An ingredient in many of these hearty stews is *hueso añejo*, a chunk of well-aged ham bone (from serrano ham), which gives the soup a subtle background flavour that is much appreciated. In Cervantes' story of Don Quixote, the knight's squire, Sancho Panza, asked to be served '*ollas podridas, que mientras más podridas son, mejor huelen*', rotten pots, which, the more rotten they were, the better they smelled. Sancho's favourite meal probably contained *añejo* bone. When *añejo* is used, the soup is often finished with a sprinkling of fresh mint, an inspired touch.

If morcilla sausage is not available, you can use black pudding, an Italian cooking sausage or even ordinary pork sausages and add a pinch of cloves and cinnamon to the stew.

230 g (8 oz) dried chickpeas, soaked overnight

340 g (12 oz) beef shin or brisket

230 g (8 oz) meaty pork spare ribs

Small piece ham bone (optional)

30 g (1 oz) salt pork (optional)

450 g (1 lb) chard or green beans

1 carrot, chopped

450 g (1 lb) pumpkin or winter squash, peeled and cut into chunks

170 g (6 oz) morcilla (blood) sausage

5 peppercorns

1 teaspoon salt

450 g (1 lb) potatoes, peeled and cut into 2.5-cm (1-inch) chunks

2 small, firm pears, peeled, cored and cut into 2.5-cm (1-inch) chunks

Chopped fresh mint (optional)

Drain the chickpeas. Pour 2 litres (3½ pints) of water into a large saucepan and add the beef, pork ribs and ham bone, if using. Bring to the boil and skim off any foam. With the water boiling, add the chickpeas. Reduce the heat, cover and simmer for 1 hour.

Chop the chard stems or French beans into 2.5-cm (1-inch) pieces. Shred the chard leaves, if using. Add to the pan with the carrot and pumpkin. Prick the morcilla several times with a skewer (so it doesn't pop open when steam accumulates) and add it to the pan. Add the peppercorns and salt. Cover and simmer for 20 minutes more.

Add the potatoes and pears. Cook for 20 minutes more. Remove several chunks of potato and pumpkin and mash them until smooth. Stir the mash into the soup to thicken it.

Let it stand for 10 minutes before serving. Cut the beef, pork rib and sausage into bite-sized pieces. Serve the meats, vegetables and broth in shallow soup plates. Garnish with chopped mint.

SERVES 6

PUMPKIN AND CHICKPEA STEW
BORONIA

This vegetarian recipe derives from a Moorish vegetable stew. The pumpkin, unlike other winter squashes, is not overly sweet. This stew is often made with ham bone and salt pork, which you can also add if you'd like a heartier dish.

540 g (19 oz) cooked chickpeas, drained and liquid reserved

450 g (1 lb) pumpkin, peeled and cut into 4-cm (1½-inch) cubes

450 g (1 lb) potatoes, peeled and cut into 4-cm (1½-inch) cubes

1 green sweet pepper, cut into 4-cm (1½-inch) strips

2 tablespoons olive oil

1 teaspoon salt

Freshly ground black pepper

450 ml (¾ pint) chickpea cooking liquid or water

1 large ripe tomato

1 garlic clove

½ teaspoon ground cumin

¼ teaspoon hot pimentón

Chopped fresh mint, to garnish

Combine the chickpeas in a large saucepan with the pumpkin, potatoes, green pepper, oil, salt, black pepper and chickpea cooking liquid. Stir to distribute the ingredients.

Remove the stem and core from the tomato. Set the whole tomato on top of the other ingredients. Bring the liquid to the boil, cover and simmer until the potatoes are tender, about 20 minutes.

Remove the tomato from the pot with a large slotted spoon. Slip off its skin and combine the pulp in a blender with the garlic, cumin and pimentón. Blend until smooth. Stir the tomato mixture into the vegetables.

Ladle the vegetables, chickpeas and some of the liquid into shallow soup plates. Garnish with a little chopped mint and serve.

SERVES 4

CHICKPEAS WITH SPINACH
GARBANZOS CON ESPINACAS

This meatless *potaje* (pottage) comes from Seville in Andalusia. It's such a popular dish that it's even served in tapa bars.

2 tablespoons olive oil

1 onion, chopped

2 garlic cloves, 1 chopped and 1 left whole

1 tomato, peeled, de-seeded and chopped

1½ teaspoons pimentón

½ teaspoon ground cumin

⅛ teaspoon ground cayenne pepper

Pinch cloves

¼ teaspoon saffron threads

8 peppercorns

600 g (21 oz) cooked chickpeas, cooking liquid reserved

280 g (10 oz) cooked and chopped spinach

Salt

In a large saucepan, heat the oil over medium heat. Add the onion and the chopped garlic and sauté for 2 minutes. Add the tomato and cook until slightly reduced, 5 minutes. Stir in the pimentón, cumin, cayenne and cloves.

In a mortar, crush the saffron and peppercorns with the remaining clove of garlic. Dissolve the spices in 3 tablespoons of water and add to the pan with the chickpeas and 450 ml (¾ pint) of their liquid, the spinach and salt to taste. Cover and simmer over medium-low heat for 20 minutes, adding additional water if necessary. The mixture should be juicy, not soupy. Serve hot.

SERVES 6 AS A MAIN COURSE; SERVES 12 AS A TAPA

Lentil Pot

Potaje de Lentejas

I just love the spicy taste that morcilla, or blood sausage, adds to this dish. If this type of sausage is hard to find, you could use black pudding, an Italian cooking sausage or even ordinary pork sausages plus an extra pinch of cloves, pepper, pimentón and cinnamon. Greenish-brown *castellana* lentils are the most widely used in Spain, but you can use brown or tiny Puy lentils as well.

450 g (1 lb) lentils

2 tablespoons olive oil

1 tomato, peeled and chopped

1 green pepper, cut in pieces

1 onion, quartered

3 carrots, sliced

2 bay leaves

1 whole head garlic, roasted and peeled
    (see page 8)

2 cloves

1 tablespoon salt

2 large potatoes, peeled and chopped

1 teaspoon pimentón

½ teaspoon ground cumin

¼ teaspoon freshly ground black pepper

Pinch ground cayenne pepper

340 g (12 oz) chorizo sausage (or any
    pork sausages)

115 g (4 oz) morcilla (blood) sausage
    (optional)

2 tablespoons Sherry vinegar or white
    wine vinegar

Combine the lentils and 2 litres (3½ pints) water in a large saucepan. Bring to the boil and skim off any foam. Add the oil, tomato, green pepper, onion, carrots, bay leaves, roasted garlic, cloves and salt to the lentils. Bring to the boil and simmer for 15 minutes.

Add the potatoes, pimentón, cumin, black pepper and cayenne. Add the sausages and cook the lentils until everything is tender, another 30 minutes. The lentils can be prepared in advance up to this point and refrigerated. Reheat.

Add the vinegar before serving.

SERVES 6

CATALAN BROAD BEANS

HABAS A LA CATALANA

Broad beans (also known as fava beans) come into season in early spring. Small and freshly picked, they can be eaten pods and all. But usually they are shelled. As the beans get older and bigger, their outer skins become tougher, so some beans may even need to be partially cooked before their skins can be slipped off. However, if you use young or frozen beans, this shouldn't be necessary. This dish is traditionally cooked in an earthenware *olla*, a deep pot. You can use any casserole dish.

85 g (3 oz) diced lean bacon

1 tablespoon olive oil

4–5 spring onions, white and green parts, or 1 small onion, chopped coarsely

2 garlic cloves, chopped

900 g (2 lb) fresh or frozen shelled broad beans

230 g (8 oz) chopped tomato, fresh or tinned

170 g (6 oz) *butifarra negra* (Catalan blood sausage) or ordinary pork sausages

1 tablespoon anise brandy (optional)

120 ml (4 fl oz) medium-dry Sherry

Pinch ground cloves

Pinch ground cinnamon

Freshly ground black pepper

1 teaspoon salt

BOUQUET GARNI

Several sprigs parsley

Several sprigs mint

1 celery stalk

1 bay leaf

2 teaspoons finely chopped fresh mint leaves

In an *olla* or deep saucepan or casserole over medium heat, fry the diced bacon in the olive oil for 1 minute. Add the spring onions and garlic and sauté for another few minutes. Add beans and sauté for 10 minutes.

Add the tomato to the pan and cook for another few minutes. Tuck the sausage into the beans. Add the brandy, if using, Sherry, 120 ml (4 fl oz) water, cloves, cinnamon, pepper and salt. Make the bouquet garni by tying together the parsley, mint, celery and bay leaf with a piece of cotton string. Add to the pan. Bring the liquid to the boil, then reduce the heat to maintain a bare simmer and cover tightly. Cook gently, stirring occasionally, for 60 to 70 minutes.

Remove and discard bouquet garni. To serve, cut the sausage into bite-sized pieces and place on top of the beans. Sprinkle chopped mint over the beans.

SERVES 6 AS A STARTER; SERVES 4 AS A MAIN COURSE

BLACK-EYED BEANS

POTAJE DE CHÍCHAROS

As far as I've been able to ascertain, in Spain black-eyed beans are not a traditional good-luck dish for New Year's Day, as they are in the American South. Nevertheless, I like to serve them on that occasion. Sometimes I prepare them as a warm salad, lightly dressed with olive oil and Sherry vinegar, to serve as a side dish with grilled quail or partridge.

To make a vegetarian version of the following recipe, omit the ham hocks and add 4 tablespoons olive oil to the pan with the black-eyed beans.

450 g (1 lb) dried black-eyed beans, soaked overnight

450 g (1 lb) ham hocks

2 bay leaves

1 onion, quartered

1 tomato, quartered

2 large carrots, peeled

1 whole head garlic, roasted and peeled (see page 8)

⅛ teaspoon ground cloves

¼ teaspoon freshly ground black pepper

Pinch saffron threads, crushed (optional)

1 teaspoon salt

Drain the black-eyed beans and combine them in a large saucepan with the ham hocks and 1.4 litres (2½ pints) of water. Bring to the boil. Add the bay leaves, onion, tomato, carrots, garlic, cloves, pepper and saffron, if using. Cover and simmer for 30 minutes.

Add the salt and simmer for 30 minutes more, until the beans and meat are tender.

To serve, cut the meat off the hocks and cut up the carrots. Mix them into the beans and serve in soup plates.

SERVES 4

ASTURIAN BEAN STEW
FABADA ASTURIANA

This dish is so good that, though it's from the northern region of Asturias, it's served everywhere in Spain. The Asturian *fabe* is a fat white bean, like a large white kidney bean. You can substitute cannellini beans, haricot beans or small white butter beans. If morcilla sausage is unavailable, you can substitute black pudding or even ordinary pork sausages.

450 g (1 lb) dried large white beans, soaked overnight

115 g (4 oz) lean bacon, in one piece

230 g (8 oz) ham

230 g (8 oz) chorizo sausage (preferably smoked Asturian)

230 g (8 oz) morcilla (blood) sausage

2 bay leaves

¼ teaspoon crushed saffron, dissolved in 1 tablespoon water

Salt and freshly ground black pepper

Drain the beans and put them in a cazuela or flameproof casserole. Blanch the bacon in boiling water for 5 minutes and drain. Add it to the beans. Add water to cover. Bring to the boil and skim off the foam.

Add the ham, chorizo, morcilla and bay leaves. Bring to the boil and skim again. Add the saffron.

Cover and simmer until beans are tender, 1 to 2 hours, adding cold water as necessary so beans are always covered with liquid. Add salt and pepper to taste. Don't stir the beans, but shake the pot from time to time.

Let the *fabada* rest for 15 minutes before serving. Remove the bay leaves and discard. Remove the bacon, ham and sausages from the beans and cut into bite-sized pieces with kitchen scissors. Return to the beans and serve.

SERVES 6

GALICIAN SOUP WITH BEANS AND GREENS
CALDO GALLEGO

In cool, green Galicia in northwest Spain, the emblematic vegetable is *grelos*. *Grelos* are the stems and flowering tops of turnip greens. They have a mild bitterness that complements cured pork. In this soup, use turnip greens or any other available greens in place of *grelos*.

115 g (4 oz) dried white beans, soaked overnight

1 bay leaf

½ onion

Ham bone or a 115-g (4-oz) piece of fresh pork

1 beef marrow bone

85 g (3 oz) lean bacon, in one piece

450 g (1 lb) turnip greens (or cabbage or chard), chopped

450 g (1 lb) potatoes, peeled and cut into chunks

1 teaspoon pimentón

Salt and freshly ground black pepper

Drain the soaked beans and combine them in a large saucepan with 2 litres (3½ pints) water. Bring to the boil and skim off the foam. Add the bay leaf, onion, ham bone, beef bone and bacon. Return to the boil and skim. Simmer for 1 hour.

Meanwhile, bring another large saucepan of water to the boil and blanch the turnip greens for 3 minutes. Drain them, add to the beans with the potatoes, and simmer for 1 hour more.

Mix a little of the stock into the pimentón, then stir the mixture into the soup. Season to taste with salt and pepper. Simmer for 30 minutes longer. Discard the bay leaf. Cut the meat off the bones and return it to the soup. Discard the bones before serving.

SERVES 8

About Pulses

Pulses – dried beans, peas and lentils – are a mainstay of Spanish cooking. In village homes, stews, soups and pottages made with pulses might be served several times a week, year round.

Pulses are an excellent source of dietary fibre and protein and are very low in fat. In Spanish dishes, they are frequently combined with small quantities of fatty meats and sausages, which add a great deal of flavour.

Hard water toughens pulses in cooking. If you have very hard water, try soaking and cooking them in bottled or filtered water. They will become tender in much less time.

Beans are less wind-producing if you drain off the soaking water and cook them in fresh water.

These are the pulses most often used in Spanish cooking:

Bean, Dried (*alubia, habichuela, judía*). Dried beans come in many colours and sizes. The most common is a large white kidney bean, rather like a cannellini bean. The *judión*, or *fabe*, is an even bigger white bean, prized for cooking in the Asturian bean dish *fabada*. In Valencia, dried lima beans or butter beans, called *garrofón*, are an essential ingredient in authentic paella. They may be white or white tipped with brown. The speckled Tolosa red bean, which has a wonderful creamy consistency, is much used in Basque dishes. The best substitute is the pinto bean. Also from the Basque country is a black bean.

Dried beans are usually soaked for 8 hours before cooking. Drain, then put them to cook in fresh, cold water. Cooking time varies with the variety – anywhere from 1 to 2 hours. Spanish housewives say you should *asustar* the beans – give them a scare while they cook: after they have come to the boil, add 120 ml (4 fl oz) of cold water to 'shock' them.

In the autumn any of these beans might be available in markets as shell beans, which are mature beans, still in their shells, before they have been dried. In the Rioja region these are called *pochas*. Shell beans don't require soaking.

Black-Eyed Bean (*chícharo, figüelo, judía de careta*). Black-eyed beans look like white beans, but have a black spot on one side. They can be used in place of other beans in popular thick stews. Soak them overnight before cooking. These beans have a dry, starchy texture, which combines very well with fat and sausages.

Broad Bean (*haba, fabe*). Broad beans are more usual in their fresh form. Though the dried bean was once a staple food in Spain, now it's mainly used as animal fodder.

Chickpea (*garbanzo*). Spain lies south of the 'great *garbanzo* divide', a line of demarcation that roughly divides olive oil–producing regions from areas further north. The chickpea plays an important role in the cooking of Spain, Greece, Turkey, North Africa and the Middle East. Aficionados can and do argue the merits of 'my mother-in-law's *garbanzos*' compared with 'your sister's *garbanzos*'. Or last Sunday's *garbanzos* compared with today's *garbanzos*.

The chickpea is a small, round, ridged, golden pea-bean. When properly prepared, it is tender and chewable, with a nutty taste that no other dried pulse can match. It has a special affinity for the strong flavours in Spanish cooking – salt pork, sausages, tomatoes, cabbage, garlic and onions.

Soak chickpeas in water overnight (for at least 8 hours), then drain them. If your water is very hard, chickpeas won't cook up tender. Use filtered water or add a pinch of bicarbonate of soda to the soaking and cooking water. Bring the cooking liquid to a rolling boil before adding chickpeas. Don't add salt until the chickpeas are nearly tender. Chickpeas cook in approximately 90 minutes.

In Spain, where chickpeas are cooked on a daily basis as part of the *cocido* (boiled dinner), housewives regularly use a pressure cooker to cut down on cooking time. All the ingredients and liquid are brought to the boil in the cooker, the soaked chickpeas are added, then the pressure lid closed. In the pressure cooker, the *cocido* takes 30 to 40 minutes to cook.

Chickpeas left over from the *cocido* can be drained and dressed with oil, vinegar, chopped parsley, onion and garlic and served as a salad.

Lentil (*lenteja*). Three main varieties of lentil are used: big, flat green ones (*castellanas*), medium brown ones and tiny brown Puy lentils (*pardinas*). The green and brown lentils will cook almost to a purée, whereas the Puy lentils keep their shape. Although they are grown widely in Spain, lentils are in such great demand that much is imported.

Lentils do not need presoaking. They cook in less time than other pulses. Allow 25 to 35 minutes, but begin testing for doneness after 20 minutes.

Peasant Soup with Wheat Kernels
Olla de Trigo

I think this is an especially tasty combination – whole grains of wheat, chickpeas and wild fennel. The wheat – newly gathered green wheat with its husk removed – is cooked slowly with fatty pork and the mild liquorice-scented fennel. Wild fennel is gathered in the spring, when the first shoots come up, and the tender stems and unfurled leaves are used.

You can use brown rice or barley instead of wheat kernels and cultivated Florence fennel instead of the stems of wild fennel. If you prefer to use wheat kernels, soak them overnight. They will be fairly chewy, even after cooking. You can also choose to eliminate some of the fat by cutting down on the amount of bacon and salt pork used.

280 g (10 oz) chopped fennel (wild stems or cultivated bulb)

60 g (2 oz) unsmoked bacon (optional)

115 g (4 oz) salt pork (optional)

170 g (6 oz) wheat kernels, soaked overnight and drained, or brown rice

230 g (8 oz) chickpeas or white beans, soaked overnight

6 lean pork chops (680 g/1½ lb)

1½ teaspoons salt

170 g (6 oz) morcilla (blood) sausage, black pudding or pork sausages

⅛ teaspoon ground cloves (optional)

⅛ teaspoon freshly ground black pepper (optional)

¼ teaspoon ground cinnamon (optional)

Chopped fennel leaves, to garnish

If you are using wild fennel shoots, strip them of outer skin and cut into short lengths.

Bring a large saucepan of water to the boil and blanch the bacon and salt pork, if using, with the wild fennel and wheat kernels for 5 minutes. Drain. Return them to the pan and cover with 2 litres (3½ pints) of fresh water. Bring to the boil.

Drain the chickpeas and add them to the boiling water. Reduce to a simmer, cover and cook for 40 minutes.

Add the chopped cultivated fennel, if using, the pork chops, salt, morcilla and rice, if using instead of wheat. If morcilla is not available, use black pudding or pork sausages and add the optional cloves, pepper and cinnamon. Return to the boil, reduce the heat and simmer, covered, for another 30 minutes.

Let the soup rest for at least 5 minutes before serving. Remove the morcilla from the pan and cut into six pieces. Remove and cut the bacon and salt pork into bite-sized pieces. Return the meat to the soup. Serve in soup bowls sprinkled with chopped fennel leaves.

SERVES 6

RED BEANS, BASQUE STYLE
ALUBIAS ROJAS A LA VASCA

The Basques love their beans, which come in several colours. Fat red beans of Tolosa are a speciality. They are deliciously creamy, yet keep their shape when cooked.

A shopkeeper in Guernica gave me his recipe for cooking beans. He recommended starting the beans at 9 in the morning to be ready for a 2 PM meal. He said not to presoak the beans because soaking causes the skins to split during cooking. When I tried his recipe with red kidney beans, smaller red beans and pinto beans, I found they cooked tender in only about 2½ hours, even without soaking. Obviously, cooking time depends on the beans. You can cook them in about 1 hour if you prefer to soak them 8 hours in advance.

Basque cooks (and Andalusian cooks, too) say you have to *asustar* the beans – give them a 'scare' with a glass of cold water several times during cooking. It's also important to make sure they are always covered with some liquid, so the skins don't split.

450 g (1 lb) dried red or pinto beans, rinsed, but not presoaked

Ham bone (optional)

1 large carrot, cut into chunks

2 bay leaves

1 small green sweet pepper, chopped

½ onion, chopped

1 tablespoon olive oil

1 leek, white and tender green parts, chopped

450 g (1 lb) potatoes, peeled and cut into 2.5-cm (1-inch) cubes

1 tablespoon salt

115 g (4 oz) chorizo sausage or any pork sausage

Cooked cabbage (optional)

Sautéed red onion slices (optional)

Mild pickled green chillies (optional)

Combine the beans in a large saucepan with 1.4 litres (2½ pints) water. Add the ham bone, if using, carrot, bay leaves, green pepper and onion. Bring the water to the boil and add the oil. Reduce the heat to a simmer, cover the pan and cook for 1 hour.

Add a glass of cold water. Simmer for another 30 minutes.

Add another glass of cold water. Add the leek, potatoes, salt and chorizo. Bring to a full boil, then reduce to a simmer and cook for another 30 to 60 minutes, until the beans are tender. Remove the bay leaves.

Serve the beans accompanied by cooked cabbage, sautéed onions and pickled green chillies, if desired.

SERVES 4

CHESTNUT AND BEAN STEW
POTAJE DE CASTAÑAS Y ALUBIAS

Dense chestnut forests cover inland regions, particularly in northwest Spain, but also in the mountains of the south. Once upon a time, chestnuts were a very important food source, though potatoes have largely replaced them.

Street-corner vendors roasting chestnuts on a brazier are one of the harbingers of autumn. The nuts are also cooked with sweet potatoes, a warming dish to carry to the cemetery on the eve of All Souls', or the Day of the Dead. In the following recipe, they are stewed with beans.

The chestnuts and aniseed lend a subtle sweetness to this stew, which some cooks like to accentuate with the addition of sugar.

310 g (11 oz) roasted, peeled (or tinned) chestnuts or 230 g (8 oz) dried chestnuts

450 g (1 lb) white beans, soaked overnight

6 meaty spare ribs (optional)

1 whole head garlic, roasted and peeled (see page 8)

1 bay leaf

1–3 tablespoons olive oil

1 onion, chopped

½ teaspoon aniseed

¼ teaspoon saffron threads

1 clove

5 peppercorns

1 teaspoon salt

1 garlic clove

If you are using dried chestnuts, soak them overnight with the beans.

Drain the beans and combine in a large saucepan with 1.4 litres (2½ pints) of water, the chestnuts and ribs, if using. Add the roasted garlic and bay leaf. Bring to the boil, skim off any foam, then cover and simmer for 1 hour.

Heat 1 tablespoon oil in a medium frying pan over medium heat (use 3 tablespoons oil if you are not using the spare ribs). Add the onion and aniseed and sauté until the onion is softened, 4 to 5 minutes. Add the contents of the frying pan to the beans and chestnuts.

Crush the saffron, clove and peppercorns in a mortar with the salt. Add the raw garlic and mash it. Dissolve this paste into some of the liquid from the pan. Stir the spice mixture into the pan. Cook for another 30 minutes, until beans are very tender.

Remove the bay leaf and serve hot.

SERVES 6

Everyday Soup Pot
El Puchero de Todos los Dias

Jimena de la Frontera is a village in southwestern Spain situated on the edge of the country's great national cork forests. I travel to Jimena several times a year to give holiday cooking courses. Carmen and Angeles help me out in the kitchen and have filled me in on local cooking lore.

Carmen used to help her husband, who was an *arriero* (mule driver), in collecting and hauling the cut cork. During the cork-cutting harvest, in midsummer, whole families move out into the cork forests, setting up encampments and cooking their meals in the open air.

The cork cutters are organized in *cuadrillas* (teams) of all men, each with a cook. They breakfast at dawn – only coffee, bread and *aguardiente* (anise brandy) – *para matar el gusanillo,* to deaden the little worm of hunger. The day's first meal comes at 11.30 or 12. It is always the same – a *puchero* (boiled dinner), with chickpeas, both fresh and salt pork fat, meaty bones and potatoes.

A large *lebrillo* (glazed earthenware bowl) is filled with pieces of bread and the stock from the *puchero* poured over. This is covered and allowed to set until the liquid is completely absorbed by the bread. It is topped by a few chickpeas, drizzled with olive oil and sprinkled with fresh mint.

The *lebrillo* is placed on a stone. One by one, each man steps forward and scoops up a portion of the thick gruel, using a spoon or the blade of his pocket knife, then steps back. The men tend to grumble a lot if the *puchero* is too thin, because then it can't be scooped up on to a knife blade.

They return to work and break again at 4.30 PM, for a gazpacho of bread, oil, tomatoes, onion, cucumber and green pepper, made in a *dornillo* (wooden bowl). The gazpacho is accompanied by *pringá,* the cooked salt pork from the *puchero,* which is spread on bread.

The evening meal, after the sun has set, consists of stock from the *puchero* with chickpeas and potatoes, accompanied by bread.

Cork comes from the outer bark of cork oak trees, which are stripped every nine years. (It does not grow hanging from the trees in bunches, like cherries, as so charmingly illustrated by Robert Lawson in *The Story of Ferdinand*, by Munro Leaf.)

Cork is packed in *quintales* of 28 kg (about 62 lb). It is baled and put into hot water, weighted to flatten it, then dried and graded according to viscosity and thickness. Not all cork becomes stoppers for fine wine. Lower-grade cork is used for insulation, floor tiles and other industrial purposes.

This *puchero* is everyday fare in village and country homes. The recipe makes enough soup to serve six to eight persons, though the other ingredients that make up the main course make four servings. The remaining stock can be used to make *sopa de picadillo*, Garnished Stock (see page 84).

½ chicken (about 680 g/½ lb)

170 g (6 oz) meaty beef shin bone

170 g (6 oz) pork spare ribs

60 g (2 oz) salt pork or pancetta

115 g (4 oz) ham bone

1 leek, white part only

1 carrot, peeled

1 turnip, peeled

1 stalk celery

140 g (5 oz) dried chickpeas, soaked for 8 hours

3 medium potatoes (450 g/1 lb), peeled

Salt

4 thick slices bread or 85 g (3 oz) medium-short-grain rice

Sprigs fresh mint, to garnish

In a large saucepan, combine the chicken, beef bone, spare ribs, salt pork, ham bone, leek, carrot, turnip and celery. Add 3 litres (5 pints) water. Bring to the boil and skim off the foam.

Drain the chickpeas and add to the boiling liquid. Reduce the heat so it bubbles gently. Cover and cook for 1 hour.

Add the potatoes and salt to taste. Simmer for 30 minutes more.

Strain 1 litre (about 2 pints) of the stock into another pan. If you are preparing the soup with bread, cut the bread into fingers and divide it between four soup plates. Ladle the hot stock over the bread. If desired, a few chickpeas can be included. Garnish with sprigs of mint. If you are using rice for the soup, bring the stock to a boil and add the rice. Simmer until the rice is tender, 16 minutes. Serve immediately, garnished with mint.

Remove the meats, vegetables and chickpeas from the soup pan. Cut the chicken and meat into four serving pieces and arrange on a serving platter. Cut up the carrot, turnip and potatoes and place on the platter with the chickpeas.

After serving the soup, serve the platter of meat and vegetables. Leftover stock can be refrigerated and skimmed of fat, then frozen for another use.

SERVES 4, PLUS 2–2.25 LITRES (3½–4 PINTS) STOCK

Spanish Boiled Dinner

El Cocido Español

Not paella, not gazpacho, but *cocido*, a meal-in-a-pot, is the true national dish of Spain. In one version or another, it is enjoyed in every region of the country. It's a family meal, perfect for a Sunday midday dinner, though a simpler version is daily fare in village homes.

At its most basic, *cocido* is identical to the *puchero* (page 107) – chickpeas, pork fat, ham bone and potatoes. The simple daily version includes a stewing hen and a small portion of beef or pork, as well as a few vegetables. The holiday version, which follows, is embellished with more meats and sausages.

In village markets where I can buy stewing hen, I also find bowls full of egg yolks – actually, they are unlaid eggs with no shells, taken from the insides of the hens. A special addition to the *cocido*, they are placed, one per person, in the soup bowl and the boiling stock poured over to poach them.

You will need your largest pan – 5.5-litre (10-pint) capacity – plus two smaller pans to prepare this recipe. Put the chickpeas to soak the night before in water three times their depth. The two kinds of sausage, chorizo and morcilla, are important ingredients. Sources for buying the sausages are found on page 342. Black pudding or ordinary pork sausages can be substituted for the morcilla. The *pelota* is a big meat dumpling – a sort of simmered meat loaf.

Serve the *cocido* in two stages. The noodle soup is the first course. Any soup pasta can be used, though thin *fideos*, rather like vermicelli, are most typical. Follow the soup with two platters, one containing all the meats and sausages, another with chickpeas and vegetables. Tomato sauce is served separately. Pickled onions or pickled mild green chillies (*guindillas*) are a good side dish.

8-cm (3-inch) piece ham bone

1 beef knuckle bone

450 g (1 lb) boneless beef brisket or
   shin meat

½ stewing hen (about 1 kg/2¼ lb)

1 (85-g/3-oz) piece unsmoked bacon

340 g (12 oz) dried chickpeas, soaked
   overnight

3 cloves

1 onion

1 leek, white part only

1 celery stalk

5 peppercorns

2 bay leaves

3 parsley stems

3 large carrots, peeled

1 large turnip, peeled

1 tablespoon salt

PELOTA

1 slice bread

Milk

1 egg, beaten

170 g (6 oz) minced beef

170 g (6 oz) minced pork

115 g (4 oz) minced pork fat

1 garlic clove, finely chopped

½ teaspoon salt

1 tablespoon chopped fresh flat-leaf parsley

Pinch ground cinnamon

Pinch freshly grated nutmeg

Freshly ground black pepper

SECOND PAN

2 teaspoons salt

8 small potatoes (680 g/1½ lb), peeled

1 small cabbage, cut into 8 wedges

230 g (8 oz) chorizo

230 g (8 oz) morcilla (blood) sausage or
   black pudding

SOUP

115 g (4 oz) soup noodles such as
   vermicelli

8 egg yolks (optional)

GARNISH

Sprigs mint

Basic Tomato Sauce (page 10)

Chopped fresh flat-leaf parsley

Combine the ham bone, beef bone, beef, stewing hen and bacon in a very large saucepan. Add 3.5 litres (6½ pints) of water and bring to the boil. When the water boils, skim off the foam that rises to the top of the pan. Return to the boil. Drain and add the chickpeas. Bring to the boil and skim again. Stick the cloves into the onion and add with the leek, celery, peppercorns, bay leaves and parsley. Simmer, covered, for 1 hour.

While the meats and chickpeas are cooking, make the *pelota*, a big meatball. Soak the bread in a little milk until softened. Squeeze it out and combine with the egg, beef, pork, pork fat, garlic, salt, parsley, cinnamon, nutmeg and pepper. Knead the mixture until smooth, then shape it into a round ball.

Add the *pelota* to the *cocido* after 1 hour. Continue simmering for 30 minutes more. Turn the *pelota*, then add the whole carrots and turnip to the pan with the salt. Simmer for another 30 minutes.

Meanwhile, start the second pan. Bring 3 litres (5 pints) salted water to the boil. Add the potatoes, cabbage and sausages. Cook until the potatoes are tender, about 30 minutes.

Strain the liquid from the first pan into a third pan. Shortly before serving, bring it to the boil and add the soup pasta. Boil for 7 to 10 minutes and remove from heat.

Serve the soup with pasta first in shallow soup plates. If desired, first place a raw egg yolk in each plate and pour over the hot soup. Garnish each serving with mint.

To serve the main course, place the chicken, beef and sausages on a serving platter and use kitchen scissors to cut them into pieces. Slice the *pelota*.

Drain and discard the liquid from the second pan. Cut carrots and turnip into pieces. On another platter, place the chickpeas, potatoes, cabbage wedges, carrots, turnip and onion. Drizzle with a little of the tomato sauce and sprinkle with chopped parsley. Serve the rest of the tomato sauce separately.

SERVES 8

5

EGG, MILK AND CHEESE DISHES

TORTILLAS AND OTHER EGG DISHES

Omelette with Broad Beans and Asparagus
(*Tortilla de Habas y Espárragos*)

Green Omelette with Spinach and Onion
(*Tortilla de Espinacas*)

Tuna and Potato Omelette (*Tortilla de Escabeche*)

Aubergine Omelette (*Tortilla de Berenjena*)

Eggs Scrambled with Green Garlic,
Mushrooms and Prawns
(*Revuelto con Ajetes, Setas y Gambas*)

Scrambled Eggs with Wild Asparagus
(*Revuelto de Espárragos Trigueros*)

Baked Eggs Flamenco (*Huevos a lo Flamenco*)

Baked Eggs and Tomatoes
(*Huevos al Horno con Tomates*)

MILK AND CHEESE

Fried Cheese (*Queso Frito*)

Rennet Custard (*Cuajada*)

Vegetable Custard (*Cuajado de Tagarninas*)

FROM THE FARMYARD

Carolina lives in the country about a mile below my house, on a *finca* (smallholding). A typical *finca* consists of irrigated gardens and fruit trees; olive and almond groves on unirrigated slopes; and perhaps a field of wheat, maize, barley or alfalfa to feed the livestock. The house is a cluster of whitewashed buildings sheltering people, animals and granary. There is a terrace on the front, shaded with a grapevine against the scorching summer sun. A gnarled old fig tree adds to the sweet shade in summer, but, in winter, drops its leaves to allow the low sun to shine on the terrace.

Carolina's family was once nearly self-sufficient, producing fresh vegetables, wheat for bread, fruit, honey from beehives, olives for oil, grapes for wine, almonds, a pig to produce a small amount of salt-cured meat and fat to last the year, a couple of goats for milk, a hutch of rabbits as an occasional source of meat, and, most important of all, chickens to provide eggs.

The chickens she let out to scratch in the dirt beneath the orange trees. The nanny goats she staked out in a clover patch every morning after milking them. The milk was boiled and used for breakfast coffee and for puddings. When there was an abundance of milk, Carolina made fresh goats' milk cheese, which she gave to her family for snacks or a light evening meal.

I still get country eggs from Carolina when I can because they have so much more flavour than those from battery chickens. Look for fresh eggs at farmers' markets if you can.

TORTILLAS AND OTHER EGG DISHES

In Spain, eggs are rarely served for breakfast. Rather they are served as a first course for a main meal or as the main dish for a light supper. They may be prepared with exquisite simplicity – fried in olive oil – or combined with other ingredients in more elaborate dishes.

The favourite egg dish is the tortilla, which is a flat, round cake made of eggs and other ingredients, usually vegetables, but also fish and meat. Tortilla is frequently called an omelette, which sounds French. But the Spanish tortilla derives from the Sephardic Jewish cookery of medieval Spain. Sephardic cooking is rich in *fritadas* (frittatas) and *cuajados*, which are nearly identical to the tortilla.

Tortillas are delicious hot out of the frying pan, but they are also consumed at room temperature. A favourite working man's mid-morning snack is a thick slab of tortilla on a split bread roll. Children seem to love tortillas, even when they are packed with vegetables. Perhaps it is because they find it so easy to pick up a slice in the fingers. Tortillas pack well, so they are favourite fare for picnics or travel.

The most famous tortilla of all, made with potatoes, is to be found in the chapter on tapas (page 22). That's because it is one of the classic Spanish tapas. Which is not to say that some of the following variations don't turn up in tapa bars as well.

OMELETTE WITH BROAD BEANS AND ASPARAGUS
TORTILLA DE HABAS Y ESPÁRRAGOS

This omelette, studded with nuggets of green, is very pretty as well as tasty. It makes a great lunch, with salad and bread to go with it.

450 g (1 lb) shelled broad beans

450 g (1 lb) asparagus, cut into 12-mm (½-inch) lengths

3 tablespoons olive oil

½ onion, chopped

2 slices bacon, chopped

2 garlic cloves, chopped

1 teaspoon salt

4 large eggs

Bring a pan of salted water to the boil and cook the beans until tender, 8 to 10 minutes; drain. Bring another pan of salted water to the boil and cook the asparagus in boiling, salted water until crisp-tender, 5 minutes; drain.

Heat the oil in a 24-cm (9-inch) frying pan and sauté the onion and bacon until the onion is softened, about 4 minutes. Add the garlic, broad beans and asparagus and continue to sauté for 5 minutes. Sprinkle the vegetables with ½ teaspoon of the salt while they are sautéing.

Beat the eggs in a bowl with remaining ½ teaspoon salt.

Drain any excess oil from the frying pan into a small bowl. Then stir the vegetables into the beaten eggs. Return the oil to the frying pan. Pour in the vegetable and egg mixture. Cook over medium heat until the bottom is set, about 5 minutes.

Place a flat lid or plate over the frying pan. Invert the omelette on to it. Then carefully slide the omelette back into the frying pan to cook on the reverse side for 2 minutes more.

Slide out on to a serving dish. Serve hot or at room temperature.

SERVES 4

GREEN OMELETTE WITH SPINACH AND ONION
TORTILLA DE ESPINACAS

A fancy way to present this omelette is layered with a potato omelette (page 22). Make two green omelettes and one potato omelette. Stack one green omelette, one potato omelette and the second green omelette on a serving dish. Spoon tomato sauce (page 10) over the top. Slice the stack like a sandwich cake, so that each wedge shows green, yellow, green.

2 tablespoons olive oil

70 g (2½ oz) chopped onion

1 garlic clove, chopped

400 g (14 oz) cooked spinach, chopped

¼ teaspoon hot pimentón

4 eggs

½ teaspoon salt

2 tablespoons grated cheese (optional)

Heat 1½ tablespoons of the oil in a 24-cm (9-inch) frying pan over medium heat. Add the onion and garlic and sauté until the onion is softened, about 4 minutes. Stir in the spinach and sauté for 2 minutes. Sprinkle with the pimentón.

Beat the eggs and salt in a mixing bowl. Add the contents of the frying pan to the eggs and stir well to blend.

Add the remaining ½ tablespoon of oil to the frying pan and heat over medium heat. Pour in the egg-spinach mixture and spread evenly. Cook until the omelette is set on the bottom, about 5 minutes. Adjust the heat as needed so the omelette doesn't brown too quickly.

Place a flat lid or plate on top of the frying pan and invert the omelette on to it. Slide it back into the frying pan to cook on the reverse side, about 2 minutes.

Slide the omelette out of the pan on to a serving dish and, if desired, sprinkle with grated cheese. Serve hot.

SERVES 4 AS A STARTER, SNACK OR TAPA

TUNA AND POTATO OMELETTE
TORTILLA DE ESCABECHE

In Madrid, this is popular fare for a picnic in the city's beautiful El Retiro park. The word *escabeche* means pickling marinade, and refers in this recipe to the tinned tuna, which is pickled in vinegar. This is the sort of easy dish a Spanish home cook could put together from staples in her cupboard.

170 g (6 oz) drained canned tuna about 1½ (200 g) tins, preferably packed in olive oil

120 ml (4 fl oz) white wine vinegar

4 tablespoons olive oil

570 g (1¼ lb) potatoes, peeled and thinly sliced

½ teaspoon salt

45 g (1½ oz) diced red sweet pepper

1 small onion, finely chopped

6 eggs

2 tablespoons chopped fresh flat-leaf parsley

In a bowl, cover the tuna with the vinegar. Let marinate, refrigerated, for 1 hour. Drain off and discard the vinegar. Flake the tuna.

Heat the oil in a 24-cm (9-inch) frying pan over medium heat. Add the potatoes and cook them, slowly, turning frequently, for 15 minutes. Sprinkle them with the salt. Add the red pepper and onion. Cook until the potatoes are fork-tender, about 10 minutes more. The potatoes should not brown.

Beat the eggs in a bowl. Add the parsley and the tuna.

Drain off excess oil from the potatoes and reserve it. Stir the potatoes into the beaten eggs.

Add a little of the reserved oil to the pan and heat it over medium heat. Pour in the egg mixture. Spread it evenly. When the eggs begin to set on the bottom, about 4 minutes, use a spatula to loosen the sides of the omelette. Then shake the pan occasionally to keep the omelette from sticking on the bottom. Cook over medium-low heat for about 4 minutes longer, or until set on the bottom and sides. The omelette does not need to brown.

When the omelette is set, cover it with a plate or flat pan lid. Hold the plate tightly and reverse the omelette on to the plate. Add a drop more oil to the frying pan, then slide the omelette back into the pan to cook on the reverse side, about 4 minutes more.

Slide out on to a serving plate. Serve hot or at room temperature.

SERVES 4 TO 6 AS A STARTER, SNACK OR TAPA

Aubergine Omelette

Tortilla de Berenjena

This tortilla, typical of Murcia, a province on the eastern coast of Spain which is known for its market gardens, can be made with courgettes in place of the aubergine. Another enticing possibility is to use tinned *piquillo* red peppers in place of the sweet peppers.

2 red sweet peppers

4 tablespoons olive oil

45 g (1½ oz) chopped onion

340 g (12 oz) chopped tomatoes

1 medium aubergine, peeled and diced

6 eggs

½ teaspoon salt

Preheat the grill. Roast the peppers under the grill, turning them, until they are charred on all sides, 25 to 30 minutes. Remove them to a plate and cover the peppers. Let stand 1 hour, then pull off the outer skins. Discard the stems and seeds and tear the peppers into strips.

Heat 2 tablespoons of the oil in a frying pan over medium-high heat and sauté the onion for 2 minutes, until softened. Add the tomatoes, peppers and aubergine and continue cooking until the aubergine is tender and most of the liquid has cooked away, about 15 minutes.

Beat the eggs and salt in a bowl. Mix the aubergine mixture into the eggs.

Wipe out the frying pan. Heat the remaining 2 tablespoons oil over medium heat, and pour in the egg mixture. Let the omelette cook until almost set, about 8 minutes. Working over a bowl to catch drips, turn the omelette out on to a plate and slide it back to cook on the reverse side, about 2 minutes. Serve hot or at room temperature.

Serves 4 to 6

EGGS SCRAMBLED WITH GREEN GARLIC, MUSHROOMS AND PRAWNS
REVUELTO CON AJETES, SETAS Y GAMBAS

Even simpler than tortilla is a *revuelto* – eggs scrambled with one or more ingredients. At my house, *revuelto* is a favourite supper dish, but it would also be wonderful at brunch.

Green garlic is the garlic equivalent of green onions – an embryonic garlic head topped by a green shoot, about 50 cm (18 inches) long. You can sprout them from garlic cloves in a flowerpot, or look for them in farmers' markets. Leeks can be substituted. If you are using leeks, chop them, then blanch them in boiling water for 1 minute and squeeze out any liquid.

115 g (4 oz) green garlic shoots
(5–6 shoots)

3 tablespoons olive oil, plus more for toast

280 g (10 oz) wild or cultivated
mushrooms, cleaned and sliced

60 g (2 oz) peeled small prawns

4 eggs, beaten with 1 tablespoon of water

½ teaspoon salt

Toast, to serve

Strip off and discard any discoloured outer leaves from the green garlic. Then chop greens and head.

Heat the oil in a large frying pan over medium heat and sauté the garlic very gently until softened, 5 minutes.

Add the mushrooms and sauté until they give up their liquid and begin to sizzle in the oil, about 5 minutes. (Some types of wild mushroom will need more time to sweat out their liquid.)

Stir in the prawns and cook for 1 minute. Then stir in the eggs and salt. Stir the mixture over medium heat until the eggs begin to set. Remove from the heat and stir until cooked through.

Serve hot, accompanied by toast. To serve as a tapa, mound the scrambled eggs on squares of toast that have been brushed with olive oil.

SERVES 4 TO 6 AS A TAPA; SERVES 2 AS A MAIN DISH

SCRAMBLED EGGS WITH WILD ASPARAGUS
REVUELTO DE ESPÁRRAGOS TRIGUEROS

This is a favourite way to cook the slightly bitter, thin stalks of wild asparagus, which come up on the edges of wheat fields in the early spring. It works equally well with regular asparagus, if you don't have access to the wild variety.

450 g (1 lb) green asparagus, trimmed and coarsely chopped

2 tablespoons olive oil

70 g (2½ oz) chopped onion

1 garlic clove, chopped

3 tablespoons chopped serrano ham or lean bacon

4 eggs, beaten with 1 tablespoon water

½ teaspoon salt

Freshly ground black pepper

4 slices bread, crusts removed, fried golden in olive oil, to serve

Bring a pan of salted water to the boil and boil the asparagus until tender, 6 minutes. Drain.

In a frying pan, heat the oil over medium heat and sauté the onion, garlic and ham until the onion is slightly softened, about 4 minutes. Stir in the asparagus and sauté gently over medium-low heat for 5 minutes.

Beat the eggs and the salt. Stir the eggs into the frying pan. Keep stirring them over medium heat until soft-set, 2½ minutes. Remove, season immediately with freshly ground black pepper, and serve with pieces of fried bread as an accompaniment.

SERVES 4 AS A STARTER OR TAPA; SERVES 2 AS A MAIN DISH

Baked Eggs Flamenco

Huevos a lo Flamenco

Served in individual cazuelas or ramekins, this colourful egg dish makes a terrific brunch.

4 teaspoons olive oil

170 ml (6 fl oz) tomato sauce (tinned or freshly made, page 10)

60 g (2 oz) chopped ham

8 eggs

4 thin slices chorizo (or substitute salami), cut in half

4 tablespoons cooked green peas

8 asparagus tips

Salt and freshly ground black pepper

Pimentón

1 tablespoon chopped fresh flat-leaf parsley

8 strips bottled pimiento

Preheat the oven to 200°C/400°F/gas mark 6.

Divide the oil between four 15-cm (6-inch) cazuelas, individual casseroles or ovenproof ramekins. Divide the tomato sauce between them. Sprinkle the chopped ham on top of the tomato sauce.

Break 2 eggs into each cazuela. Put 2 halves of chorizo on either side of the eggs. Sprinkle with peas. Arrange 2 asparagus tips in each cazuela. Sprinkle each with salt and pepper, a pinch of pimentón, and parsley. Cross 2 strips of pimiento on top of each.

Bake until the egg whites are set, but yolks are still runny. This takes about 8 minutes in an earthenware cazuela (the eggs will continue to cook after removing from oven), but only about 6 minutes in a metal pan. The eggs can also be baked in a shallow baking pan and served on to plates at the table. Serve immediately.

SERVES 4

BAKED EGGS AND TOMATOES
HUEVOS AL HORNO CON TOMATES

This makes a delicious brunch dish. Serve it with plenty of crusty bread.

680 g (1½ lb) ripe tomatoes (about 6–8 medium)

4 tablespoons chopped fresh flat-leaf parsley

½ teaspoon dried oregano, crumbled

2 garlic cloves, chopped

½ teaspoon salt

Freshly ground black pepper

3 tablespoons olive oil

6 eggs

6 anchovy fillets, drained

Preheat the oven to 190°C/375°F/gas mark 5.

Slice the tomatoes about 6 mm (¼ inch) thick. Place them in an overlapping layer in a 24 x 33-cm (9 x 13-inch) baking pan. Scatter the parsley, oregano, garlic, salt and pepper over the tomatoes. Drizzle with the oil.

Bake the tomatoes for 10 minutes and remove the pan from the oven. Break the eggs on to the tomatoes. Place the anchovy fillets between the eggs.

Return the pan to the oven until the egg whites are set, but the yolks are still liquid, 4 to 8 minutes, depending on the size and initial temperature of the eggs.

To serve, use a spatula to loosen the sides and cut into squares.

SERVES 6

Milk and Cheese

Even today a flock of goats often traverses the rocky hillside facing my house, led by their goatherd, Salvador. With their bells tinkling, I can hear them coming from a long way off. When I have out-of-town visitors and the goats mosey by, I like to joke that they were sent by central casting. With the blue Mediterranean out in the distance, the olive trees all around, the bees humming over the wild thyme and the goats grazing on the slopes, it's a pretty complete picture of Mediterranean life.

For many years, there were several herds that went out every morning from the village. As they passed through the streets, housewives would come out with their pails and the goatherd would milk the goats at their doorstep. The warm milk was carried to the kitchen and brought to the boil three times in a special milk-boiler. It was then ready to be poured into coffee, whisked into thick drinking chocolate or cooked in a sweet pudding.

During the milking season, the goatherds made cheese with the excess milk, which I used to buy at a neighbourhood shop. It was a small round of very white curds, marked by the woven esparto grass moulds in which it was pressed. The cheese was soft and fresh, very mild in flavour and lightly salted.

No herds are stabled in the village anymore, and local cheese is no longer produced. Salvador's goats have a barn in the country, in the hills far below my house. He milks the goats each morning and delivers the milk to a refrigerated lorry, which takes it to a dairy in the city. The dairies produce cheeses using pasteurized milk. They are similar to the ones I used to buy in my neighbourhood shop.

While milk and cheese are important additions to the diet in every region of Spain, they are not extensively used in cooking. Of course, milk goes in breakfast coffee or, for children, cocoa or other breakfast drink, but it is not widely consumed as a beverage. In the traditional kitchen, when milk was abundant, it was made into cheese. As cheese, milk could be kept for longer periods. An important food, cheese is served with bread, for breakfast, a snack, a tapa and supper.

How Cheese is Made

Mari Carmen is an artisanal cheesemaker in a small village in the Basque country. She makes prizewinning Idiazábal cheese, a traditional cheese made from the milk of latxa sheep. She and her husband, Florencio, live in a sixteenth-century tower house, where the kitchen is the centre of life. He tends a herd of three hundred black-faced, long-haired latxa sheep, and she makes her wonderful cheese from their milk.

The sheep are milked twice a day. The traditional wooden *kaikua* (milking jugs) have been replaced with stainless steel ones. The milk is kept in a holding tank for 24 hours. It is then heated gently – hot water circulates around the tank – to a temperature of about 22°C (71–72°F) and left to set for an hour, then reheated to 30°C (86°F). Next the *cuajo*, or curdling agent, is added.

Cuajo is rennet. It comes from the stomachs of baby animals, where it produces enzymes that allow the suckling to digest its mother's milk. The *cuajo* is dried and powdered and dissolved in water before being added to the milk for cheese-making. Mari Carmen uses calves' rennet, rather than that from lambs, because she says it makes a milder cheese. The mild ones win the prizes, she says, but the sharp ones sell first.

The milk is stirred for 7 minutes to dissolve the rennet. It is then allowed to rest until it clabbers, or curdles. This requires close watching – and experience. It can vary from 10 to 15 minutes, depending on the ambient temperature.

At this point the cheese is 'like a giant yogurt', Mari Carmen explains. The next step is to cut the curds with a lyre into bits about the size of grains of wheat. The curds are stirred for 20 minutes, then warmed again to 38°C (100°F). This keeps the cheese from turning bitter and wrinkled.

The curds are then pressed for 15 minutes to release the whey. Next they are cut into pieces with a knife and pressed into plastic moulds, with cotton stretched across the tops. These are stacked on a press to further press out the whey.

The pressed cheeses are turned out of the moulds and drained. Six litres of milk (6¼ quarts) make about 1 kg (2 lb 3 oz) of cheese.

The fresh cheeses are submerged in a cold brine for 10 hours. After removal from the brine, they are allowed to air-dry for two days.

During the maturing process – which in former times was dependent on weather conditions, but now is thermostatically controlled – the cheeses are kept under 15°C (60°F) at the beginning, then under 10°C (50°F). They must be turned every 15 days. Cheeses are aged for a minimum of three months and up to one year.

Some cheeses get washed and brushed to reduce exterior mould. Some Idiazábal cheeses are also smoked over alder and beech wood. Originally a way of stopping mould, smoking gives the cheese another taste dimension.

Living with latxa sheep is no lark, says Mari Carmen. In fine weather, they feed in the green pastures all around. In winter, they are stabled below the house and must be given fodder. 'We are slaves to the sheep', she sighs.

The basic method of making cheese is very similar everywhere in Spain, whether the cheese is made of sheep's, cows' or goats' milk. It is in the maturing process, where special bacteria contribute to the process, that cheeses acquire their identities.

FRIED CHEESE
QUESO FRITO

Slices of cheese, lightly breaded and fried, are delectable – crisp on the outside, melting on the inside. The fried cheese can be served as a tapa or with greens as part of a salad. I also like it with fresh pears or with thin slices of quince jelly. A semi-cured sheep's milk cheese, such as Manchego, is ideal in this preparation, while a lightly smoked Idiazábal adds flavour nuances. Any medium-firm cheese that melts without becoming stringy can be used.

250–280 g (9–10 oz) semi-cured goats' or sheep's milk cheese (8-cm/3-inch wedge)

4 tablespoons plain flour

1 egg, beaten

5 tablespoons fine dry breadcrumbs

Olive oil, for frying

Hot pimentón (optional)

Remove the rind from the cheese and cut into triangles 1 cm (⅜ inch) thick. Dredge the slices in flour, dip in beaten egg then coat with breadcrumbs.

Heat oil to cover the bottom of a frying pan over medium-high heat. Fry the slices of cheese in two or three batches. Turn when they are browned on the bottom. They need only about 30 seconds per side.

Drain briefly on kitchen towels and serve hot.

SERVES 6 AS A STARTER; SERVES 12 AS A TAPA

RENNET CUSTARD
CUAJADA

Cuajada is an interesting 'custard' with no eggs. It is set using rennet. This velvety-smooth custard is excellent for breakfast with fruit, as a dessert with honey or as a savoury appetizer with fresh herbs. It can be made with whole or semi-skimmed milk.

900 ml (1½ pints) milk

85 g (3 oz) non-fat dry milk powder

1 teaspoon vanilla extract (optional)

1¾ rennet tablets

honey (optional)

Have ready six 170 ml (6 fl oz) glass or earthenware cups or pots.

Scald the milk. Remove from heat and beat in the milk powder until smooth. Add the vanilla, if using. Cool the milk to lukewarm (43°C/110°F).

Dissolve the rennet tablets in 2 tablespoons of water. Stir the rennet into the warm milk. Stir it once and immediately pour into the six cups.

Let the cups stand undisturbed for 15 minutes. Cover the tops with clingfilm and refrigerate for 6 hours.

Serve the custards accompanied by honey, if desired. Each person sweetens the custard to taste.

SERVES 6

VEGETABLE CUSTARD
CUAJADO DE TAGARNINAS

I first tasted this custard, made with wild thistle greens, in La Mancha, Spain's central high plateau region. But it wasn't until I visited Fernando and Maria, who tend a herd of a couple hundred goats up in the mountains in southern Spain, that I learned to recognize this unusual wild vegetable.

Maria was doing the milking the day I visited, while her husband had taken the mule in search of some special fodder to cure an ailing goat. Maria told me she hadn't left the *cortijo*, a simple country cottage built up against great grey stones, in many months, as the work was too demanding. Solar panels provided enough electricity to power a black-and-white TV and butane gas ran a refrigerator.

Milking takes so much time that Maria said she never cooks anything much for the midday meal – *huevos fritos* or *huevos revueltos* (fried eggs or scrambled eggs), because eggs are quick. Sometimes she scrambles them with a wild thistle that comes up in the early spring.

When Fernando returned he picked some of the wild thistle, *tagarninas* (*Scolymus hispanicus*), to show me. After winter rains the first leaves come up, forming a flat rosette about 60 cm (2 feet) across. Later in the summer the plant sends up tall stalks on which bloom yellow flowers.

He pulled the whole plant up by the roots and, with bare hands, stripped off the prickly leaves, leaving the slender stems. The stems are chopped and blanched, then mixed with eggs for an omelette or scramble.

This custard is so delicious that I suggest you try it, substituting chopped asparagus for the wild thistle. The custard can also be baked in individual dishes. It makes a wonderful luncheon dish, much appreciated by vegetarian guests.

450 g (1 lb) cut asparagus (2.5-cm/ 1-inch lengths)

1 tablespoon olive oil

1 garlic clove, chopped

3 tablespoons tinned tomato sauce

½ teaspoon salt

Freshly ground black pepper

5 eggs, beaten

Pinch dried thyme

670 ml (1¼ pints) milk

2 teaspoons cornflour

Preheat the oven to 180°C/350°F/gas mark 4. Butter a 2-litre (3½-pint) pudding basin or mould.

Bring a pan of salted water to the boil and cook the asparagus until it is tender, about 7 minutes. Drain it well and set aside.

Heat the oil in a frying pan over medium-high heat and sauté the garlic for about 1 minute. Stir in the asparagus and sauté for 5 minutes. Remove from the heat and stir in the tomato sauce. Season with salt and pepper.

In a large bowl, beat the eggs with the thyme. Set aside. In a saucepan combine the milk and cornflour. Cook over medium heat, stirring constantly, until the milk thickens slightly, about 10 minutes.

Whisk a little of the hot milk mixture into the eggs, then add the remaining milk. Stir in the asparagus.

Pour into the pudding basin or mould. Cover the basin with aluminium foil and put it into a bain marie of hot water and place in the oven. Bake until the custard is set, or when a skewer comes out clean, about 40 minutes.

Remove the basin from the bain marie and let it rest for 5 minutes. Then loosen the sides with a knife, and pour off any liquid which has accumulated in the bottom of the basin. Place a platter on top and invert the custard on to the platter. Serve hot or at room temperature.

SERVES 6 AS A STARTER

Get to Know the Cheeses of Spain

The cheeses of Spain are becoming more widely distributed in places like the United States and are acquiring many aficionados. Although some are produced in such small quantities that they are little commercialized, others are enjoyed around the world. The cheeses described below are some of the ones you might find in a shop that carries imported cheeses, as well as some lesser-known varieties worth seeking out if you are travelling in Spain.

Cheese in Spain is usually served as a tapa, an aperitif with wine, in a sandwich as a snack, but hardly ever as a cheese course following the meal. A few bland cheeses are favoured for dessert, served with fruit, honey and nuts.

The cheeses that have *denominación de origen* or designation of origin (DO), are marked like this: ⓓⓞ.

Burgos. A soft, compact fresh white ewes' milk cheese, often served for dessert with honey, fruit and nuts. As the Spanish say, *Uvas y queso saben de beso* (grapes and cheese taste like a kiss).

Cabrales. Cabrales is the name of a town in Asturias, in northern Spain. The cheese is usually made from cows' milk, though it may contain small quantities of ewes' and goats' milk, too. Aged in caves, the cheese is off-white, with blue-green veins. It has a lovely creamy consistency and a bit of a 'bite'. Traditionally, Cabrales were wrapped in fig or mulberry leaves, but leaf-wrapping has been phased out. Use this cheese like any fine blue cheese. It's exceptional mashed with white wine or cider as a dip for chicory or spooned over grilled steak. ⓓⓞ

Cantabria. A cows' milk cheese, soft, buttery and pleasant, from Santander in northern Spain. ⓓⓞ

Gallego. Various cows' milk cheeses made in Galicia are grouped under this label. They are usually pale yellow, mild in flavour and neither soft nor hard.

Liébana. From the Picos de Europa, the mountains in Cantabria (northern Spain), a cheese made from ewes', cows' and goats' milk. There are several different varieties, including fresh, matured and smoked cheeses. ⓓⓞ

Ibérico. Made from a mixture of cows', ewes' and goats' milks, somewhat in the same style as Manchego. Available semi-cured and cured, this is a good everyday cheese, especially when sliced as an aperitif or grated and used in cooking. ⓓⓞ

Idiazábal. A hard cheese made in the Basque country from the milk of ewes of the long-haired latxa breed. It is smooth and sharp. Some – but not all – of these cheeses are smoked. A grilled ham and smoked Idiazábal sandwich is quite sensational. ⓂⒾ

La Serena. A ewes' milk cheese from Extremadura. Soft and creamy with a subtle bitterness due to the use of vegetable coagulant from a wild cardoon. ⓂⒾ

Mahón. Made in the Balearic island of Minorca, primarily of cows' milk. It is available both fresh and aged. The aged cheese is hard, somewhat like Parmesan. Both are good to use in cooking. Some Mahón cheeses are oiled and coated with pimentón, giving them an amber skin. ⓂⒾ

Majorero. A goats' milk cheese from Fuerteventura in the Canary Islands. Fresh, semi- and fully matured varieties are available. ⓂⒾ

Manchego. Recognized as one of the world's great cheeses, this is Spain's best-known cheese. It is made in the central region of Spain known as La Mancha, Don Quixote's stamping grounds, from the milk of ewes of the Manchega breed. The cheese is marketed fresh, semi-cured, ripe and well aged. The very well-aged, or *viejo*, cheese is sharp and splintery. It has a tantalizing strong nose, a bit of a bite and a smooth finish. Semi-cured Manchego is mild and smooth, fitting easily into any sort of meal. Serve it as an aperitif, as well as in sandwiches and gratinéed foods. ⓂⒾ

Picón Bejes-Treviso. A strongly flavoured blue cheese from the Picos de Europa region of Cantabria in northern Spain, made from a mixture of cows', ewes' and goats' milk, and matured in caves.

Roncal. This cheese comes from the Roncal Valley in Navarre, in northern Spain, where it is made from milk from sheep of the latxa and rasa breeds. It is one of Spain's most highly regarded cheeses, with a sharp yet mellow flavour, white curds and a hard rind. ⓂⒾ

Tetilla. This Galician cheese, made of cows' milk, is named for its shape, a lovely rounded breast. It is yellow on the outside, paler on the inside, very smooth and with a salty tang. ⓂⒾ

Torta del Cásar. Made in Extremadura from the milk of Merino sheep, which were once renowned for their wool. An unusual cheese, it is slightly runny and mildly acidic.

Zamorano. A ewes' milk cheese from the province of Zamora in Castilla-Leon. Mature cheeses have a hint of piquancy. The milk comes from the Churra breed of sheep, which is also appreciated for the quality of its meat. ⓂⒾ

6

VEGETABLES

COLD DISHES WITH VEGETABLES

Artichoke Salad, Tarragona Style
(*Ensalada Tarragonense*)

Garlic Coleslaw with Pomegranate Seeds
(*Ensalada de Col*)

Cauliflower Salad with Lemon Dressing
(*Ensalada de Coliflor al Limón*)

Green Bean and Potato Salad
(*Ensalada de Judías Verdes y Patatas*)

Roasted Onion Salad (*Ensalada de Cebollas Asadas*)

Minted Broad Bean Salad (*Ensalada de Habas*)

Tomatoes and Peppers with Tuna (*Titaina*)

HOT VEGETABLE DISHES

Green Beans with Garlic Sauce
(*Judías Verdes en Salsa*)

'Land Fish' (Fried Aubergine) (*Pez de Tierra*)

Aubergine, Moorish Style (*Berenjena a la Morisca*)

Jaén-Style Spinach with Crispy Croûtons
(*Espinacas a la Jinense*)

Cauliflower, Mule-Driver's Style
(*Coliflor al Ajo Arriero*)

Cauliflower with Almond Sauce
(*Coliflor con Salsa de Almendras*)

Asparagus in Cazuela (*Cazuela de Espárragos*)

Artichokes, Córdoba Style
(*Alcachofas a la Cordobesa*)

Courgette and Potato Gratin, Balearic Style
(*Tumbet Balear*)

Courgette Timbale with Cheese
(*Cuajado de Calabacines*)

Pumpkin Sauté (*Calabaza Frita*)

Summer Vegetable Stew (*Pisto*)

Chard with Raisins and Pine Kernels
(*Acelgas con Pasas y Piñones*)

Medley of Vegetables (*Menestra de Verduras*)

Vegetable Pizzas (*Coques de Verdures*)

Vegetable Mélange with Wild Mushrooms
(*Menestra con Setas*)

Spanish Chips (*Patatas Fritas*)

Double-Mashed Potatoes (*Patatas Revolconas*)

Poor Folk's Potatoes (*Patatas a lo Pobre*)

Widowed Potatoes (*Viudo*)

Potatoes, La Rioja Style (*Patatas a la Riojana*)

FROM THE VEGETABLE GARDEN

The best view in my house is from the kitchen window. From there I look down on soft rolling hills, voluptuous curves that are thrown into relief as the sun passes from east to west. In the spring, when rains are sufficient, the hills turn briefly green, then gold. By late summer they are dried and withered. A wide river valley cuts through the hills, separating them from the coastal ridge. Some of the slopes are planted with olives, while those near the river are thick with avocado trees.

Hidden in the folds of the hills, once watered by springs and irrigation ditches and now by drip irrigation, are small fields – *huertas* – that produce two, three and even four crops a year in this frostfree region of southern Spain.

I am not a gardener, but I closely watch the seedlings, flowerings and harvestings in the *huerta* next to my land. Antonio, the man who farms this plot, plants the fields, which are terraced on the hillside. It's not his land; he farms it on some arrangement with the owner. He has a weekday job and tends the garden on weekends, often bringing along his wife and small children to lend a hand and enjoy the peace and quiet of the country. Antonio is generous with the produce. I can help myself to tomatoes, peppers, beans, aubergines and melons in the summer; cabbages and tiny radishes in the fall; broad beans, chard, peas, new potatoes and strawberries in the spring; plus three kinds of lettuce most of the year.

The village market was, until recent years, a real farmers' market, supplied by locals like Antonio. Fruits and vegetables were seasonal and grown locally. In the spring, I would buy artichokes and asparagus day after day, knowing that a month later they would be gone until the following year. At the height of summer, when the tomatoes were luscious, I would make gazpacho and tomato salads daily.

Now, of course, modern technology and transportation bring fruits and vegetables from every corner of the globe. New farming methods allow tomatoes grown under plastic to ripen in January. Now that ordinary homes have refrigerators with freezer compartments, frozen vegetables also extend the seasons' supply. Still, there is nothing so delicious as those vegetables grown almost on my doorstep.

WHERE ARE THE VEGETABLES?

✳

Some of my American friends who visit Spain are puzzled because they are not served vegetables accompanying their restaurant meals. 'Where are the vegetables?' they ask. The markets are full of fabulous vegetables. But, eating in restaurants, you could feel deprived.

This perceived lack of vegetables is often due to the fact that vegetables are rarely served as a side dish. A Spanish meal is not like a typical American or British dinner – a piece of meat or fish plus potatoes plus vegetable. Although restaurants that cater to foreigners have learned how to pile some beans, peas and carrots next to the steak, this is not Spanish. Instead, most authentic restaurant menus have a whole section of vegetable entrées. They are meant to be ordered as a first course or as a main course for a light meal. So, you start your Spanish dinner with a first course of salad, vegetable or soup, then follow it with meat or fish, which is accompanied only by potatoes and a little garnish of lettuce.

In home cooking, vegetable dishes often become the main dish for a light supper or for a Lenten (non-meat) meal. Many of them are prepared with exquisite care. Likewise, traditional Spanish meals are incredibly rich in salads, raw and cooked, and in gazpachos, most of which are vegetable based. Tapas also include vegetables and salads, as do the hearty soups and stews that are such an important part of the Spanish diet. If you have some gazpacho or soup for lunch, a couple of salads as tapas and a first course of asparagus, vegetables along with the meat course are hardly essential.

Despite the abundance of vegetables in Spanish cuisine, vegetarians will have a hard time negotiating Spain's menus. This is because many basic vegetable preparations are *salteado con un poco de jamón* (sautéed with a little ham). Although they are very good, they are not vegetarian. Many *tortillas* (vegetable omelettes) (see chapter 5) make good vegetarian choices.

I have included recipes here for strictly vegetarian dishes as well as vegetable preparations that are usually cooked with some meat or fish. You can serve them as side dishes, if you wish, but many are best, Spanish style, as starters or light supper dishes. Look for more vegetable and salad recipes in chapter 2 (tapas), chapter 4 (soups and one-pot meals) and chapter 5 (with eggs).

COLD DISHES WITH VEGETABLES

ARTICHOKE SALAD, TARRAGONA STYLE
ENSALADA TARRAGONENSE

In this simple salad, artichokes and celery are dressed with a distinctive romesco sauce made from ground almonds and dried sweet peppers. The name 'Tarragona style' has nothing to do with the herb tarragon. Rather, Tarragona is a city in Catalonia that is famous for its exceptional romesco. If time is short or fresh artichokes are not available, tinned artichoke can be used instead.

In Spain, this is the sort of cold dish that is served as *primer plato* (a first course) at dinner. However, I like to enjoy it all by itself as a lunch dish.

6 small globe artichokes or 3 large ones

6 celery stalks, cut diagonally into 7-cm (2½-inch) pieces

2 teaspoons sweet pimentón

½ teaspoon hot pimentón or pinch ground cayenne pepper

24 almonds, blanched and skinned (see page 6)

4 tablespoons olive oil

4 tablespoons chopped fresh flat-leaf parsley

3 garlic cloves

½ teaspoon salt

2 tablespoons white wine vinegar

85–115 g (3–4 oz) torn lettuce or batavia

1 egg, hard-boiled and sliced

1 teaspoon chopped fresh mint leaves

1 tablespoon chopped spring onion, white and green parts

Bring a large pan of salted water to the boil. Meanwhile, trim off the outer leaves of the artichokes and cut the artichokes in half, if small, or in quarters, if large. Then cut them crosswise just above the heart, discarding the upper leaves. Rub the artichoke pieces with a cut lemon. Add the pieces to the boiling water and cook until just tender, about 10 minutes. Drain. When cool, remove the fuzzy choke from each piece.

Bring another large pan of salted water to the boil. Blanch the celery for 6 minutes. Drain and refresh under cold water. Combine the two kinds of pimentón in a small bowl and mix with 4 tablespoons water until smooth.

In a small pan over medium heat, toast the almonds in 2 teaspoons of the oil until golden, 3 to 4 minutes. Remove from the heat.

In a food processor, chop the parsley, then add the garlic and process until finely chopped. Add the toasted almonds and process until fine. Add the salt, vinegar and 120 ml (4 fl oz) water and continue to process until the mixture is quite smooth. Then add the pimentón paste and the remaining oil. This makes 240 ml (8 fl oz) of dressing. (The dressing can be served with other vegetables and salads.)

Place the artichokes and celery pieces in a bowl and pour over the dressing. Allow to marinate for 1 hour at room temperature.

On a large platter prepare a bed of lettuce or batavia. Arrange the artichokes and celery on top. Garnish with the egg, mint and chopped onion.

SERVES 6 AS A STARTER

Garlic Coleslaw with Pomegranate Seeds
Ensalada de Col

On an autumn trip through Extremadura in western Spain, I discovered a bounty of salads garnished with ruby-red pomegranate seeds. They seemed to be everywhere: on lettuce, mixed greens, even on cabbage slaws like this one. The seeds are not only beautiful, they add a delightful sweet-tart crunch, too.

The bright flavours of this salad make it a good choice to serve before roast pork or roast chicken for an autumn menu.

½ cabbage (680 g/1½ lb)

1 teaspoon salt

½ teaspoon pimentón

⅛ teaspoon cumin seeds

Freshly ground black pepper

3 garlic cloves, sliced

3 tablespoons olive oil

3 tablespoons white wine vinegar

Pomegranate seeds or chopped apple

Shred the cabbage, then chop it finely. Wash it well and drain. Place in a salad bowl and sprinkle with salt, pimentón, cumin seeds and pepper. Toss well.

In a small pan over medium heat, fry the sliced garlic in the olive oil just until the garlic is lightly golden, about 3 minutes. Pour the hot oil and garlic over the cabbage and toss. Add the vinegar to the same pan with 1 tablespoon water. Heat it and pour over the cabbage. Let the cabbage marinate at least 30 minutes before serving.

If pomegranate is available, serve the salad topped with its seeds. Otherwise, sprinkle chopped apple on the salad. Serve at room temperature.

SERVES 6 AS A SIDE DISH

CAULIFLOWER SALAD WITH LEMON DRESSING

ENSALADA DE COLIFLOR AL LIMÓN

Make this cauliflower to serve on the buffet for a party. It can be prepared a day in advance and marinated, refrigerated. Garnish at serving time.

680 g (1½ lb) cauliflower (about 1 medium head)

4 tablespoons chopped fresh flat-leaf parsley

2 garlic cloves, finely chopped

1 tomato, chopped

1 spring onion, chopped

3 tablespoons olive oil

4 tablespoons fresh lemon juice

½ teaspoon salt

Lettuce to garnish

1 egg, hard-boiled and sliced

Bring a large pan of salted water to the boil. Separate the cauliflower into florets. Add them to the boiling water and boil until just tender, about 5 minutes. Drain and refresh under cold water.

When cauliflower is cool, arrange it on a serving platter.

In a small bowl, combine the parsley, garlic, tomato, onion, oil, lemon juice and salt. Stir to combine. Spoon the dressing over the cauliflower. Tuck lettuce leaves around the salad and garnish with sliced egg.

If you are preparing the cauliflower in advance, omit the tomato from the dressing. Place the cauliflower in a covered container and combine with the dressing. Before serving, add the chopped tomato and spread out the salad on the serving dish.

SERVES 6 AS A SIDE DISH; SERVES 10 TO 12 AS A TAPA

Green Bean and Potato Salad

Ensalada de Judías Verdes y Patatas

If you are not serving this salad to vegetarians, you might add slivered *salchichón* (similar to salami). The salad makes a good side dish for a summer barbecue with grilled meat. Making it a day in advance gives the beans and potatoes time to absorb the marinade, but do save a little chopped fresh mint to sprinkle on the finished salad before serving.

680 g (1½ lb) French beans

2 medium potatoes (340 g/¾ lb)

2 garlic cloves, finely chopped

1 spring onion, chopped

½ red sweet pepper, roasted and diced (see page 7)

¼ teaspoon crumbled dried oregano

2 teaspoons chopped fresh mint

Crushed red chilli flakes

4 tablespoons olive oil

4 tablespoons white wine vinegar

Salt and freshly ground black pepper

Lettuce leaves

2 eggs, hard-boiled and sliced

Black olives

Bring a large pan of salted water to the boil. Trim the beans, but leave them whole. Add to the boiling water and cook to desired degree of doneness (crisp-tender or well done), 5 to 8 minutes. Drain and refresh under cold water.

Bring another large pan of water to the boil. Add the potatoes and cook until tender, 15 to 20 minutes. Drain. When cool enough to handle, peel and cut the potatoes in lengthwise wedges.

Combine the beans and potatoes in a bowl. Add the garlic, onion, roasted pepper, oregano, mint, red chilli flakes, oil, vinegar and salt and pepper. Combine gently and let the ingredients marinate at room temperature for at least 1 hour, or up to 24 hours in the refrigerator.

Place lettuce leaves on a serving platter. Arrange the beans and potatoes on top of the lettuce. Spoon over all the remaining dressing. Garnish with the eggs and a few olives.

Serves 6 as a starter

ROASTED ONION SALAD

ENSALADA DE CEBOLLAS ASADAS

The sweet and sour flavours of these marinated onions go well with grilled meat. They can be presented on a bed of greens or as a side dish, much like a relish. I serve it as one of the trimmings with a festive roast turkey dinner.

900 g (2 lb) onions (5–6 medium)

2 tablespoons olive oil

2 tablespoons Sherry vinegar

1 tablespoon seedless raisins

1 tablespoon capers

Salt and freshly ground pepper

Salad leaves, to serve (optional)

Preheat the grill. Place the whole, unpeeled onions on a grill pan. Grill for 10 minutes, then turn the onions and grill for 10 minutes more. The onion skins should be browned. Remove and let the onions cool.

Peel and discard the onion skins. Cut the onions into quarters or sixths and place in a bowl. Add the oil, vinegar, raisins, capers and salt and pepper.

Let the onions marinate at room temperature for at least 1 hour, or up to 24 hours in the refrigerator. To serve, line a serving dish with salad leaves, if desired, and spoon the onions over.

SERVES 6 AS A STARTER OR SIDE DISH

MINTED BROAD BEAN SALAD

ENSALADA DE HABAS

This salad is a Catalan inspiration. It's a dish for springtime when fresh broad beans become available. I like the fresh taste that the mint leaves contribute.

4 sprigs plus 2 tablespoons fresh mint

Salt

450 g (1 lb) small shelled broad beans

4 tablespoons extra virgin olive oil

3 tablespoons Sherry vinegar

200 g (7 oz) shredded iceberg lettuce

4 tablespoons julienned serrano ham

Finely chopped spring onion (optional)

Bring 1 litre (about 2 pints) of water to the boil. Remove the pan from the heat. Add the 4 sprigs of mint, cover, and let the mint infuse for 30 minutes. Discard the mint.

Add salt to the water and bring to the boil. Add the broad beans and cook them for 2 minutes. Drain and refresh in cold water.

In a bowl, combine the oil and vinegar. Add the beans. Cover and let them marinate for at least 1 hour.

Immediately before serving, spread the lettuce on a serving platter. Chop the remaining 2 tablespoons of mint and stir it into the beans. Spread the beans on top of the lettuce. Scatter the ham strips and spring onion, if using, on top.

SERVES 6 AS A STARTER

TOMATOES AND PEPPERS WITH TUNA
TITAINA

This dish comes from Valencia, where it is made with *tollina* (dry salt tuna), which adds texture as well as flavour. Here, the recipe is adapted to use tinned tuna. Or you could omit the tuna and serve the slowly cooked vegetables as a side dish with grilled fresh tuna steaks.

3 tablespoons olive oil

4 tablespoons pine kernels

1 red sweet pepper

1 green sweet pepper

800 g (1¾ lb) large tomatoes

½ teaspoon sugar

¼ teaspoon ground cinnamon

Pinch freshly grated nutmeg

Freshly ground black pepper

½ teaspoon salt

200-g tin water-packed tuna, drained

Heat the oil in a cazuela or frying pan over high heat and toast the pine kernels. Skim them out when they are golden-brown, leaving the oil in the pan.

Cut the peppers into 2.5-cm (1-inch) strips, then cut the strips into 4-cm (1½-inch) pieces. Sauté the peppers slowly in the oil in the cazuela for 10 minutes over medium heat while preparing the tomatoes.

Peel the tomatoes. Cut them in half crosswise, then scoop out and discard seeds. Cut the halved tomatoes into quarters. Add the tomatoes to the peppers. Season with sugar, cinnamon, nutmeg, pepper and salt. Simmer for 15 minutes.

Add the tuna and simmer for 15 minutes more. Most of the liquid from the vegetables should have cooked away. Add the pine kernels.

Serve warm or at room temperature.

SERVES 4 AS A STARTER OR SIDE DISH

Hot Vegetable Dishes

Green Beans with Garlic Sauce
Judías Verdes en Salsa

This is the sort of substantial vegetable dish that a Spanish *ama de casa* (housewife) might serve her family as a first course in place of a soup or salad. If you prefer to serve it as a side dish, pair it with simple, unsauced food, such as sautéed chicken breast or grilled steak.

450 g (1 lb) green beans, preferably the wide, flat romano variety (or runner beans, if in season)

1 slice white bread, crusts removed

2 tablespoons white wine vinegar

1 garlic clove

¼ teaspoon pimentón

3 tablespoons olive oil

¼ red sweet pepper, slivered

Salt and freshly ground black pepper

2 eggs, hard-boiled and quartered

Bring a large pan of salted water to the boil. Top and tail the beans, then cut into 5-cm (2-inch) lengths. Add to the boiling water and cook until crisp-tender, 7 to 8 minutes. Drain, saving 120 ml (4 fl oz) of the liquid. Refresh the beans in cold water.

Sprinkle the bread with the vinegar and let it stand until softened. Squeeze out any excess liquid. Combine the bread, garlic, pimentón and half of reserved bean liquid in a blender and blend until smooth.

Heat the oil in a frying pan over medium heat and sauté the beans with the slivered red pepper for 5 minutes. Add the garlic paste from the blender and the remaining bean liquid. Season with salt and pepper. Cook for 5 minutes more over medium heat.

Serve garnished with eggs. Serve hot or at room temperature.

Serves 4 as a starter or side dish

'Land Fish' (Fried Aubergine)

Pez de Tierra

Aubergine prepared this way is sometimes called *pez de tierra* ('land fish') because it resembles fried fish fingers or small, whole fried fish. Another popular dish is *boquerones de la tierra*, or 'land anchovies', which are cooked green beans that have been floured and fried. Any leftover 'land fish' can be topped with tomato sauce and cheese and baked at 350°F until the cheese is melted.

1 medium aubergine (280–340 g/10–12 oz)
45 g (1½ oz) plain flour
¼ teaspoon ground cumin
⅛ teaspoon freshly ground black pepper
340 ml (12 fl oz) olive oil, for frying
Salt

Peel the aubergine and cut it as for chips, in strips about 9 cm (3½ inches) long by 2 cm (¾ inch) wide. Combine the flour, cumin and pepper in a bowl. Add the aubergine strips and toss to coat them with flour.

Heat the oil in a deep frying pan or deep-fat fryer until it is shimmering but not smoking (182°C/360°F). Fry the aubergine pieces in two batches until golden-brown. They take only 2 minutes. Remove, drain on kitchen towels and sprinkle with salt.

Serve hot.

Serves 4 as a starter or side dish

AUBERGINE, MOORISH STYLE
BERENJENA A LA MORISCA

When the Moors conquered Spain in 711 AD, they brought along many new vegetables, including aubergine (but not tomatoes, which came later from the New World). It remains part of their culinary legacy, as do the lively spices in this dish, which are much like those used in North African cooking today. This makes a good side dish with roast lamb or chicken, or it can be served as a vegetarian main course if it is served with rice or another grain.

900 g (2 lb) aubergine (3 medium), peeled and cut into 2.5-cm (1-inch) cubes

1 tablespoon salt

2 tablespoons olive oil

70 g (2½ oz) chopped onion

4 garlic cloves, sliced

200 g (7 oz) chopped tomatoes

½ teaspoon crushed red chilli flakes, or to taste

Freshly ground black pepper

1 teaspoon ground cumin

1 tablespoon fresh lemon juice

1 tablespoon chopped fresh flat-leaf parsley or fresh coriander leaves

Bring a large pan of water to the boil. Add the aubergine with the salt and boil for 8 minutes. Drain in a colander. Press the aubergine gently to express any excess liquid.

Heat the oil in a frying pan over medium heat and sauté the onion and garlic for 5 minutes. Add the aubergine and sauté for 5 minutes more. Add the tomatoes, red chilli flakes, black pepper and cumin. Let bubble gently for 10 minutes, until the vegetables are very thick.

Stir in the lemon juice. Garnish with parsley. Serve hot or at room temperature.

SERVES 6 AS A SIDE DISH

Jaén-Style Spinach with Crispy Croûtons
Espinacas a la Jinense

Jaén is the province in Andalusia that produces more olive oil than anywhere else in the world. Rolling hills, as far as the eye can see, are tufted with the trees. The fruity, sweet-acrid smell of fresh-pressed oil coats the countryside like a light dressing. The oil imbues foods with rich flavour.

This way of preparing spinach is good enough to be the main attraction. Serve it for lunch with cheese and cold cuts or an omelette.

900 g (2 lb) fresh spinach, washed, or 400 g (14 oz) frozen spinach

4 tablespoons olive oil

6 garlic cloves

1 slice stale bread

1 teaspoon pimentón

1 tablespoon white wine vinegar

2 tablespoons chopped onion

1 teaspoon salt

Freshly ground black pepper

¼ teaspoon caraway seeds

60 g (2 oz) croûtons, cut into 2-cm (¾-inch) cubes

Cook the spinach with the water clinging to it over high heat until wilted, about 3 minutes. Remove and drain well. Chop the spinach.

Heat 2 tablespoons of the oil in a cazuela over medium-high heat. Fry 2 cloves of the garlic with the slice of bread, turning until bread is toasted on both sides, 2 to 3 minutes. Remove and grind them in a mortar or blender with the pimentón and vinegar (add a little water if necessary to run the blender).

In the oil remaining in the cazuela, sauté the onion over medium heat until softened, about 5 minutes. Add the spinach, the bread-garlic paste, salt, pepper, caraway and 240 ml (8 fl oz) water. Simmer for 15 minutes.

Chop the remaining 4 garlic cloves. Heat the remaining 2 tablespoons of oil in a small frying pan over medium heat and fry the croûtons and garlic until golden, about 5 minutes. Pour over the spinach and serve.

Serves 6 as a side dish

CAULIFLOWER, MULE-DRIVER'S STYLE
COLIFLOR AL AJO ARRIERO

Before there were lorries and trains, muleteers once transported wool and wheat from inland regions to the seaboard for shipping abroad and carried salt fish and other imports to the interior. En route, they stopped at rustic wayside inns, where the wine was rough and the food was simple. You can expect to find garlic in any dish prepared 'mule-driver's style'. This is a wonderful side dish with pork or chicken. It can be prepared in the same manner using broccoli.

1 head cauliflower, separated into florets

5 tablespoons olive oil

1 teaspoon salt

4 garlic cloves, chopped

1 tablespoon pimentón

1 tablespoon white wine vinegar

Pinch ground cayenne pepper

Bring a large pan of salted water to the boil. Add the cauliflower and boil until tender, 7 to 8 minutes. Drain, saving 4 tablespoons of the cooking water. Place the cauliflower in a serving bowl and keep warm.

Heat the oil and salt in a small saucepan over medium heat. Add the chopped garlic to the hot oil. Remove from heat and stir in the pimentón, vinegar, cayenne and the reserved cooking water. Pour this mixture over the cauliflower. Serve immediately, hot or warm.

SERVES 6 AS A SIDE DISH

CAULIFLOWER WITH ALMOND SAUCE
COLIFLOR CON SALSA DE ALMENDRAS

✳

In Spain, traditional Christmas feasts usually include two or three different vegetable dishes, which are often served as distinct courses. Among the most favoured holiday vegetables are cauliflower and cardoons, both of which can be prepared in this savoury almond sauce.

If you are using cardoons, trim the stems, cut them into 8-cm (3-inch) pieces, and cook in boiling water with a squeeze of lemon juice until fork-tender, about 40 minutes.

1 head cauliflower, separated into florets
Salt
60 g (2 oz) almonds, blanched and skinned (see page 6)
2 tablespoons olive oil
2 garlic cloves, sliced crosswise
2 tablespoons plain flour
120 ml (4 fl oz) white wine
340 ml (12 fl oz) Simple Stock (page 82)
Freshly ground black pepper
Pinch pimentón

Cook the cauliflower in boiling salted water until tender, 7 to 8 minutes. Drain and refresh in cold water. Set aside.

Slice 2 tablespoons of the almonds into slivers. Heat the oil in a frying pan over medium heat and toast the slivered almonds and sliced garlic until golden, about 2 minutes. Skim them out and reserve.

Stir the flour into the oil remaining in the pan and cook for 1 minute. Combine the remaining almonds in a blender or food processor with the wine and process until you have a smooth paste.

Stir the almond paste into the pan with the stock. Season with salt and pepper. Cook for 5 minutes over medium heat, stirring frequently.

Immediately before serving, put the cooked cauliflower in the sauce and heat thoroughly. Serve the cauliflower in sauce, sprinkled with the reserved slivered almonds and garlic and a sprinkling of pimentón.

SERVES 6 AS A SIDE DISH

Asparagus in Cazuela
Cazuela de Espárragos

This is the sort of vegetable dish that, with the addition of eggs, makes a substantial main course. In Spanish homes it might be served as the main dish for a Lenten (non-meat) meal, perhaps preceded by a fish soup. I am more likely to serve it for lunch or a light supper.

This version calls for the eggs to be baked on top of the asparagus, but another variation of the dish calls for the eggs to be beaten together and poured over the asparagus, then baked until set. Without the eggs, the asparagus makes a good side dish with fish or chicken.

800 g (1¾ lb) green asparagus, trimmed

3 tablespoons olive oil

2 garlic cloves, sliced

1½ slices white bread (about 45 g/1½ oz), crusts removed

½ teaspoon pimentón

½ teaspoon ground cumin

Pinch ground cloves

Freshly ground black pepper

1 tablespoon white wine vinegar

Salt

4 eggs

Bring a large pan of salted water to the boil. Slice the asparagus stalks into short lengths and blanch them for 3 minutes. Drain, reserving 280 ml (½ pint) of the liquid. Refresh the asparagus in cold water and drain again.

Heat the oil in a frying pan over medium heat and fry the garlic and the slice of bread until they are toasted, about 2 minutes. Remove them. Add the asparagus to the pan and sauté it for 3 minutes.

In a blender, combine the garlic, bread, pimentón, cumin, cloves, pepper, vinegar and half of the reserved liquid. Blend until smooth. Add this mixture to the asparagus with salt to taste. Cover and simmer for 10 minutes, adding the remaining liquid as needed.

Preheat the oven to 190°/375°F/gas mark 5.

Spoon the asparagus and sauce into a cazuela or casserole or divide the mixture between four individual ramekins. If you are using a cazuela, break the four eggs on top of the asparagus. If you are using ramekins, break one egg into each. Bake until the whites are set, but the yolks are still runny, 5 to 8 minutes.

Let sit for 1 minute before serving.

Serves 4 as a main dish

Artichokes, Córdoba Style
Alcachofas a la Cordobesa

My children were always crazy about artichokes, so one day I bought a whole crate of them at the wholesale market in a nearby town. We ate them in dozens of different ways. My children's favourite method was simply dipping the leaves of a steamed artichoke in homemade mayonnaise, but I enjoyed some of the more substantial preparations, such as this one. It makes a fine supper dish served with nothing more than salad and bread.

If you are using large artichokes for this dish, cut the trimmed bottoms in half. If you are using large potatoes, cut them into 5-cm (2-inch) chunks. Frozen artichoke hearts can be substituted for the fresh ones.

about 16 small globe artichokes

1 lemon, cut in half

3 tablespoons olive oil

3 garlic cloves

450 g (1 lb) small new potatoes, peeled

¼ teaspoon saffron threads

4 peppercorns

2 teaspoons salt

1½ tablespoons plain flour

450 ml (¾ pint) Simple Stock (see page 82) or water

Finely chopped fresh mint, to garnish

Trim the artichokes, discarding the tough outer leaves. Cut them in half crosswise and discard the tops. Rub the trimmed artichokes with the cut lemon and drop them into a bowl of water into which a squeeze of lemon has been added. This keeps cut surfaces from turning dark.

Heat the oil in a cazuela over medium heat and fry the garlic cloves until they are golden, about 2 minutes. Skim them out and reserve. Drain the artichokes. Add the potatoes and artichoke bottoms to the oil and sauté gently, about 3 minutes.

In a mortar or blender, crush the saffron with the peppercorns and salt. Add the fried garlic and crush it, then add the flour and combine to form a smooth paste. Add some of the stock or water and stir until smooth. Stir this into the artichokes with the remaining liquid. Cover and simmer until potatoes and artichokes are tender, about 20 minutes. Serve sprinkled with chopped mint.

Serves 4 as a main dish

COURGETTE AND POTATO GRATIN, BALEARIC STYLE
TUMBET BALEAR

Layers of courgettes, potatoes and roasted sweet pepper make this zesty vegetable dish especially satisfying. It can also be made with aubergine in place of the courgettes.

5 tablespoons olive oil

280 g (10 oz) chopped tomatoes

½ teaspoon crumbled dried basil

½ teaspoon sugar

3 teaspoons salt

680 g (1½ lb) potatoes, thinly sliced

2 courgettes (680 g/1½ lb), sliced crosswise into 6-mm (¼-inch) slices

1 onion, sliced

1 tablespoon fine dry breadcrumbs

4 eggs, beaten with 1 tablespoon water

1 red sweet pepper, roasted, peeled and cut into strips (see page 7)

Preheat the oven to 180°C/350°F/gas mark 4.

Heat 1 tablespoon of the oil in a saucepan over medium heat and add the tomatoes, basil, sugar and 1 teaspoon of the salt. Cook the tomatoes for 10 minutes until the liquid is reduced.

In a large frying pan, heat the remaining oil and fry the potato slices slowly, turning to cook evenly, until they are fork-tender, about

15 minutes. They do not need to brown. Sprinkle the potatoes with 1 teaspoon of the salt while they are cooking. Remove the potatoes from the pan and reserve.

Add the courgettes and onion to the oil remaining in the pan and sauté over medium heat until the courgettes are fork-tender, about 10 minutes. Sprinkle with the remaining 1 teaspoon salt.

Oil a 24 × 33-cm (9 × 13-inch) baking pan or casserole and dust with the breadcrumbs. Spread the potatoes in the bottom of the pan. Pour over a quarter of the beaten eggs. Spread the courgettes and onion over the potatoes. Add another quarter of the eggs. Lay strips of roasted pepper over the courgettes and pour a quarter of the eggs over. Top with the tomato sauce. Pour the remaining egg over the casserole.

Bake for 25 minutes. Let set for 5 minutes before serving.

SERVES 6 AS A STARTER; SERVES 4 AS A MAIN DISH

COURGETTE TIMBALE WITH CHEESE

CUAJADO DE CALABACINES

A Sephardic (Spanish Jewish) speciality, this timable is an excellent way to use extra courgettes from prolific summer gardens. Aubergine and spinach are also prepared in this manner. If you are using aubergine, peel it, cut it into chunks, then cook it in boiling water for 10 minutes. Drain and squeeze out any excess liquid. For spinach, cook briefly and drain well.

900 g (2 lb) courgettes

½ onion

2 teaspoons salt

1 garlic clove, crushed

115 g (4 oz) grated cheese, such as semi-cured Manchego or any firm, flavourful cheese

3 eggs

120 ml (4 fl oz) milk

4 tablespoons fine breadcrumbs

¼ teaspoon freshly ground black pepper

Grate the courgettes and onion. Place in a colander and sprinkle with the salt. Let stand for 1 hour. Squeeze out as much excess liquid as possible.

Preheat the oven to 180°C/350°F/gas mark 4. Oil a 20-cm (8-inch) cake tin.

Beat together the garlic, cheese, eggs, milk, breadcrumbs and pepper. Stir in the grated courgettes.

Pour into the prepared cake tin. Bake until a skewer comes out clean, about 35 minutes.

Serve hot or cold.

SERVES 4 AS A STARTER; SERVES 8 AS A SIDE DISH

PUMPKIN SAUTÉ

CALABAZA FRITA

Rosario was one of my early guides in the kitchen. She grew up in the *campo* (in the country), on a small farm. We often cooked together, making bread and goats' milk cheese. When I told her I was making this pumpkin sauté, she suggested preparing it without the bread. Her version is much more modern, but I still prefer the thick, garlicky sauce that only the traditional recipe can produce.

This dish is best with fresh pumpkin, but you could use any winter squash. Although, traditionally, it is served as a first course, rather like a soup, I like it as a side dish. It's great with roast turkey, pork chops and baked ham.

1 (900 g/2-lb) pumpkin

3 tablespoons olive oil

1 slice bread, crusts removed

3 garlic cloves

1 tablespoon white wine vinegar

1½ teaspoons dried oregano

¼ teaspoon hot pimentón (optional)

2.5-cm (1-inch) piece lemon zest, finely chopped

½ teaspoon salt

Cut the top from the pumpkin. Scrape out and discard the fibres and seeds. Peel the pumpkin. Cut the flesh into 2-cm (¾-inch) cubes.

Heat the oil in a cazuela or deep frying pan over medium-high heat. Brown the bread and garlic and remove. Combine them in a blender with the vinegar, oregano, pimentón, if using, and 4 tablespoons water. Set aside while you cook the pumpkin.

Add the cubed pumpkin to the oil in the pan and sauté it for 2 minutes over medium heat. Add the lemon zest and salt. Reduce the heat, cover the pan, and let the pumpkin cook slowly for 10 minutes.

Purée the bread mixture in the blender. Add to the pumpkin with 120 ml (4 fl oz) water. Cook for 5 minutes more over medium heat.

SERVES 6 AS A SIDE DISH

SUMMER VEGETABLE STEW
PISTO

This is a splendid dish, whether it is served hot or cold. It has many permutations – a side dish with meat or fish, a starter, a sauce cooked with chicken or lamb, paired with fried eggs for a light main dish or as a topping for Vegetable Pizzas (see recipe on page 159).

It also has other names – *samfaina* in Catalonia and *alboronía* in La Mancha – denoting its Moorish origins.

680 g (1½ lb) aubergine (about 2 medium), peeled and cut into 2.5-cm (1-inch) cubes

Salt

3 tablespoons olive oil

1 onion, chopped

2 garlic cloves, chopped

1 green sweet pepper, cut into 2.5-cm (1-inch) squares

600 g (21 oz) chopped tomatoes

450 g (1 lb) courgettes, cut into 2.5-cm (1-inch) cubes

1 teaspoon crumbled dried oregano

Freshly ground black pepper

⅛ teaspoon cumin seeds

Chopped fresh flat-leaf parsley

White wine vinegar (optional)

Place the aubergine in a colander and sprinkle it liberally with salt. Let it drain for 1 hour.

In a casserole, heat the oil and sauté the onion and aubergine for 5 minutes. Add the garlic and green pepper and sauté for another minute, then add the tomatoes and courgettes. Sauté over medium heat for another 5 minutes.

Season with 1 teaspoon salt, oregano, black pepper and cumin seeds. Cover and cook over low heat until the vegetables are soft, about 20 minutes. It shouldn't be necessary to add additional liquid, but stir frequently so that they don't scorch.

Serve hot or at room temperature, garnished with chopped parsley. If you are serving it at room temperature, a touch of vinegar is a good addition.

SERVES 6 AS A SIDE DISH

CHARD WITH RAISINS AND PINE KERNELS
ACELGAS CON PASAS Y PIÑONES

I serve this as a side dish with roast pork loin (see chapter 10), but it also can be used as a topping for a Vegetable Pizza (page 159). This is best made with sweet Málaga muscatel raisins, which must be de-seeded. You can substitute any seedless dark raisin. Spinach can be substituted for the chard, if you prefer.

3 tablespoons olive oil

2 tablespoons pine kernels

2 garlic cloves, chopped

680 g (1½ lb) fresh chard, washed, trimmed and chopped

4 tablespoons de-seeded raisins

½ teaspoon salt

Freshly ground black pepper

Heat the oil in a deep frying pan over medium heat and fry the pine kernels for a few seconds, until they are toasted. Remove the pan from the heat, skim out the pine kernels and reserve.

Return the pan to medium heat and add the garlic. When the garlic begins to turn golden, after about a minute, add the chopped chard. Sauté the chard for 5 minutes.

Add 120 ml (4 fl oz) water, raisins, salt and pepper. Cook, covered, for 10 minutes. Remove the cover and cook for another 5 minutes, until most of the excess liquid has evaporated.

Toss reserved pine kernels with the chard.

SERVES 6 AS A SIDE DISH

MEDLEY OF VEGETABLES
MENESTRA DE VERDURAS

This vegetable medley can be served as a first course, a side dish or as a topping for Vegetable Pizzas (opposite). In the spring, fresh artichokes are perfect for this vegetable melange, but you can use tinned or bottled artichoke bottoms, if you prefer. Peas, chard stems and tiny broad beans are other possible additions.

6 medium globe artichokes

Salt

450 g (1 lb) asparagus, trimmed and cut into 2.5-cm (1-inch) lengths

3 tablespoons olive oil

1 onion, chopped

2 garlic cloves, chopped

115 g (4 oz) mushrooms, sliced

200 g (7 oz) chopped tomato

4 tablespoons white wine

Freshly ground black pepper

1 tablespoon chopped green fennel leaves or flat-leaf parsley

If you are using fresh artichokes, cut off the stems and trim off the tough outer leaves. Cut off and discard the top two-thirds of the artichokes. Cut the artichokes in eighths. Cook them in boiling salted water with a squeeze of lemon juice until a leaf pulls off easily, about 10 minutes. Drain. Scrape out any fuzzy choke. Cook the asparagus in boiling, salted water until tender, 6 to 7 minutes. Drain and refresh in cold water.

Heat the oil in a frying pan over medium heat and sauté the chopped onion, garlic and mushrooms until softened, about 5 minutes. Add the tomato and sauté for 5 minutes.

Add the cooked artichokes and asparagus to the pan. Add the wine and season with salt, pepper and fennel. Simmer over medium heat until most of the liquid has evaporated.

Serve hot.

SERVES 6 AS A STARTER OR SIDE DISH

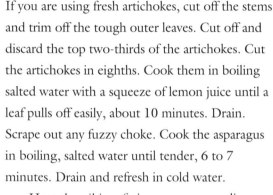

VEGETABLE PIZZAS

COQUES DE VERDURES

Coques are the Catalan version of pizza – slabs of dough baked with toppings. They seldom include cheese, which makes them rather different from the ubiquitous 'Italian' pizza. They may also be prepared as small, individual pies, with the dough doubled over the filling to create a pasty.

For this recipe, I've suggested making three pizzas with each of three vegetable toppings: *pisto*, with aubergine and tomatoes; *acelgas*, chard with raisins and pine kernels; and *menestra*, vegetable medley. Of course, you can also choose your favourite and use it for all three of the *coques*. For the base, use your favourite pizza dough recipe, the Empanada Dough, or purchased frozen pizza bases.

3 (25-cm/10-inch) pizza bases, or 1 recipe Empanada Dough (page 196), rolled into 3 (25-cm/10-inch) rounds

1½ tablespoons olive oil

½ recipe (about 450 ml/¾ pint) Summer Vegetable Stew (page 156)

½ recipe (about 450 ml/¾ pint) Chard with Raisins and Pine Kernels (page 157)

½ recipe (about 450 ml/¾ pint) Medley of Vegetables (page 158)

Tinned tuna or sardines, well drained (optional)

A few olives (optional)

Preheat oven to 200°C/400°F/gas mark 6.

Place the pizza bases on baking sheets. Brush each with ½ tablespoon oil. Spread each with a vegetable mixture. Tuna or sardines go well with the topping of *pisto*. The olives match up with the *menestra*.

Bake for 10 minutes, until crust is lightly golden.

Serve hot or at room temperature.

SERVES 6, ALLOWING ½ PIZZA PER PERSON

Vegetable Mélange with Wild Mushrooms
Menestra con Setas

One day in early spring, I set off on my first mushroom-hunting expedition. Our group included several adults and several children, under the direction of Salvador, a firewood cutter, who was well acquainted with the woods and their secret treasures. He took us to a pine forest not far off a main national highway; the sandy soil was soft underfoot from rains a few days before. Within minutes, Salvador pulled up several *boletos* (boletus, also known as ceps or porcini). He stopped long enough to show them to me and then headed off on his own.

I started off slowly, eyes to the ground, dodging low-hanging pine branches, which snagged my hair. The eye is at first too quick, too far-ranging, to spot these sly, secret growths. It takes a certain myopic concentration to begin to understand their mysterious presence.

Stopping to turn and look under each pine, I saw, right at my feet, a rise in the thick, springy carpeting of pine needles. I brushed off the needles and there it was, a big *boleto*. I squatted beside it, pondering its strange origins. Gestating in darkness, mushrooms choose their particular moment to push up through heavy, damp earth and a dense layer of pine needles to shine in the light of day. Unlike other plants, fungi contain no chlorophyll and are not nurtured by the process of photosynthesis. Light and air are, to them, a mere curiosity. I picked it and wandered on, deeper into the woods, holding my talisman before me.

The *boletos* were not the only mushrooms I discovered. There was an incredible variety – tiny white ones, like underground pearls, popping up through the pine needles to encircle a tree. Brown shiny ones, like chocolate drops, and among them, pale, beige and white 'flowers', presumably the same mushroom fully opened, a delicate spiral that looked as if it would waft away in a breeze – until I touched it and found it had the same spongy density as its neighbours. I left undisturbed the many varieties I couldn't identify. Even armed with a book, which provided descriptions and photos, I felt a little chill of terror at the thought of confusing a possibly deadly poisonous fungus with the edible ones.

When we regrouped, the morning's 'catch' was spread on a big tarpaulin for inspection. There were hundreds of mushrooms, mainly *boletos*, but also some big field mushrooms (same variety as cultivated mushrooms). There were none of the prized chanterelles Salvador had brought back the previous week. Some of the *boletos* were bigger than a child's face.

At home I sliced my share of the mushrooms, put them in a frying pan with olive oil and sautéed them, draining off the liquid they exuded until they started to stick to the pan. Then, I added more oil, garlic, parsley, salt and pepper, and finally a little dry Sherry.

I was totally unprepared for the eating of them; they were nothing like cultivated mushrooms. The flavour was darker, duskier, muskier, woodsier. The opposite of ethereal, they were the essence of earth. Appealing, evocative and as magical as the hunt itself.

I think of those wild mushrooms when I make this *menestra*, a vegetable stew that can be served as a starter or a side dish. In southern Spain, the *menestra* invariably contains tomato sauce, while in the north it does not. The vegetables vary with the season – peas, broad beans, artichokes, slender green beans, borage, cauliflower or asparagus. Use any mushrooms in season.

450 g (1 lb) wild mushrooms, cleaned

230 g (8 oz) shelled green peas

12 (10-cm/4-inch) asparagus tips

3 chard stems, cut in half

6 small onions

6 baby carrots

3 tablespoons olive oil

2 garlic cloves, sliced crosswise

85 g (3 oz) lean bacon, diced

4 tablespoons chopped fresh flat-leaf parsley

120 ml (4 fl oz) white wine

Salt and freshly ground black pepper

3 eggs, hard-boiled and quartered

If the mushrooms are very large, quarter or slice them. Flat ones, such as oyster mushrooms or chanterelles, can be left whole. Set aside.

Cook each of the vegetables – peas, asparagus, chard stems, onions and carrots – separately in lightly salted water until just tender, 5 to 15 minutes. Drain and refresh in cold water and set aside.

In a cazuela or deep frying pan, heat the oil over medium heat and fry the garlic just until golden, 1 minute. Skim out and set aside.

Add the bacon and the mushrooms to the oil and sauté over medium heat until the mushrooms have sweated out their liquid. The timing depends on the variety of mushrooms. Some require as long as 20 minutes.

When mushrooms are again sizzling in the oil, add all of the cooked vegetables, except the asparagus. Continue to sauté the mixture for another 5 minutes.

Add the parsley and wine and cook until the liquid has evaporated, about 5 minutes. Season with salt and pepper. Arrange the asparagus tips around the edge of the vegetables. Sprinkle with the fried garlic bits. Garnish with the quartered eggs.

SERVES 6 AS A STARTER OR SIDE DISH

SPANISH CHIPS
PATATAS FRITAS

These crispy fried potatoes are much like chips, but, fried in olive oil, they take on a Mediterranean flavour. They accompany meat dishes of all kinds, including stews, and are often added right to the sauce.

900 g (2 lb) baking potatoes (4 medium)
Olive oil, for frying
Salt

Peel the potatoes. Wash and pat them dry. Cut them lengthwise into 12-mm (½-inch) wide slices. Cut the slices into strips 12 mm (½ inch) wide.

Pour enough oil into a large, deep frying pan to fill it to a depth of 2.5 cm (1 inch). Heat until the oil is shimmering but not smoking (182°C/360°F). Add the potatoes and fry them until lightly golden, about 12 minutes.

Drain briefly on paper towels and sprinkle with salt. Serve hot.

SERVES 4 AS A SIDE DISH

DOUBLE-MASHED POTATOES
PATATAS REVOLCONAS

Pimentón – Spanish for paprika – is probably the most important spice in present-day Spanish cooking. Pimentón comes from the capsicum pepper – the pepper discovered by Columbus on his first trip to the New World. He was looking for the Indies, the source of 'pepper' (*pimienta*). When he found the hot-tasting capsicum, Columbus called it *pimiento*.

Extremadura, in the west of Spain, is the land of the conquistadores. The capsicum pepper, brought back from the New World, was first cultivated in monasteries there. Today, Extremadura produces smoke-dried pimentón de la Vera (DO), which may be sweet (*dulce*), bittersweet (*agri-dulce*) or hot (*picante*). The smokiness adds a flavour dimension and some interesting dishes can be created simply by substituting it for paprika. (Sources for pimentón de la Vera are listed at the back of the book.)

Serve these potatoes as a first course or as a supper dish, accompanied by fried eggs. They are also good as a side dish with pork chops or roast chicken.

1.4 kg (3 lb) baking potatoes
1 bay leaf
5 tablespoons olive oil
4 garlic cloves, peeled
1 tablespoon sweet pimentón de la Vera
Pinch hot pimentón
½ teaspoon ground cumin
1 teaspoon salt
2 slices bacon, diced

Peel the potatoes, cut them into chunks, and transfer them to a large pan with the bay leaf. Cover with water and place the pan over medium heat. Boil until fork-tender, about 15 minutes. Drain, saving 240 ml (8 fl oz) of the cooking liquid. Mash the potatoes with a potato masher or wooden spoon, adding half of the reserved liquid.

Heat the oil in a large frying pan over medium heat and fry the garlic until golden, 1 to 2 minutes. Remove the garlic with a slotted spoon and transfer to a blender with the pimentón, cumin, salt and remaining liquid. Blend until smooth.

Add the bacon to the oil in the pan and fry, stirring, until crisped. Add the mashed potatoes to the oil in the pan and sauté, stirring, for 1 minute more. Pour in the garlic mixture and mash it into the potatoes. Reheat, turning the potatoes in the oil. Serve immediately.

SERVES 6 AS A STARTER OR SIDE DISH

POOR FOLK'S POTATOES

PATATAS A LO POBRE

Poor in meat, but rich in flavour, this rustic vegetarian dish is frequently found as a side dish with fish, poultry or meat. I serve it on the buffet table, alongside Herb-Roasted Marinated Pork Loin (page 262). The potatoes can be peeled and sliced in advance – leave them covered with water until you are ready to assemble the casserole.

5 tablespoons olive oil

1.4 kg (3 lb) baking potatoes, peeled and sliced 6 mm (¼ inch) thick

2 teaspoons salt

1 onion, sliced

1 green sweet pepper, cut into strips

1 large tomato, quartered and sliced

3 tablespoons chopped fresh flat-leaf parsley

3 garlic cloves, chopped

¼ teaspoon crumbled dried thyme

½ teaspoon pimentón

5 tablespoons white wine

Preheat the oven to 180°C/350°F/gas mark 4.

Pour half the oil into a 3-litre (5-pint) cazuela or other flameproof casserole. Arrange half the potatoes in the casserole and sprinkle with 1 teaspoon of the salt. Top with half the onion, pepper, tomato, parsley and garlic.

Add the remaining potatoes, sprinkle with the remaining 1 teaspoon salt and the remaining onion, pepper, tomato, parsley and garlic. Sprinkle with thyme and pimentón. Pour the remaining oil, wine and 5 tablespoons water over the vegetables.

Place the cazuela over medium heat on the hob, until the liquid begins to simmer. Then cover the casserole with a lid or foil and bake until potatoes are fork-tender, about 45 minutes.

Let the casserole rest for 10 minutes before serving.

NOTE: This casserole can be cooked entirely on the hob, but you will need to use more oil and more liquid. Don't stir the potatoes, but shake the cazuela occasionally. The bottom layer may form a crust – a delicious bit to scrape up.

SERVES 6 TO 8 AS A SIDE DISH

WIDOWED POTATOES

VIUDO

'Widowed potatoes' is the name given to potatoes bereft of meat, but often cooked with salt cod or other fish. Surprisingly, tinned sardines are a perfect addition. Serve these potatoes as a starter or light supper dish with bread to sop up the juices.

3 tablespoons olive oil

1 green sweet pepper, chopped

1 onion, chopped

230 g (8 oz) tinned chopped tomato
   (plus juice)

1.4 kg (3 lb) baking potatoes, peeled and
   cut into 2.5-cm (1-inch) chunks

1 whole head garlic, roasted and peeled
   (see page 8)

1 bay leaf

2 teaspoons salt

1 teaspoon pimentón

Freshly ground black pepper

2 (225 g) tins sardines, drained (optional)

Heat the oil in a cazuela over medium heat and sauté the green pepper and onion until softened, about 5 minutes. Add the tomatoes with their juice, potatoes, garlic, bay leaf, salt, pimentón, black pepper and 450 ml (¾ pint) water.

Bring to the boil, then cover and simmer until potatoes are fork-tender, about 35 minutes.

If you are using the sardines, add them to the casserole and heat thoroughly.

Spoon into bowls, with all the liquid, and serve hot.

SERVES 6

POTATOES, LA RIOJA STYLE
PATATAS A LA RIOJANA

La Rioja cooks say you shouldn't cut the potatoes with a knife, but rather cut them slightly, then break them into pieces. Supposedly, the rough broken surfaces release more potato starch, which is what thickens the cooking liquid. This dish is often served instead of soup as a first course.

La Rioja is Spain's best-known wine-producing region, so I would definitely serve these potatoes with a young Rioja red.

1.5 kg (3½ lb) baking potatoes

4 tablespoons olive oil

1 onion, chopped

1 small green sweet pepper, cut into 2.5-cm (1-inch) pieces

1 teaspoon pimentón

1 bay leaf

1 teaspoon salt

340 g (12 oz) soft chorizo, cut into 8 pieces

Peel the potatoes and cut and break them into 4-cm (1½-inch) chunks.

Heat the oil in a cazuela or casserole over medium heat and sauté the onion until softened, about 5 minutes. Add the potatoes and turn them in the oil for another 5 minutes. Add the green pepper, pimentón, bay leaf, salt and 450 ml (¾ pint) water. Bring to the boil, then lower the heat so potatoes cook gently for 10 minutes.

Add the chorizo to the potatoes and continue to cook for another 25 minutes, or until the potatoes are tender.

Let the dish rest for 10 minutes before serving. The cooking liquid should be thickened to a sauce consistency. Remove the bay leaf and serve.

SERVES 4 AS A STARTER

7

Paella and Other Rice Dishes

RICE FOR EVERY OCCASION

Paella is happy food. It's fiesta food, what you eat on Sundays for lunch when all the relatives come, or what you cook over an open fire on a country outing. In Spain, it's an occasion much like the backyard barbecue – the guys take charge. At the beach, Spanish families on holiday order a paella in advance at a *chiringuito* (beach shack), and arrive, fifteen or twenty people with kids in tow, to sit down to a midday feast.

But there are rice dishes beyond paella. Everyday rice. And likewise, there are paellas that do not include rice, but rather pasta.

PAELLA HOW-TO

The Pan. Paella is specifically a wide, shallow two-handled pan that allows rice to be cooked quickly over a fast-burning wood fire. The pan, made of rolled steel, comes in sizes from 25 cm (10 inches) up to around 1 metre (about 3 feet). The depth varies from 4 to 5 cm (1½– 2 inches). A 30-cm (12-inch) pan, measured across the top of the pan, serves two to three; a 35-cm (14-inch) pan is about right to serve four to five; a 45-cm (18-inch) pan serves six to eight. Good kitchenware shops sell paella pans or they can be mail-ordered from the sources given at the end of the book (see page 342).

It is difficult to manage a paella pan larger than 35 cm (14 inches) on the hob. If you are preparing in larger quantities, I suggest that you do one of the following:

1. Cook two or more 35-cm (14-inch) paellas on the hob

2. Move the operation outdoors over a wood fire, charcoal barbecue or special large gas burner

3. Use a deeper pan, such as a flat-bottomed wok, instead of a paella pan (see the recipe for Rice in a Frying Pan, page 178)

4. After the sautéing step and once the liquid comes to the boil, finish cooking the paella in an oven preheated to 180°C/350°F/ gas mark 4

With frequent use, a paella pan becomes seasoned, so it only needs washing and drying. However, it may rust if it is not used for a period of time, in which case scour it well before the next use.

The Rice. Use Spanish medium-short-grain rice, preferably the kind that has the Valencia or Calasparra DO (designation of origin). Spanish rice has a white *perla* (pearl), where the starch is concentrated. Its great virtue is as a flavour conductor, soaking up the savoury juices with which the rice cooks – chicken, rabbit or seafood, the herbal essence of snails, fresh vegetables, the heady scent of saffron.

You will sometimes see bomba rice recommended for paella. Bomba is one of the medium-short-grain varieties grown in Spain. It is especially esteemed for *caldoso* (soupy) rice dishes, because the kernel of starch doesn't burst open and make the rice sticky. You don't have to seek it out for paella.

If real Spanish rice is not available, the closest equivalent is a medium-short-grain rice, such as arborio or carnaroli. Long-grain 'American', 'pilaff' or converted rice is not a substitute.

Allow about 100 g (3½ oz) of uncooked rice per person. For paella, the volume of liquid is double the volume rice, so 2 cups rice requires 4 cups liquid. Other rice dishes that are not cooked in a paella may be cooked with a larger proportion of liquid to rice. Do not wash the rice before cooking.

Rice is usually – but not always – added to the paella once the liquid has come to the boil.

Stir in the rice, bring the liquid to a full boil – then never stir the paella again! This is a hard but firm rule. Stirring releases the rice starch and makes a gummy paella.

The Cooking Liquid. Simple, country paellas are made with only water – and the result is very tasty. Restaurant cooks usually use stocks, which enhance the finished flavour of the rice.

I like to make a simple stock using the bony parts of a chicken, prawn shells and liquid from steaming open the mussels.

Colour it Yellow. Paella is always a sunny, golden colour. Although the colouring agent of choice is saffron (*azafrán*), this expensive spice is not used at all in most family paellas. Most paellas are coloured with powdered artificial yellow colouring. This is true in many restaurants as well, though good ones use some real saffron for its inimitable flavour.

I suggest you do the same, using a bit of saffron and a bit of food colouring. Crush a few threads of saffron in a mortar. If you don't have a mortar, use the end of a knife handle to crush the saffron in a teacup. Stir 3 tablespoons of water or white wine into the saffron. Then supplement the golden colour with a pinch of powdered yellow colouring or 5–6 drops of yellow food colouring. Do not, however, substitute that other yellow spice, turmeric, because it's too strongly flavoured for paella. If neither saffron nor yellow colouring is available, the best substitute is a big spoonful of pimentón (spanish paprika), which adds both colour and flavour.

Adding Meat and Seafood. Although the authentic Valencia paella contains no seafood (see page 174), it's fairly typical in much of Spain to combine chicken or rabbit with prawns, squid, clams and mussels. Other versions may include fish as well or pork, sausages and chicken livers. But no matter what other ingredients you add, the rice should predominate. If you are calculating 100 g (3½ oz) of rice per person, allow approximately 230 g (8 oz) per person of combined chicken, meat and seafood.

Cut the chicken, rabbit or other meat into small pieces, so that they cook fully in the time it takes to cook the rice.

How to Cook it. Paella is best cooked over a wood fire. Fast-burning twigs bring the liquid to the boil. As the fire burns down, the rice cooks gently and the smoke adds a flavour dimension. If you are cooking over a wood fire, it's most important to level the pan, supporting it equally on a tripod or stones around the fire.

Of course, building a wood fire is not always practical. You can prepare fine paella on the hob – the only limitation is size. A gas barbecue is not successful, because it is not possible to set the pan close enough to the heat source, so it doesn't quite reach the hot temperatures needed to bring the liquids to the boil. The paella can be cooked over a charcoal fire if you lay a deep bed of coals, positioning the pan only 10 or 13 cm (4 or 5 inches) over the fire. In Spain, big paellas are usually made outdoors on concentric gas cooking rings hooked up to camping gas. These are available from sources in the UK. (See the Sources list at the end of the book.)

Don't cover the paella pan during cooking. Traditional paellas are never oven-cooked. However, restaurants that must turn out several dozen paellas in an afternoon usually resort to finishing in the oven, to free hobs for the next round. It's also an option if you are using a pan too large to manoeuvre on the hob.

The Sofrito. The *sofrito* is the mixture of sautéed ingredients – meat, seafood, peppers, beans, tomatoes – that flavours the paella. Olive oil is the essential starting point of a good *sofrito*. Then, patience, so flavour develops slowly. Use a medium fire, so the chicken browns very slowly. It should be nearly cooked by the time the liquid and rice are added.

Fresh green beans, broad beans, peas and globe artichokes add a special flavour. Broad beans and artichokes will darken the *sofrito*, so I prefer to par-boil them, then add to the rice towards the end of the cooking time.

Timing. Allow 20 to 30 minutes for the *sofrito*. Then add the liquid and bring it to a full boil. Add the rice. Cook it over a hot fire for the first 5 minutes, then reduce the heat to medium. The rice should cook in 20 minutes from the time it was added to the pan. It will be tender, but very slightly chewy. Let the paella rest for 5 to 10 minutes before serving.

Fiesta Paella with Chicken and Shellfish

Paella con Pollo y Mariscos

A *romería* is a pilgrimage to a country shrine, a grand occasion for a fiesta with singing and dancing and paella cooked outdoors. In the autumn there is a *romería* on the banks of the river that cuts through the valley below me. A parade of riders on horseback and decorated carts pulled by oxen or tractors leaves from town to arrive at the riverside to claim campsites for the day. Elegant horsemen, with women in *traje flamenco* (flouncy, ruffled flamenco dresses) mounted behind them, parade their horses around the area.

Among the trees, where children run and play, family groups get their fires burning brightly to make big paellas. The men do the cooking, while the women unpack food to nibble on while the rice cooks. Olives, potato omelettes, sliced ham and sausage are spread out on a folding table. There's plenty of wine, cold beer and soft drinks for the children. After the feasting, some take up their guitars and singers and dancers gather to clap and stomp and twirl. The fiesta is in full swing!

Paella in southern Spain, where I live, usually contains chicken or rabbit plus prawns, mussels and squid. The top is gaily garnished with strips of red pimiento, green peas and pink prawns. Real fiesta food.

With paella, you want a happy wine. Serve a young red (*tinto joven*) or chilled rosé (*rosado*).

12 mussels, scrubbed

450 g (1 lb) king prawns

4 tablespoons olive oil

680 g (1½ lb) chicken legs and breasts, cut into small pieces

115 g (4 oz) pork, cut into 2.5-cm (1-inch) cubes

340g (12 oz) squid, cleaned and cut into rings

1 green sweet pepper, cut into 2.5-cm (1-inch) squares

2 garlic cloves, finely chopped

1 large tomato, peeled, de-seeded and chopped

60 g (2 oz) frozen green peas, thawed, or par-boiled broad beans

2 small globe artichokes, quartered and par-boiled (optional)

900 ml (1½ pints) chicken stock or water

370 g (13 oz) Spanish medium-short-grain rice

¼ teaspoon saffron threads, crushed

½ teaspoon pimentón

4 drops yellow food colouring in 2 tablespoons water

Freshly ground black pepper

1 bay leaf

2 teaspoons salt, or to taste

1 tinned or bottled red pimiento, drained and cut into strips

½ lemon, to garnish

Place the mussels in a pan with 4 tablespoons water. Cover the pan and cook over a hot fire, shaking the pan until the mussel shells open, 3 to 4 minutes. Discard the empty half shells of the mussels. Strain the liquid and reserve it.

Cook 4–5 unpeeled prawns in boiling water to cover for 1 minute. Reserve them and add the liquid to the mussel liquid. Shell the remaining prawns and set them aside. (If you are preparing a stock in which to cook the rice, the prawn shells can be boiled with the bony backs and wings of the chicken. Add the mussel and prawn liquid to the stock or water.)

Heat the oil in a 35-cm (14-inch) paella pan over medium heat. Sauté the chicken and pork until they are lightly browned, about 10 minutes. Add the squid and continue sautéing 5 minutes more.

Add the green pepper and garlic and sauté for 2 minutes more. Add the tomato and increase the heat so it quickly loses its liquid. Stir in the peeled prawns, peas and artichokes, if using, and sauté 5 minutes more.

Pour in the 900 ml (1½ pints) stock or water and turn up the heat to high. When the liquid is boiling, add the rice.

Combine the saffron, pimentón and food colouring. Dribble this into the pan. Add the black pepper, bay leaf and salt (if the stock was salted, less will be needed). Stir to distribute all the ingredients. Cook over high heat for 5 minutes.

Lower the heat so liquid is barely simmering, and cook for 10 minutes more. Do not stir the paella. Arrange the mussels and cooked prawns on top of the rice. Garnish with strips of pimiento.

Cook for 5 to 6 minutes more, until the rice is tender and all the liquid is absorbed.

Let the paella set for 5 to 10 minutes before serving. Place a half-lemon in the centre or lemon wedges around the edges. Many people like to add a squeeze of lemon to their serving of paella.

SERVES 4 TO 5

VARIATION: Here's an alternative method for a 45-cm (18-inch) paella pan to serve 6 to 8. Increase the quantity of rice to 540 g (19 oz); increase the liquid to 1.15 litres (2½ pints). Preheat the oven to 180°C/350°F/gas mark 4. Prepare the *sofrito* on the hob. Add the liquid to the paella pan and bring to the boil. Add the rice and bring again to the boil. Very carefully place the pan in the oven and bake for 20 minutes.

PAELLA, VALENCIA STYLE
PAELLA VALENCIANA

Valencia is Spain's third largest city, a bustling metropolis that sparkles with Mediterranean light. You needn't travel far out of the city to arrive at a very different world – the wetlands of the Albufera. The Albufera is a lake separated from the sea by sand and silt. It is a region rich in wildlife – ducks, mallards, herons, eels, frogs – and it is also where rice has been cultivated since the epoch of the Moors.

The people of the Albufera traditionally lived by hunting, fishing and rice growing. The original paella was a dish cooked by the rice reapers, who made their midday meal from the foods that were hunted, fished, foraged and grown – rice, eels, wild duck, wild rabbit, snails, frogs' legs – cooked over a wood fire in a shallow, flat-bottomed pan.

When I visited the Valencia region, I sampled many varieties of paella and other rice dishes and asked advice from many cooks. The best counsel I received was from Santos, who drove me around the back roads through the shimmering rice paddies: 'Practise every Sunday.' Paella is to be enjoyed week after week, and it just gets better the more you practise.

This is the recipe for paella where it grows, in the rice fields of Valencia. If snails are not available, omit them. Chicken breast can be substituted for the duck.

140 g (5 oz) fresh giant lima beans or use
    dried butter beans, soaked overnight

280 g (10 oz) sliced wide, flat green beans
    (5-cm/2-inch pieces), or use runner
    beans

2 chicken thighs (280 g/10 oz)

½ rabbit, cut into 4 serving pieces

1 boneless duck breast (280 g/10 oz), cut
    into 4 pieces (or substitute chicken
    breast)

Salt

4 tablespoons olive oil

2 garlic cloves, finely chopped

1 tomato, peeled and chopped

6 drops yellow food colouring dissolved in
    2 tablespoons water

¼ teaspoon saffron threads, crushed

1 teaspoon pimentón

900 ml (1½ pints) chicken stock or water

12 cooked or tinned snails, in their shells

Sprig fresh rosemary

370 g (13 oz) Spanish medium-short-grain
    rice

Lemon wedges

If you are using dried butter beans, soaked overnight, cook them in boiling water for 5 minutes. Drain, refresh under cold water and set aside.

Blanch the green beans in boiling water for 1 minute. Drain, refresh in cold water and set aside.

Cut the chicken thighs in half along the bone, making four pieces. Lightly salt the chicken, rabbit and duck.

Place a 35-cm (14-inch) paella pan on the hob and heat the oil over medium heat. Sprinkle 1 teaspoon salt into the oil, then add the chicken, rabbit and duck. Brown slowly for 10 to 15 minutes, turning occasionally. Then add the fresh limas or par-boiled butter beans and the blanched green beans. Continue sautéing these ingredients for 5 minutes more.

Add the garlic and, when it begins to turn golden, about 1 minute, the tomato. Keep frying the mixture for another 5 minutes.

In a small bowl, combine the yellow food colouring, saffron and pimentón. Stir until spices are dissolved. Dribble this mixture into the pan.

Add the stock and turn the heat to high. Add the snails and rosemary. When the liquid is boiling, add the rice, stirring to distribute it evenly. Continue to cook over high heat for 6 minutes. Remove the rosemary.

Turn down the heat to medium. Cook for 14 minutes more, without stirring. (The total cooking time once the rice is added is 20 minutes.) The liquid should be mostly absorbed, and the rice al dente.

Let the paella set for 8 minutes before serving. Garnish with lemon wedges.

SERVES 4

FISH WITH PASTA IN PAELLA
PESCADO CON FIDEOS EN PAELLA

This is paella made with pasta instead of rice. It is prepared in a paella pan or in a cazuela. *Fideos* are vermicelli noodles, broken into short lengths. Now they are manufactured in 12-mm (½-inch) elbows with a pinhole through the middle. The pasta is cooked right in the pan or casserole, with only enough liquid to keep it juicy.

The fish should be solid-fleshed, so it doesn't disintegrate, and cut either in thick crosswise steaks or fillets. Good choices are monkfish, halibut, turbot or bream.

6 tablespoons olive oil

400 g (14 oz) chopped tomatoes

100 g (3½ oz) chopped green sweet pepper

3 garlic cloves, chopped

1 tablespoon pimentón

Salt

1 small squid (280 g/10 oz), cut into squares

1.8 litres (3¼ pints) Simple Fish Stock (page 88) or water

1.13–1.4 kg (2½–3 lb) firm-fleshed fish, cut into thick steaks or fillets

230 g (8 oz) small sea crayfish (langoustines) or king prawns

450 g (1 lb) pasta (*fideos* or spaghetti broken into short lengths)

¼ teaspoon saffron threads, crushed to a powder

¼ teaspoon ground cumin

Freshly ground black pepper

115 g (4 oz) peeled prawns

Sprigs of mint, to garnish

Garlic Mayonnaise, for serving (recipe follows)

To make the *sofrito*, heat 3 tablespoons of the oil in a large saucepan over medium heat and sauté the tomatoes, green pepper and garlic until softened, 5 minutes. Stir in the pimentón. Add 2 teaspoons salt, squid and stock. Bring to the boil and simmer, covered, for 20 minutes.

Increase the heat and return the liquid to the boil. Add the fish. Simmer until the fish flakes when probed with a skewer, 5 to 10 minutes, depending on thickness of the fish. With a skimmer, remove the fish to a platter. Reserve the cooking liquid and keep it hot.

In a cazuela or a 35-cm (14-inch) paella pan, heat the remaining 3 tablespoons oil over medium heat and sauté the unpeeled crayfish or king prawns, turning to cook on both sides, for about 4 minutes. Remove and set aside.

Add the pasta to the pan and toast it in the oil, stirring constantly, until lightly golden. Add 1 litre (about 2 pints) of the reserved liquid in which the fish was cooked and bring to the boil. Mix the saffron, cumin and black pepper in an additional 120 ml (4 fl oz) of the reserved liquid and stir it into the pasta. Taste for salt, adding more if necessary.

Cook the pasta over high heat for 5 minutes. Stir in the peeled prawns. Arrange the cooked fish and sautéed crayfish on top of the pasta. Cook for another 2 minutes, or until the pasta is tender.

Let the pasta set for 5 minutes before serving. Garnish with mint sprigs. Serve accompanied by the garlic mayonnaise.

SERVES 4 TO 6

GARLIC MAYONNAISE I
ALIOLI I

Another version of *alioli* is found on page 180. They can be used interchangeably. This one does not have raw eggs. Refrigerated, the sauce keeps for 2 days.

120 ml (4 fl oz) bottled mayonnaise

4 garlic cloves, crushed

120 ml (4 fl oz) olive oil

1 tablespoon fresh lemon juice

Salt

In a bowl, whisk the mayonnaise until smooth. Add the garlic, then slowly stir in the oil. Stir in the lemon juice and add additional salt, if necessary.

MAKES ABOUT 240 ML (8 FL OZ)

RICE IN A FRYING PAN
ARROZ EN PEROL

I once arrived in Córdoba on a fine October day to find it was a local holiday, the feast of San Rafael. The whole town closed up shop and headed for the hills for a midday cookout. The special dish they prepared for the feast was *arroz en perol*, rice cooked, not in the flat paella pan, but in a deep two-handled frying pan, over a fire of thyme, rosemary and wild oak.

A *perol*, made of rolled steel, is lightweight and easy to manage over a wood fire. In the kitchen, use a flat-bottomed wok or any deep (8–10-cm/3–4-inch) frying pan.

680 g (1½ lb) rabbit or chicken, cut into small serving pieces

Salt and freshly ground black pepper

3 tablespoons olive oil

70 g (2½ oz) chopped onion

100 g (3½ oz) sliced mushrooms

70 g (2½ oz) chopped green sweet pepper

3 garlic cloves, chopped

Crushed red chilli flakes

200 g (7 oz) chopped tomato

⅛ teaspoon dried thyme, crumbled

4 tablespoons chopped fresh flat-leaf parsley

1 bay leaf

115 g (4 oz) chopped asparagus

900 ml (1½ pints) Simple Stock (recipe page 82) or water

370 g (13 oz) Spanish medium-short-grain rice

Saffron threads, crushed, and/or yellow food colouring (see Colour it Yellow, page 170)

Season the rabbit with salt and pepper. Heat the oil in a deep frying pan over medium heat and add the meat. Brown the meat slowly, turning occasionally.

When the meat is partially browned, about 10 minutes, add the onion, mushrooms, green pepper, garlic and red chilli flakes to taste. Continue stirring and browning the meat.

Add the tomato and continue cooking over medium heat. Add the thyme, parsley, bay leaf, asparagus and stock. Bring to the boil and stir in the rice.

Mix the saffron and/or yellow food colouring into 3 tablespoons water. Dribble it into the rice and stir to combine.

Cook over high heat for 6 to 7 minutes. Then lower the heat and cook for 14 to 15 minutes more, without stirring, until all the liquid is absorbed and rice is done.

Let the rice set for 5 to 10 minutes before serving.

SERVES 4

STARBOARD RICE WITH FISH ON THE SIDE
ARROZ A BANDA

Originally, this was a fishermen's dish cooked on board a trawler. Some of the day's catch was boiled in a pan, then skimmed out and rice was added to cook in the tasty stock. The rice was served first, followed by the boiled fish. The dish has since achieved near-cult status, especially in Alicante, where the rice is usually prepared in a paella pan, instead of a fisherman's kettle, and served in solitary splendour, accompanied by a pungent *alioli* (garlic sauce).

The success of this rice dish depends on the flavour of the fish stock. In Spain, bony (and cheap) rockfish such as gurnard, weever and scorpion fish would be used. In England, I suggest making a fish stock, adding squid, prawns or crab shells plus mussel stock.

3 tablespoons olive oil

3 garlic cloves, chopped

100 g (3½ oz) chopped tomato

30 g (1 oz) peeled prawns

370 g (13 oz) Spanish medium-short-grain rice

1.8 litres (3¼ pints) Simple Fish Stock (page 88)

¼ teaspoon crushed saffron threads

1 teaspoon pimentón

1 tablespoon white wine

1 teaspoon salt

900 g (2 lb) fish fillets or fish steaks (monkfish, halibut, turbot, bream, sea bass, etc.)

Garlic Mayonnaise II (recipe follows)

Heat the oil in a 24–28-cm (9–11-inch) paella pan over medium heat. Add the garlic, then the tomato and prawns. Stir in the rice and sauté for 2 minutes.

Add half of the fish stock. Increase the heat and bring the liquid to the boil. Mix the saffron and pimentón in the wine. Add to the pan with the salt. Cook the rice over high heat for 5 minutes. Reduce the heat to medium-low and cook until rice is done, another 15 minutes.

While the rice is cooking, bring the remaining fish stock to the boil in another pan. Add the fish. Simmer until they are just done, 5 to 12 minutes, depending on thickness of the fish. Skim out the fish and keep warm on a platter while the rice finishes cooking.

Serve rice in the paella pan with the platter of fish. Pass the garlic sauce separately.

SERVES 4

Garlic Mayonnaise II
Alioli

If raw egg could be a health hazard in your area, choose the other version of *alioli*, garlic sauce, which appears on page 177.

2 cloves garlic, chopped

1 egg, at room temperature

170 ml (6 fl oz) extra virgin olive oil

1 teaspoon salt

2 tablespoons fresh lemon juice or vinegar

Put the garlic and egg in a blender and pulse until garlic is finely chopped. With the motor running, pour in the oil in a slow trickle, allowing it to be absorbed by the egg before adding more. Blend in all the oil. The sauce will emulsify and thicken. Blend in the salt and lemon juice.

The sauce will keep, refrigerated, for up to 2 days.

Makes 240 ml (8 fl oz)

Squid and Black Rice
Arroz Negro con Calamares

What makes black rice black? The question stirs up passions. Jordi from Barcelona swears that black rice is not made with squid ink, but from very patiently cooking the *sofrito*, the slow, slow, frying of onions, garlic and tomatoes until the point when 'you're scared they're going to burn'. Then you add a little water and repeat the process, over and over, until the *sofrito* is nearly black.

On the other hand, Amalia from Alicante said the rice should be made with tiny cuttlefish, sautéed whole, which release their ink in cooking. The recipe I've given here is adapted, with the black ink from squid to colour the rice.

This rice dish can be made in a paella pan or a cazuela. Note that the procedure is somewhat different from that for paella – the rice is added to the *sofrito*, then boiling liquid is added to the rice.

The ink from one good-sized fresh squid (340–450 g/12–16 oz) is sufficient to colour the rice. Frozen squid does not work, because the ink dries up. However, if you can purchase tiny sachets of frozen ink, you can use them with frozen squid.

12 mussels

900 ml (1½ pints) Simple Fish Stock (page 88)

1 fresh squid (340 g/12 oz), cleaned, ink sac reserved (see page 9)

230 g (8 oz) monkfish fillets

4 tablespoons olive oil

4 whole king prawns

1 onion, chopped

2 garlic cloves, chopped

1 large tomato, peeled, seeded and chopped

2 teaspoons pimentón

370 g (13 oz) Spanish medium-short-grain rice

Salt and freshly ground black pepper

Garlic Mayonnaise (pages 177 and 180), to serve

Combine the mussels in a pan with 4 tablespoons water. Cover and cook over high heat, shaking the pan, until mussel shells open, about 3 minutes. Discard the empty half shells. Reserve the mussels. Strain the liquid and add it to the fish stock. Pour the fish stock into a pan ready to be heated.

Put the ink sac from the squid in a small bowl and add 4 tablespoons of the fish stock to it. Mash the ink sac to release the ink. Set aside.

Cut the cleaned squid into rings or squares. Cut the monkfish into 4-cm (1½-inch) chunks.

Heat the oil in a 30-cm (12-inch) cazuela until quite hot. Sauté the prawns, for about 2 minutes per side, until they are pink and slightly curled. Remove the prawns and reserve them.

Add the squid to the oil and sauté for 2 minutes over high heat. Add the onion and garlic and continue cooking over high heat.

Add the monkfish and cook for another minute over high heat. Stir in the tomato and pimentón and continue to cook for 5 minutes.

Bring the reserved fish stock to the boil.

Stir the rice into the cazuela and cook for 1 minute. Stir in 900 ml (1½ pints) boiling fish stock. Cook for 5 minutes over high heat. Season with salt and pepper.

Use a small sieve to strain the ink mixture into the rice. Stir to mix it well. Lower the heat to medium and simmer the rice for 5 minutes more. Arrange the cooked mussels and prawns on the top of the rice. Don't stir it again. Simmer for 10 minutes more. If you have refrained from stirring, the surface of the rice should be very black; the rice will be grey-black.

Remove from the heat and let the rice rest for 10 minutes. The rice will continue to cook from the heat of the cazuela.

Serve hot, passing garlic mayonnaise on the side.

Serves 4

RICE WITH 'PARTRIDGE'
ARROZ CON 'PERDIZ'

This recipe name is a bit of a joke because there is no bird in this dish at all. The 'partridge' is a whole head of garlic, set in the middle of the rice. This vegetarian dish is prepared for meatless meals during Lent.

155 g (5½ oz) dried chickpeas, soaked overnight

1 bay leaf

1 whole head garlic, unpeeled

1 tablespoon pimentón

2 teaspoons salt

3 tablespoons olive oil

½ onion, chopped

1 garlic clove, peeled and chopped

200 g (7 oz) chopped tomatoes

140 g (5 oz) diced courgettes

1 medium potato, peeled and thinly sliced

370 g (13 oz) medium-short-grain rice

Pinch saffron threads, crushed (optional)

1 tomato, sliced

Bring 1.4 litres (2½ pints) of water to the boil in a large pan. Drain the chickpeas and add them to the boiling water with the bay leaf. Boil gently, uncovered, for 40 minutes.

Add the whole head of garlic to the chickpeas. Dissolve the pimentón in a little water and stir into the chickpeas with 1 teaspoon of the salt. Cook for another 40 minutes, until the chickpeas are tender. Drain the chickpeas, reserving the cooking liquid and the garlic.

Preheat the oven to 190°C/375°F/ gas mark 5.

In a cazuela, heat the oil over medium-high heat and sauté the onion and chopped garlic until the onion is softened, about 5 minutes. Add the chopped tomatoes, courgettes and potato and continue sautéing for another few minutes. Then stir in the rice and the cooked chickpeas.

Bring 1 litre (about 2 pints) of the liquid in which the chickpeas were cooked to the boil. Add it to the rice with the remaining 1 teaspoon salt and saffron, if desired. Place the head of garlic in the centre and the slices of tomato around it. Carefully place the cazuela in the oven.

Bake the rice for 18 to 20 minutes.

Let the rice rest for 5 minutes before serving. Each person can squeeze some of the soft garlic on to a serving of rice.

SERVES 6

8

SEAFOOD

SHELLFISH

Clams with Beans (*Almejas con Faves*)

Clams with Artichokes and Sherry
    (*Almejas con Alcachofas*)

Crab Gratin (*Txangurro*)

Cuttlefish or Squid with Broad Beans
    (*Chocos con Habas*)

Galician Mussel Stew with White Wine
    (*Guiso de Mejillónes, a la Gallega*)

Scallop Gratin, Galician Style
    (*Vieiras a la Gallega*)

Savoury Scallop Pie (*Empanada de Zamburiñas*)

Empanada Dough (*Masa para Empanadas*)

Stuffed Squid in Tomato Sauce
    (*Calamares Rellenos*)

Squid in their own Ink
    (*Chipirones en Su Tinta*)

FIN FISH

Baked Sea Bream with Potatoes (*Pescado al Horno*)

Sea Bream Baked in a Salt Crust (*Dorada a la Sal*)

Pan-Roasted Whole Sea Bream (*Besugo al Horno*)

Sea Bream with Sherry Sauce, Rota Style
    (*Hurta a la Roteña*)

Sea Bream Grilled on its Back (*Besugo a la
    Espalda*)

Halibut with Onion Confit (*Mero Encebollado*)

Hake in Green Sauce, Basque Style
    (*Merluza a la Vasca*)

Whole Hake with Mushroom Stuffing
    (*Merluza Rellena*)

Mackerel in Oregano Marinade
    (*Caballa en Escabeche*)

Monkfish in Pimentón Sauce (*Rape al Pimentón*)

Monkfish in Almond Sauce
    (*Rape an Salsa de Almendras*)

Sardines Baked with Pine Kernels and Clams
    (*Moraga de Sardinas al Horno*)

Sea Bass with Canary Island Coriander Sauce
and 'Wrinkly' Potatoes (*Samcocho con
Mojo Verde y Papas Arrugadas a lo Canario*)

Sea Bass with Caper Dressing
(*Lubina a la Plancha con Aliño
de Alcaparras*)

Sea Bass in Saffron Sauce (*Lubina en Amarillo*)

Grilled Swordfish Steaks
with Lemon-Parsley Dressing
(*Pez Espada a la Plancha*)

Swordfish in Tomato Sauce, Málaga Style
(*Pez Espada a la Malagueña*)

Pot-Roasted Tuna with White Wine
(*Atún Mechado*)

Basque Tuna and Potato Stew (*Marmitako*)

Mixed Fish Fry, Málaga Style
(*Fritura de Pescaditos Malagueña*)

SEAFOOD STEWS AND CASSEROLES

Catalan Seafood Casserole with Red Pepper Sauce
(*Romesco de Pescados y Mariscos*)

A Fine Kettle of Fish (*Caldeirada*)

SALT COD

Catalan Salad with Salt Cod, Tuna and Anchovies
(*Xató*)

'Cobblestones' (Cod and Bean Salad) (*Empedrado*)

Cod Fritters with Molasses
(*Tortillitas de Bacalao con Miel de Caña*)

Piquillo Peppers Stuffed with Cod
(*Pimientos de Piquillo Rellenos*)

Cod and Potato Purée, Mule-Driver's Style
(*Bacalao al Ajo Arriero*)

Codfish in Biscay Red Pepper Sauce
(*Bacalao a la Vizcaina*)

Codfish Topped with Peppers, Bilbao Style
(*Bacalao a la Bilbaina*)

AT THE FISH MARKET

In my first days in the village – this was in 1966 – I would awake each morning to the cries of the fishmongers echoing through the narrow white streets of the *pueblo* (village), '*Que bueno, que fresco, tres duritos el kilito*', and throw open the shutters to watch as the women gathered to haggle over their few pesetas' worth of fish.

I loved the fish markets from the very first day. I slowly learned to recognize the different fish and attempted to translate the names into English, a difficult job even for someone who knows her fish – and I didn't. I grew up in midwestern America eating frozen halibut. I first tasted fresh shrimp when I was twelve, on a family vacation to Biloxi, Mississippi. What a revelation!

So I plunged in with gusto. My first fresh fish purchased at the village market was large, ugly, scaly and red. I brought it home and put it on the table. Now what?

My maid (yes, in 1966, when the cost of living in Spain was incredibly low, I had a maid who did the laundry by hand and scrubbed the floor tiles on her hands and knees) showed me how to scale it with a sharp knife and clean it. I baked it with olive oil and lemon and it was delicious, my first home-cooked fish.

The fishmongers at the markets became my friends and adversaries. One fat fishmonger, Calabaza ('pumpkin'), whose raspy voice was the loudest in the market, would threaten to pull me in with a fishy hand. 'Bonito, cheap,' he would tell me. His daughter, the prettiest girl in the village, stood behind him scaling fish.

I knew it wasn't bonito. Mackerel or chub? 'Well, you tell me which you like best,' he replied. I didn't know, so he wouldn't say. I would buy the lovely blue and striped fish, so fresh they were rigid, and grill them for lunch.

Another fishmonger, this one on the coast, would fillet sole with a rapid, deft hand, which, as I watched him wielding the knife, was missing the middle finger. Over the years I watched his prices, chalked up on a board, steadily creep up.

He would give me my change for a kilo of fish, point to the chalkboard, and say, 'Seventy pesetas.' Counting the change, I would discover he had collected only sixty pesetas. As I looked up, he would give me a wink.

Another time I had been complaining about the skyrocketing price of prawns, but ordered a kilo anyway. I watched the scales and when it reached a kilo, he added, not the usual two or three extra, but a good 250 g more. Good public relations.

One day a lady fishmonger reached out and took my arm. '*Señora, mire, las conchas buenas, finas.*' ('Look at these fine clams!') I looked. Beautiful big, glossy shells on the counter. While I watched, feeling them, turning them over, the things began to move. Shells opened slowly, just a peek, and a pink tongue oozed out.

I jerked my hand away, squealing, 'But they're alive!' Well, of course they're alive, she assured me. She smacked her lips to indicate how delicious. She didn't say anything about slitting their necks, so I bought a few dozen.

At home I rinsed them off and left them by the sink while my guests and I sipped chilled white wine. We heard little clacking sounds. Impatient perhaps? Well, let them wait a little longer. Then, suddenly, clank, clackety, clack. I ran to look and the whole lot of them had thrown themselves off the counter and were marching across the kitchen floor. Back to the sea! Back to the sea! We're outta here! A one-legged march, shells humping along.

I gathered them up, put the water on to heat and threw them in. A few clacks and all was silent. Shells opened silently.

They were not good. They were tough and rubbery, those big Venus-shell clams. I later took instruction at a tapa bar. These clams must be prised open and served raw on the half shell with, perhaps, just a squeeze of lemon. You know they're fresh when the drop of lemon causes them to shudder, just before you pop them into the mouth.

Thus proceeded my education in the cooking of foods from the sea. The fish market continues to be my passion and seafood my favourite dish.

SHELLFISH

CLAMS WITH BEANS
ALMEJAS CON FAVES

This dish is typical of fishing villages in Asturias and Cantabria on the north Bay of Biscay coast. Clams and beans may seem a strange combination, but they go together very well. This dish makes a very satisfying lunch with a salad and bread to accompany it.

230 g (8 oz) cannellini beans, soaked overnight

1 onion, peeled and quartered

2 garlic cloves, peeled

1 bay leaf

Sprig parsley

3 tablespoons olive oil

1 teaspoon salt

900 g (2 lb) clams for steaming, washed in several changes of water

¼ teaspoon saffron threads

1 tablespoon dried breadcrumbs

Salt and freshly ground black pepper

Pinch dried thyme

Drain the soaked beans. Combine them in a large pan with enough water to cover, with the onion, 1 garlic clove, bay leaf and parsley. Bring to the boil, then simmer, covered, for 30 minutes. Add 120 ml (4 fl oz) cold water and the oil and salt and cook for 30 minutes more, or until beans are tender.

Scrub the clams and rinse under running water. Combine them in a pan with 120 ml (4 fl oz) water. Cover and steam them open over high heat, shaking the pan until the clam shells open, about 3 minutes. Discard any clams that do not open. Remove from the heat. Strain the liquid and reserve it. Shell the clams, discarding the shells.

Crush the saffron in a mortar with the remaining garlic clove and the breadcrumbs. Mix to a paste with a little of the liquid from the beans. Season with salt and pepper and a pinch of thyme.

Add the clams to the strained beans with the breadcrumb mixture and reserved clam liquid. Simmer for 10 minutes. Serve immediately

SERVES 4 AS A STARTER OR LIGHT SUPPER DISH

CLAMS WITH ARTICHOKES AND SHERRY

ALMEJAS CON ALCACHOFAS

Although this dish can be made with frozen artichokes and tinned clams, it is tastiest when both are fresh. When cooking fresh artichokes, use glass, stainless steel or enamel cookware so they don't darken.

Should you have any leftovers, this makes a fine pasta sauce.

900 g (2 lb) clams for steaming, washed in several changes of water

1 kg (2¼ lb) globe artichokes

Sliced lemon

Salt

4 teaspoons plain flour

3 tablespoons olive oil

70 g (2½ oz) finely chopped onion

2 garlic cloves, peeled and sliced

120 ml (4 fl oz) dry Sherry

4 tablespoons chopped fresh flat-leaf parsley

Combine the clams with 280 ml (½ pint) of water in a deep frying pan. Cover and steam them over high heat, shaking the pan, just until clam shells open, about 3 minutes. Discard any clams that do not open. Shuck the clams, discarding the shells. (If you are using tinned clams, you should have about 240 ml/8 fl oz of clam meat plus liquid.)

Strain the clam liquid and reserve it.

Trim the artichokes, rubbing the cut surfaces with lemon. Cut off the stems. Remove several layers of the outer leaves. Cut off and discard the top ⅔ of the leaves, reserving the bottoms. Cut the bottoms into quarters or eighths (depending on size of artichokes). With the tip of a knife, nip out the fibrous choke.

Place the artichoke bottoms in a pan with water to cover, salt and half of the flour. Bring to the boil and boil for 5 minutes. Remove from the heat and leave the artichokes to cool in the liquid.

In a cazuela, heat the oil over medium heat and add the onion and garlic. Sauté for a few minutes, until the onion is softened. Drain and add the artichokes and sauté for 5 minutes. Sprinkle with the remaining flour and stir.

Add the Sherry and 240 ml (8 fl oz) of reserved clam liquid. Add half of the chopped parsley. Let bubble gentle over medium heat, stirring occasionally, for 10 minutes. Add the clams to the artichokes and heat thoroughly. Sprinkle with the remaining parsley.

SERVES 6 AS A STARTER

CRAB GRATIN

TXANGURRO

Txangurro is the Basque word for the spider crab. Once cooked, the flaked crab meat is mixed with a brandy-enriched sauce, then spooned into the crab shells and browned under the grill or in a hot oven. Typically it is served as a first course, but, with a side dish of steamed rice, it is filling enough for a main course.

As there really is not a great deal of meat in a crab, I suggest you use already-shelled fresh or frozen crab meat. However, should you have fresh crabs, boil them for 15 minutes, then plunge them into cold water to stop the cooking. Clean and remove the crab meat from the shells, discarding the stomach and spongy gills. Crack the claws and extract the meat. Clean the shells and reserve.

4 tablespoons olive oil

2 medium onions, chopped (about 300 g/10½ oz)

1 carrot, diced

2 garlic cloves, chopped

680 g (1½ lb) chopped tomatoes

4 tablespoons brandy

120 ml (4 fl oz) dry Sherry

340 g (12 oz) fresh or frozen crab meat, drained and liquid reserved

½ teaspoon hot pimentón or ½ teaspoon paprika with a pinch of cayenne

½ teaspoon salt

2 tablespoons chopped fresh flat-leaf parsley

1 bay leaf

45 g (1½ oz) crumbled stale breadcrumbs

1 tablespoon butter

Heat the oil in a deep frying pan over medium heat and sauté the onion, carrot and garlic for 5 minutes. Add the tomatoes and sauté over high heat for 5 minutes more. Add 3 tablespoons of brandy, the Sherry, 4 tablespoons liquid from the crabs, the pimentón, salt, parsley and bay leaf. Bring to the boil, then simmer for 40 minutes.

Discard the bay leaf. Purée the sauce in a blender, then strain it. Return the sauce to the pan and stir in the crab meat. Add the remaining 1 tablespoon brandy. Simmer for 5 minutes.

Preheat the oven to 200°C/400°F/gas mark 6.

Spoon the mixture into the crab shells or oiled ramekins. Sprinkle with breadcrumbs and dot with butter. Bake until the top is lightly golden, about 20 minutes. Serve hot.

SERVES 4 AS A STARTER; SERVES 8 AS A TAPA

CUTTLEFISH OR SQUID WITH BROAD BEANS
CHOCOS CON HABAS

Pepa was a fisherman's wife. She had an amazing repertoire of dishes that were made with whatever was left from the day's catch plus whatever vegetables were to hand in her tiny kitchen garden. She cooked mackerel with *pisto* (courgettes and tomatoes), sardines with spinach and little cuttlefish with spring broad beans.

Tiny (5-cm/2-inch) cuttlefish can be cooked whole. However, as these are not likely to be available, I have substituted squid for this dish, cleaned and cut into 5-cm/2-inch squares.

3 tablespoons olive oil

115 g (4 oz) chopped spring onion

4 garlic cloves, chopped

4 tablespoons chopped fresh flat-leaf
    parsley

2 teaspoons pimentón

900 g (2 lb) medium squid (about 4),
    cleaned (see page 9) and cut into 5-cm
    (2-inch) pieces

450 g (1 lb) shelled broad beans

1 teaspoon salt

Freshly ground black pepper

Heat the oil in a cazuela over medium-high heat and sauté the onion and garlic until softened, 5 minutes. Stir in the parsley, pimentón and squid. Continue to sauté for 5 minutes.

Add 340 ml (12 fl oz) water. Bring to the boil, cover and simmer for 15 minutes.

Add the broad beans, salt and pepper. Simmer until squid and beans are quite tender, about 30 minutes more. Serve hot.

SERVES 4

GALICIAN MUSSEL STEW WITH WHITE WINE
GUISO DE MEJILLÓNES, A LA GALLEGA

In Galicia, in northwest Spain, the picturesque little port of Meloxo has a busy fishing harbour in a protected cove on one of the Atlantic *rias* (estuaries). Just around the curve of coast, facing out to the open ocean, is another sight altogether. Here rafts are anchored far out into the bay. Small boats work around the flats.

These are some of Galicia's mussel 'farms', which harvest 90 per cent of all the mussels sold in Spain and a good share of those marketed abroad as well. I talked to some of the 'mussel men', members of a cooperative who cultivate this crop, who explained how the mussels are planted and harvested.

Tiny baby mussels – each the size of a grain of rice – are removed from rocks at sea and carried to the floating mussel beds, latticed flats called *bateas*. There they are wrapped in fine cotton threads and attached to ropes suspended from the flat into the water to a depth of 12 metres (about 40 feet). Each flat can have a maximum of five hundred mussel ropes.

After that, the mussels do their own thing, drifting in the tides, riding the waves, feeding on what the ocean brings them, more or less as they would if they were still attached to rocks. Although these are sometimes called mussel 'farms', the mussels aren't fed like barnyard chickens. They eat only ocean plants. There is considerable variation between the different flats. The ones further out to sea might produce twice the number of mussels as those closer to shore.

After a period of four to six months, when the mussels are ten times their initial weight, the mussel men haul up the ropes, grade and divide the mussels, then restring them to continue their growth.

Mussels are harvested year-round. However, during their spawning period in April and May, they are likely to be scrawny specimens. After that, they begin feeding again and plump up. A good mussel, whatever its size, should have about 15 per cent of its weight as flesh.

By the time they weigh 15 kg (33 lb) per metre of rope – at about two years after seeding – they are ready for harvesting. The ropes thick with mussels are hauled up.

'Now we do it with cranes,' explained Manuel. 'But before it was hard work. All the men had back trouble.' And muscles.

Mussel farming is a family business, with each family running one, two or three of the mussel farming beds.

The rights to mussel flats are owned as property, which can be passed from father to son. If one wants to retire and no family is taking his place, the concession can be sold. Several of the men said their sons were studying to become biologists, teachers and computer technicians and probably wouldn't follow in the family business.

After harvesting, the mussels are graded by size. They are then deposited in purification tanks for at least 12 hours, where they are sluiced in clean (chlorinated) water, before shipping to market. An in-house biologist (or a mussel veterinarian) monitors the water and inspects the catch daily.

I sampled a selection of the plump, briny molluscs in three or four delicious ways, with a chilled Galician white wine (the Albariño wine region reaches practically to the shores of the *rias*). This mussel stew was one of the best.

1.4–1.8 kg (3–4 lb) fresh mussels, scrubbed and debearded

2 bay leaves

5 tablespoons olive oil

1 onion, chopped

1 small green sweet pepper, chopped

2 garlic cloves, chopped

60 g (2 oz) chorizo sausage, chopped (optional)

1.4 kg (3 lb) potatoes, peeled and sliced

140 ml (¼ pint) white wine

1 teaspoon pimentón

Pinch dried thyme

Freshly ground black pepper

Chopped fresh flat-leaf parsley

Combine the mussels in a large pan with the bay leaves and 240 ml (8 fl oz) water. Cover and place over high heat. Shake the pan several times, until the mussel shells have opened, 5 to 7 minutes; discard any that don't open. Remove from the heat. Drain the mussels, saving the liquid. When the mussels are cool enough to handle, remove the mussels from the shells and discard the shells.

Heat the oil in a cazuela or large heavy pan and sauté the onion, green pepper, garlic and sausage, if using, until the onion is softened, 5 minutes. Add the potatoes, wine, pimentón, thyme and black pepper. Salt is not needed, as the mussel liquid is salty.

Strain the mussel liquid through a fine sieve and add 240 ml (8 fl oz) of it to the potatoes. Cover and cook for 10 minutes over low heat, then add the mussels. Cook for 10 minutes more, or until the potatoes are fork-tender.

Let rest for 5 minutes. Serve sprinkled with chopped parsley.

SERVES 6

SCALLOPS GRATIN, GALICIAN STYLE
VIEIRAS A LA GALLEGA

Scallops are emblematic of Galicia, on the north Atlantic coast. In medieval times, pilgrims to Galicia's famous shrine of St James in Santiago de Compostela collected scallop shells to wear on their belts to prove they had completed the arduous journey.

In the winter, I buy fresh scallops, still in their shells and with the delicate red coral intact, in my local fish market. I have adapted this recipe to use frozen scallops as well.

450 g (1 lb) fresh or frozen scallops, thawed

1 tablespoon fresh lemon juice

4 tablespoons olive oil

1 onion, finely chopped

1 garlic clove, finely chopped

3 slices bacon, chopped

4 tablespoons white wine

2 teaspoons sweet pimentón or paprika

Pinch hot pimentón or cayenne

2 tablespoons chopped fresh flat-leaf parsley

Salt and freshly ground black pepper

4 tablespoons fine dry breadcrumbs

Pat the scallops dry. If they are very large, they can be sliced in half horizontally. Place them in a bowl with the lemon juice.

Heat 3 tablespoons of the oil in a frying pan over medium heat. Sauté the onion, garlic and bacon until the onion is softened, about 15 minutes.

Add the wine and cook until partially reduced, about 1 minute. Remove the frying pan from the heat and stir in the two kinds of pimentón, parsley, salt and pepper.

Divide the scallops between six scallop shells or individual ramekins. Put a spoonful of the onion mixture on to each shell. Sprinkle with the breadcrumbs. Drizzle the remaining 1 tablespoon of oil over the scallops.

Set the shells or ramekins in a grill pan and place under the grill until the scallops are bubbling and the tops are lightly browned, about 8 minutes.

SERVES 6 AS A STARTER

SAVOURY SCALLOP PIE
EMPANADA DE ZAMBURIÑAS

In Galicia, the region in the top northwest corner of Spain, *empanada*, a savoury pie filled with shellfish, pork loin, chicken or sardines, is baked in huge dimensions, to be cut in thick wedges. I especially liked this one filled with *zamburiñas* (tiny scallops). It was wonderfully good, full of sea flavour and juicy enough to balance the thick crust.

Empanada has become a favourite snack food in every region in Spain. It's sold by the slice at deli takeaway counters and bakeries. It makes great party food and is easy to pack on a picnic. *Empanada* can be served hot from the oven or at room temperature.

Instead of scallops, this *empanada* can be filled with mussels or with tinned clams that have been well drained. Other versions are made with sliced pork loin, chicken breast or even tinned sardines.

1 recipe Empanada Dough (recipe follows)

8 tablespoons flat-leaf parsley leaves

4 garlic cloves

2 green sweet peppers, cut into chunks (about 450 g/1 lb)

4 onions, cut into chunks (about 1 kg/2¼ lb)

5 tablespoons olive oil

Pinch saffron threads, dissolved in a little water (optional)

85 g (3 oz) serrano ham or lean bacon, julienned

Freshly ground black pepper

Salt

680 g (1½ lb) frozen queen scallops, thawed, or large scallops, quartered

2 *guindillas* (pickled mild green chillies), chopped

1 egg, beaten with 2 teaspoons water

While the dough is rising, prepare the filling. Combine the parsley and garlic in a food processor and process until chopped. Add half the peppers and onions and process until the onions are chopped. Repeat with the remaining peppers and onions.

Heat the oil in a large frying over high heat. Sauté the onion mixture for a few minutes. Add the saffron, if using. Lower the heat to medium and continue to cook for 30 minutes, until the onions are very soft and reduced to a jamlike consistency. Add the ham to the mixture and remove from the heat. Season with black pepper and a little salt (the ham and shellfish will contribute salt).

Preheat the oven to 190°C/375°F/gas mark 5. Knock back the dough. Divide it in half. Leave one piece covered. Knead one ball of dough briefly. Then pat, roll and stretch out the dough to a diameter of 40 cm (16 inches) and about 1 cm (⅜ inch) thick. Fit the dough into a 30-cm (12-inch) pie pan, pizza pan or paella pan.

Spread the dough with half of the onion mixture. Place the scallops on top and cover with the remaining onion mixture. Scatter the chopped chillies over the filling.

Roll out the second piece of dough to the same size. Fit it on top of the *empanada*. Use a knife to trim off any dough that extends over the pan rim. Pinch and roll the edges to seal the top and bottom crusts. Roll the excess dough into long ropes. Use them to decorate the top of the *empanada*. Cut a steam vent in the centre. Brush the dough with the beaten egg.

Bake for 35 to 40 minutes, until the crust is golden-brown.

Let the *empanada* cool for at least 15 minutes before slicing. Serve warm or at room temperature.

SERVES 12 AS A TAPA; SERVES 6 AS A LUNCHEON MAIN COURSE

EMPANADA DOUGH

MASA PARA EMPANADAS

1 packet active dried yeast

1 teaspoon sugar

340 ml (12 fl oz) warm water (43°C/110°F)

800 g (1¾ lb) strong or plain flour

2 teaspoons salt

120 ml (4 fl oz) olive oil

To make the dough, dissolve the yeast and sugar in 120 ml (4 fl oz) of water. Set aside for 5 minutes, until bubbly.

Combine the flour and salt in a large bowl. Make a well in the centre and pour in 240 ml (8 fl oz) water, the oil and the yeast mixture. Use a large wooden spoon to stir the dough until combined.

Turn the dough out on to a board and knead it for 8 minutes. The dough will be sticky at first, but becomes smooth and elastic. Sprinkle with additional flour, if necessary. Form into a smooth ball.

Put the dough in an oiled bowl, turning to coat it with oil, which keeps the surface from drying. Cover the bowl with a damp cloth and put it in a warm place to rise until doubled in size, about 2 hours.

MAKES ENOUGH DOUGH FOR 1 LARGE EMPANADA

STUFFED SQUID IN TOMATO SAUCE
CALAMARES RELLENOS

The squid's pouch-shaped body makes it a natural for stuffing, and I've sampled dozens of different versions. One is a meat stuffing, the same mixture as for *albóndigas* (meatballs) (page 45). This stuffing, with ham, chopped hard-boiled eggs and breadcrumbs, is my favourite. The squid is simmered until very tender in a wine-flavoured tomato sauce. Serve this dish as a first course or make it a main course by serving it with rice.

2 squid, each 20–25 cm (8–10 inches) long (about 800 g/1¾ lb), cleaned (see page 9)

115 g (4 oz) serrano ham, chopped

8 tablespoons fine fresh breadcrumbs

1 garlic clove, finely chopped

2 tablespoons chopped fresh flat-leaf parsley

2 eggs, hard-boiled and chopped

Pinch freshly grated nutmeg

Freshly ground black pepper

½ teaspoon salt

Pinch cloves

4 tablespoons olive oil

Plain flour

70 g (2½ oz) chopped onion

45 g (1½ oz) chopped green sweet pepper

1 garlic clove, chopped

450 g (1 lb) chopped tomatoes

120 ml (4 fl oz) white wine

1 bay leaf

½ teaspoon salt

Cut the tentacles and wing flaps from the cleaned squid, chop and place in a bowl with the ham, breadcrumbs, garlic, parsley, eggs, nutmeg, black pepper, salt, cloves and 1 tablespoon of the oil. Mix well and stuff the squid pouches with the mixture. Close the ends with cocktail sticks.

Dredge the squid in the flour, shaking off the excess. Heat the remaining 3 tablespoons oil in a large frying pan or cazuela over medium heat and brown the squid on all sides, about 5 minutes. Remove.

Add the onion, green pepper and garlic to the oil and sauté until the onion is softened, without letting it brown, 4 minutes. Add the tomatoes and sauté over high heat for 5 minutes. Then add the wine, bay leaf and salt.

Return the squid to the pan. Lower the heat and simmer until the squid are very tender, about 1 hour.

Remove the bay leaf. Slice the squid crosswise 2.5-cm (1-inch) thick. Serve with the sauce.

SERVES 4 AS A STARTER OR MAIN DISH

SQUID IN THEIR OWN INK
CHIPIRONES EN SU TINTA

When I was still a secondary school student in Illinois, my parents made a trip to Spain and returned with many tales to tell, including one about eating squid served in its own ink. Squid? Oh, weird. In black ink? Weirder yet. Nevertheless, I was attracted by foods so unusual. Perhaps that enticement was part of what brought me to these shores.

In the late summer, baby squid measuring just 5–8 cm (2–3 inches) come into the market. In Andalusia, they are usually floured and fried whole or grilled on an oiled griddle and served sprinkled with olive oil, garlic and parsley. But in the Basque country they are cooked in a sauce coloured black with their own ink. Frozen squid cannot be used, because freezing dries up the ink. Some speciality fish shops may sell packets of frozen ink – a useful ingredient for black rice or black pasta also. This dish can also be made with large squid. In that case, the body pouch is opened up and cut into 8-cm (3-inch) squares.

This dish is usually served as a tapa or a starter. It often comes with cooked white rice that has been pressed into a small (5-tablespoon) mould and unmoulded on to each serving of the squid and black sauce or with triangles of bread fried in olive oil.

24 (8-cm/3-inch) squid (about 570 g/
    1¼ lb), cleaned and ink sacs reserved
    (see page 9)

3 slices lean bacon (30 g/1 oz)

45 g (1½ oz) plain flour

4 tablespoons olive oil

2 garlic cloves

1 sprig parsley

1 onion, cut into several pieces

2 tomatoes (340 g/12 oz), peeled

2 tablespoons brandy or dry Sherry

4 tablespoons white wine

Salt and freshly ground black pepper

Poke the tip of the squid with a fingertip and turn them inside-out. Wash the squid, drain and pat dry.

Wash and drain the squid tentacles and fins. Pat them dry. Then chop them coarsely. Chop the bacon and combine with the chopped tentacles.

Place the flour in a shallow bowl. Stuff the squid body pouches with the chopped mixture, using a finger to poke the stuffing in. Pinch the opening closed and lay each stuffed squid in the flour. Gently turn them in the flour to coat all sides. Transfer to a plate, patting off any excess flour.

Heat 2 tablespoons of the oil in a frying pan over medium heat. Fry the squid in two or three batches, adding an additional tablespoon of oil after the first batch is fried. Turn the squid in the oil until golden on all sides. They do not need to be crisp. The coating of flour helps to prevent them from spattering in the oil. Transfer them to a cazuela or frying pan.

In a food processor, chop the garlic and parsley. Add the onion and process until finely chopped.

Wipe out the frying pan in which you fried the squid. Add the remaining 1 tablespoon oil to the pan. Sauté the chopped onion mixture over medium heat until the onion is softened, about 5 minutes.

While onion is cooking, chop the tomato in the food processor. Add the tomato to the pan.

Sauté over medium heat for 5 minutes, until the tomatoes have sweated out their liquid. Add the brandy and continue cooking, stirring frequently. Let the mixture just begin to thicken and stick, then add 4 tablespoons water. Cook for 25 minutes. Purée the sauce in the processor and return it to the pan.

Using the back of a spoon, crush the ink sacs reserved in the bowl. Dissolve the ink in the white wine. Sieve this into the sauce in the frying pan and simmer for 5 minutes over medium-low heat, stirring. Season with salt and pepper. Add additional water if the sauce is too thick.

Pour the sauce over the squid in the cazuela. Heat thoroughly, about 5 minutes.

SERVES 4 AS A TAPA; SERVES 2 AS A MAIN COURSE

FIN FISH

In the following dishes, I recommend that you prepare fresh fish in the Spanish way. Salt the fish liberally and allow it to sit for 15 to 30 minutes. Then drain it, rinse and pat dry with kitchen towels. Fresh fish contains a lot of moisture that seeps out in cooking; salting eliminates the excess. It won't cause the fish to become dry; overcooking is what makes for dry fish. Frozen fish, however, should never be salted, as it has already lost excess moisture in the thawing process.

In Spain, small and medium-sized fish are often cooked whole after they have been gutted and scaled. This has two advantages. First, the fish is less likely to be overcooked, as can happen with fillets. And, second, it is easy to remove bones from cooked fish, while filleting an uncooked fish is tedious. You can substitute fillets, if you prefer, but adjust the cooking time so the fish doesn't dry out.

In Spain, several varieties of sea bream are among the favoured fish but if your fishmonger does not have them, use another firm-fleshed fish instead. The second favourite fish (actually, it's a toss-up) is *merluza* (hake), but if it's not available when you want it, cod, whiting or haddock will do.

For a solid-fleshed fish for stews, use monkfish, halibut or turbot.

Ask your fishmonger for the necessary trimmings for making fish stock – you can use head, bone and trimmings from any white fish, but not from oily fish such as mackerel, herring, salmon, etc. Bits from monkfish, cod, whiting and haddock are all suitable.

Fish is often served without any side dish other than potatoes, so other flavours and textures don't compete with the delicacy of the fish or its sauce. You can serve salad or a vegetable dish as a first course.

BAKED SEA BREAM WITH POTATOES
PESCADO AL HORNO

This is typically made with a large whole sea bream (*besugo*), cooked in a rectangular metal pan called a *besuguera*, which goes from the hob to the oven. As served at *chiringuitos* (beach shacks) on the Málaga and Cádiz coasts, the fish is baked whole, head intact. However, if your sea bream has already been beheaded, that's fine, too. A whole fish weighing around 2 kg (4–5 lb) will serve 6 people. If you are using smaller fish, start the potatoes and other vegetables baking for 20 minutes, then top with fish.

1 whole sea bream (about 2 kg/ 4–5 lb), gutted and scaled

Salt

5 tablespoons olive oil

900 g (2 lb) potatoes, peeled and thinly sliced

5 garlic cloves, chopped

3 tablespoons chopped fresh flat-leaf parsley

1 green sweet pepper, chopped

Freshly ground black pepper

1 onion, sliced

2 tomatoes, sliced

2 bay leaves, broken into pieces

120 ml (4 fl oz) dry white wine

Rub the fish inside and out with salt and set aside for 30 minutes. Rinse it and pat dry.

Preheat the oven to 180°C/350°F/gas mark 4.

Pour 2½ tablespoons of the oil into a large casserole and add half the sliced potatoes. Scatter over half the garlic, parsley and green pepper. Sprinkle with salt and black pepper. Add all the sliced onion, most of the tomatoes, then the remaining potatoes, garlic, parsley and green pepper. Sprinkle with salt and black pepper.

Place the fish on top of the potatoes and top with the remaining slices of tomato. Drizzle with the remaining 2½ tablespoons oil. Tuck in the pieces of bay leaf. Pour the wine over and place over medium heat until the liquid begins to simmer. Then cover the pan with aluminium foil and bake until the potatoes are tender, about 40 minutes. Remove the foil during the last 15 minutes. Serve hot.

SERVES 6

SEA BREAM BAKED IN A SALT CRUST
DORADA A LA SAL

Baking fish in salt seals in the moisture, producing deliciously juicy fish with all the flavour intact. The method does not make salty fish. You have to start with a whole, very fresh fish; don't remove the head and don't scale the fish.

This is a very simple preparation, but it does require some cautionary notes. Many recipes recommend that the fish not be gutted, so that no salt gets inside the fish. However, if the fish was caught with the use of strong-smelling chum, the guts can contain rotting bait that gives the fish a bad flavour. If possible, have the fishmonger gut the fish through the gills. If this is not possible, ask him to make the smallest possible incision on the fish belly to gut the fish.

The fish usually selected for baking in salt are *dorada* (gilthead bream) and *lubina* (sea bass). Any large bream or bass or other firm-fleshed fish is suitable.

The first time you prepare this, use all the salt called for in the recipe. The next time you may be able to use less, depending on the size of the baking pan and the size of the fish.

The real art is in the serving. Crack the salt crust by hacking it along one side. Lift it off in one piece, if possible. The fish skin should come off with the salt. If it does not, lift it off. Break the salt away from the edges of the fish. Then use a large spoon to lift out the flesh. Place it on a serving dish or on individual plates. Lift out and discard the backbone. Spoon out the remaining flesh. Discard all the salt.

1 whole fish (around 2 kg, 4–5 lb), gutted (as described) but unscaled

about 2.5 kg (6 lb) coarse rock salt

Garlic Mayonnaise II (page 180)

Preheat the oven to 200°C/400°F/gas mark 6.

Pat the fish dry. Mix the salt with 5 tablespoons water. Spread a layer of the salt in the bottom of a shallow roasting pan or oven pan long enough to hold the fish. Place the fish on top. Mound the remaining salt over the fish, patting it down over the fish to completely enclose it.

Bake the fish for 50 to 60 minutes. As it's not possible to test for doneness, judge the time according to the fish's weight. A whole fish weighing 2 kg (4½ lb) requires 55 minutes.

Serve immediately, opening as described above. Accompany the fish with the garlic mayonnaise.

SERVES 6

VARIATION: Smaller fish can be prepared in the same way. Bake a fish weighing 570 g (1¼ lb) at the temperature given above for 30 minutes.

PAN-ROASTED WHOLE SEA BREAM
BESUGO AL HORNO

Besugo (red sea bream) is traditionally part of the Christmas Eve dinner. A *besuguera* is a shallow rectangular metal pan just right for baking a *besugo*. Usually the fish is served in the same pan in which it is baked.

1 whole fish (about 1.8 kg/4 lb), gutted and scaled

Salt

1 lemon

3 tablespoons olive oil

6 garlic cloves, chopped

4 tablespoons chopped fresh flat-leaf parsley

70 g (2½ oz) fine dry breadcrumbs

1 teaspoon pimentón

1 bay leaf, broken into pieces

60 g (2 oz) peeled small prawns (optional)

120 ml (4 fl oz) white wine

Sprinkle the fish inside and out with salt and set aside for 30 minutes. Rinse it and pat dry.

Preheat the oven to 190°C/375°F/gas mark 5.

Cut half of the lemon into slices. Cut 4 or 5 deep slits in the skin of the fish and insert a lemon slice in each.

Pour the oil into an ovenproof pan large enough to hold the fish. Place the fish in the pan. Combine the garlic, parsley, breadcrumbs, pimentón and 1 tablespoon of lemon juice. Spread this mixture over the fish. Tuck pieces of bay leaf and the prawns, if using, around the fish. Pour the wine around the fish.

Bake the fish for 10 minutes. Baste it with liquid in the pan and bake until the fish flakes easily, 15 to 20 minutes longer.

Serve hot, directly out of the pan.

SERVES 4 AS A MAIN DISH; SERVES 8 AS PART OF A LARGE HOLIDAY MEAL

SEA BREAM WITH SHERRY SAUCE, ROTA STYLE
HURTA A LA ROTEÑA

Rota is an Atlantic port near Cádiz, within the Sherry triangle, and where, incidentally, there is a US naval base. Quite a few Americans received their introduction to Spanish food (and flamenco) while stationed there. The *hurta* (red-banded sea bream) is especially esteemed, but the dish can be made with any solid-fleshed fish. Use fillets at least 2.5 cm (1 inch) thick.

1 kg (2¼ lb) sea bream fillets

4 tablespoons olive oil

220 g (7½ oz) chopped onions

400 g (14 oz) chopped green sweet pepper

3 garlic cloves, sliced

680 g (1½ lb) chopped tomatoes

1 teaspoon salt

Freshly ground black pepper

1 bay leaf

120 ml (4 fl oz) plus 1 tablespoon dry or medium-dry Sherry

Chopped fresh flat-leaf parsley

If fish is fresh, salt it lightly and set aside for 15 minutes. This draws out excess moisture. Frozen fish does not require this step, as it loses moisture in thawing.

Make the *sofrito*. Heat 3 tablespoons of the oil in a frying pan over medium heat and sauté the onions, green pepper and garlic for 3 minutes. Add the tomatoes and sauté over high heat for 5 minutes. Season with salt, pepper and bay leaf. Add 120 ml (4 fl oz) of the Sherry and simmer the sauce, covered, for 30 minutes. Uncover and simmer for 5 minutes more, or until the sauce is very thick.

Preheat the oven to 200°C/400°F/gas mark 6.

In a non-stick frying pan, heat the remaining 1 tablespoon of oil over medium heat. Pat the fish fillets dry. Fry them for about 30 seconds on each side in the oil. They do not need to brown. Remove and place in a cazuela large enough to hold them in a single layer.

Pour the *sofrito* over the fish. Add remaining 1 tablespoon of Sherry. Bake until the fish flakes easily, 12 to 20 minutes, depending on thickness of the fillets.

Sprinkle with chopped parsley and serve in the same cazuela.

SERVES 6

SEA BREAM, GRILLED ON ITS BACK
BESUGO A LA ESPALDA

Originally a style of grilling *a la brasa*, over hot coals, this is easy to do under the grill or on an iron griddle. *Besugo* is the red sea bream, but any large sea bream could be prepared this way. Smaller fish, one per serving, can be prepared in the same manner.

1 whole sea bream (about 900 g/2 lb) (with or without head)

Salt

2½ tablespoons olive oil

1 teaspoon coarse salt

2 garlic cloves, sliced crosswise

Red chilli flakes, tiny chillies, or 3–4 crosswise slices of dried red chilli, such as cayenne

1 teaspoon white wine vinegar

Have the fish gutted, scaled and split open along the belly. Butterfly the fish, leaving the backbone in. The head is usually left on, split open so that it lies flat. Open the fish out flat, salt it lightly, and let it rest 30 minutes at room temperature.

Grease a non-ridged grill pan with fat or oil, and sprinkle with coarse salt. Preheat the pan under the grill for 12 minutes.

Pat the fish dry with kitchen towels. Brush skin and flesh sides with ½ tablespoon of olive oil. Lay the fish, skin side down, on the hot grill pan and grill 10 cm (4 inches) from the flame for about 10 minutes. Don't turn the fish. Test to see if the flesh is opaque. When the fish is cooked, you should be able to lift out the spine and discard it.

While the fish is cooking, in a small pan place 2 tablespoons of oil, sliced garlic and red chilli flakes. Heat until the oil begins to sizzle and garlic begins to turn golden, less than 1 minute. Remove from heat and immediately add the vinegar and 1 teaspoon of water.

Transfer the grilled fish to a heated platter and serve it, on its back, with the garlic oil spooned over it.

SERVES 2

Halibut with Onion Confit
Mero Encebollado

Use thickly cut fish steaks or fillets for this flavourful dish. The fish can be turbot, halibut, monkfish or salmon. A Chardonnay from the Somontano wine region (Aragon) would complement the dish nicely.

4 tablespoons olive oil

4 large onions, halved and sliced

½ red sweet pepper, julienned

3 garlic cloves, chopped

Salt and freshly ground pepper

140 ml (¼ pint) white wine

900 g (2 lb) halibut steaks or fillets

60 g (2 oz) plain flour

Pinch dried thyme

1 tablespoon capers

Heat 2 tablespoons of the oil in a frying pan over medium heat and sauté the onions, red pepper and garlic for 5 minutes. Then sprinkle with ½ teaspoon salt, black pepper and half of the wine. Reduce the heat, cover the pan and let the onions cook until reduced to a marmalade consistency, about 25 minutes.

Place the fish steaks on a platter and sprinkle with salt. Set aside for 15 minutes. Drain off accumulated liquid and pat the fish dry.

When the onion confit is done, spread it in a baking pan large enough to hold the fish in one layer.

Preheat the oven to 190°C/375°F/gas mark 5.

Combine the flour, a pinch of salt and thyme in a shallow pan. Dredge the fish in it, patting off any excess.

Heat the remaining 2 tablespoons oil in a clean frying pan over medium-high heat. Fry the fish quickly until lightly browned on both sides, about 4 minutes. As they brown, place them on top of the onions in the baking pan.

Scatter the capers on top and pour over the remaining wine. Bake, uncovered, until fish flakes easily, 10 to 15 minutes, depending on thickness of the pieces of fish.

Serve the fish hot, accompanied by the onion confit.

Serves 6

HAKE IN GREEN SAUCE, BASQUE STYLE
MERLUZA A LA VASCA

The Basques, seafaring folk who inhabit the northern part of the country on the Bay of Biscay, are undoubtedly the best fish cooks in Spain. Early on in my food career, I received an introduction to Basque gastronomy from Doña Pia, a Basque woman who ran an impressive restaurant in the village where I live.

Doña Pia was built like a top – of large girth, with tiny feet and a tiny knot of a bun on top. She would sit in the kitchen with her feet up on a stool and command operations all around her. (A telling tale about Basque women: When one day the devil decided he wanted to learn the Basque language, he hid himself behind the door in a Basque kitchen to listen. At the end of a whole year, he had learned two words in Basque, 'Yes, ma'am'.)

This was my favourite dish in her restaurant. She always used impeccably fresh hake – the head waiter would even bring the whole fish to the table to exhibit the line still hooked in its mouth, proving that it was *de anzuelo* (hooked on a long line rather than a net). This makes a difference, because hake (a relative of cod) is an especially delicate fish.

Fresh cod, haddock or halibut can be substituted if hake is not available.

Salt

1.4 kg (3 lb) hake, cut into crosswise steaks 2.5 cm (1 inch) thick

2 tablespoons plain flour

5 tablespoons olive oil

6 garlic cloves, sliced crosswise

140 ml (¼ pint) white wine

12 hard-shell clams for steaming

12 small peeled prawns

3 tablespoons chopped fresh flat-leaf parsley

6 cooked or tinned spears of white asparagus (optional)

1 egg, hard-boiled and chopped

Salt the fish and set aside for 15 minutes. Pat dry and dust with the flour.

Heat the oil in a cazuela or frying pan over medium heat. Add the garlic and fish. Let them cook without browning for 2 minutes on each side. Sprinkle with any remaining flour. Then add the wine, ½ teaspoon salt, clams and prawns.

Cook the fish, bubbling gently, shaking and rocking the casserole, until the fish is just flaky and the clam shells have opened, 6 to 7 minutes. The sauce should be slightly thickened.

Add the parsley, asparagus, if using, and egg. Serve hot, from the same cazuela.

SERVES 6

Whole Hake with Mushroom Stuffing
Merluza Rellena

Having tried stuffed hake several times in restaurants, I was eager to make it at home. Unfortunately, I didn't know where to begin. Luis, one of the fishmongers at the market where I shop regularly, gave me complete instructions and dressed the fish ready for stuffing. He opened up the fish along the belly, lifted out the spine and trimmed the fins. Then he removed a thin slice from the thickest part of the fish, making a slightly larger cavity for the stuffing and evening out the thickness of the fish. He instructed me to mince the removed slice of flesh and add it to the stuffing mixture. The resulting fish is nearly bone free (only a line of bones attached to the back fins remains), moist and deeply flavourful.

You can prepare this with just about any large fish, with the head intact or removed. Salmon is a good choice.

You will need needle and thread to sew up the fish.

1 whole fish (1.5–1.8 kg/3½–4 lb), spine removed

Salt and freshly ground black pepper

20 g (¾ oz) fresh breadcrumbs

240 ml (8 fl oz) dry white wine

4 tablespoons olive oil

4 tablespoons finely chopped onion

4 tablespoons chopped lean bacon

115 g (4 oz) finely chopped mushrooms

1 garlic clove, finely chopped

85 g (3 oz) chopped white fish

45 g (1½ oz) chopped prawns

2 tablespoons chopped fresh flat-leaf parsley

1 tablespoon capers

1 egg, beaten

120 ml (4 fl oz) Simple Fish Stock (page 88)

Open up the fish and sprinkle it with salt and pepper. Set aside for 30 minutes. Pat dry.

Soften the breadcrumbs in 2 tablespoons of the wine.

Preheat the oven to 200°C/400°F/gas mark 6. Have ready needle and thread to sew up the fish.

Heat 2 tablespoons of the oil in a frying pan over medium heat and sauté the onion, bacon, mushrooms and garlic until softened, about 5 minutes. Stir in the chopped fish and sauté for 1 minute. Then add the prawns and breadcrumbs and sauté for 1 minute more. Remove from heat and add the parsley and capers. Season to taste with salt. Mix in the egg.

Spread the stuffing on one half of the fish. Fold over the other half to enclose it. Sew up the fish from tail to head.

Pour 1 tablespoon of the oil into a baking pan large enough to hold the fish. (A shallow pan is better than a deep roasting pan for removing the fish.) Place the fish in the pan and drizzle with the remaining 1 tablespoon oil.

Bake for 5 minutes. Then pour over the remaining wine and fish stock. Bake for 20 to 25 minutes more, then test by poking with a fork in the thickest section. The fish is done when it just flakes easily.

Transfer the fish to a serving platter or chopping board. It can be served whole, or cut into crosswise slices and placed on individual dinner plates. Strain the liquid remaining in the pan. Spoon a little of it over the fish and serve the rest separately.

SERVES 6

Adobo and Escabeche, Two Tangy Marinades

Adobo is a tangy mixture of spices and vinegar used to marinate fish or meat before cooking. Pork and solid-fleshed fish such as shark are good candidates for *adobo* marinades. *Escabeche* is a marinade for cooked food. Game birds (especially partridge), poultry and fish are pickled in *escabeche*. Before the days of refrigeration, both marinades were used to conserve foods, so the vinegar content was very high.

Adobo marinades invariably contain wine vinegar (Sherry vinegar gives an added depth of flavour), oregano, garlic and pimentón. The food to be marinated is submerged in the mixture for 24 hours (for fish) to several days (for meat). Then it is drained and fried, grilled or roasted.

Escabeche marinades usually are made from vinegar and wine cooked with olive oil, garlic, onion, pepper and herbs. Cooked foods are added to the marinade and gently heated, then allowed to cool. The olive oil rises to the top and seals the food. Foods in *escabeche* can be served at room temperature or warmed slightly.

MACKEREL IN OREGANO MARINADE
CABALLA EN ESCABECHE

Escabeche was a traditional way of preserving fish before the days of refrigeration. (For more about *escabeche*, see page 209.) Although the recipe can be prepared with almost any fish, it is usually made with those of the 'blue' family – mackerel, tuna, sardines or trout. Serve this as a first course.

680 g (1½ lb) mackerel fillets

60 g (2 oz) plain flour

4 tablespoons olive oil

1 carrot, sliced

½ onion, cut in wedges

1 bay leaf

½ teaspoon dried oregano

⅛ teaspoon cumin seeds

¼ teaspoon black peppercorns

Slivers of dried red chilli, such as cayenne (optional)

½ teaspoon pimentón

2 teaspoons salt

170 ml (6 fl oz) white wine vinegar

Lettuce

Olives

Tomatoes

Sliced hard-boiled egg

Extra virgin olive oil

Split the fish fillets lengthwise, eliminating any bones, then cut them in half crosswise, making about 16 pieces. Dust them with flour, shaking off the excess.

Heat the oil in a frying pan over medium heat. Fry the fish in two batches, turning the fish to brown well on both sides, about 4 minutes. Keep the heat moderate so the oil and flour do not burn. Remove the fish from the pan and reserve.

Strain the remaining oil into a saucepan. Add the carrot, onion, bay leaf, oregano, cumin seeds, peppercorns, chilli, if using, pimentón, salt, vinegar and 450 ml (¾ pint) water. Bring to the boil and simmer for 3 minutes.

Place the fried fish in a nonreactive bowl or jar, then cover with the hot marinade. Let cool, then cover tightly and refrigerate for at least 24 hours.

To serve, remove pieces of fish from the marinade. Serve them on a bed of lettuce, garnished with olives, tomatoes and sliced egg. Drizzle with a little olive oil.

SERVES 6 AS A FIRST COURSE

MONKFISH IN PIMENTÓN SAUCE
RAPE AL PIMENTÓN

This can be made with any solid-fleshed fish, such as monkfish. If you like experimenting with unusual fish, try it with skate or chunks of eel. Serve with lots of bread or add boiled potatoes to the cazuela to soak up the savoury sauce. The name of this fish in Spanish is pronounced rah´-pay.

680–900 g (1½–2 lb) monkfish fillets

Salt

2 slices bread, crusts removed

4 garlic cloves

2 tablespoons pimentón

1 teaspoon dried oregano

240 ml (8 fl oz) Simple Fish Stock
    (page 88)

3 tablespoons olive oil

Boiled potatoes (optional)

2 teaspoons Sherry vinegar
    or sour orange juice

Chopped fresh flat-leaf parsley

Cut the fish fillets into 8-cm (3-inch) pieces. Sprinkle with salt and set aside for 15 minutes. Drain off the accumulated liquid and pat dry.

Soak the bread in water to cover until softened. Squeeze it out and combine in a blender with the garlic, pimentón, oregano and fish stock. Blend until smooth.

Heat the oil in a cazuela or frying pan over medium heat. Sauté the pieces of fish for about 1 minute on each side. The fish does not need to brown. Pour over the blended pimentón sauce. Simmer the fish in the sauce for 10 minutes. If sauce thickens too much, add additional stock or water.

Add the cooked potatoes, if using, and cook for another 5 minutes or until the fish just flakes easily. Add the vinegar or orange juice and cook for 2 minutes more.

Sprinkle with parsley. Serve from the cazuela.

SERVES 4

Monkfish in Almond Sauce

Rape en Salsa de Almendras

Almond trees grow on a terraced hillside just beyond my property. In January, when winter mists still cling to the mountainside, the pale pink blossoms appear, covering the earth in little drifts. By September the nuts begin to fall.

I learned that almonds are not just for snacking and sweets. In Spanish cooking, they are used extensively to give body and flavour to sauces and soups. This fish dish is one I first enjoyed in Málaga and much later found to be typically Catalan. The Catalans call the almond sauce *picada*.

680 g (1½ lb) monkfish tail or fillets, sliced about 2.5 cm (1 inch) thick

Salt

3 tablespoons plain flour

4 tablespoons olive oil

24 almonds, blanched and skinned (see page 6)

2 garlic cloves

1 sprig parsley

1 bread slice, crusts removed

½ teaspoon saffron threads, crushed

120 ml (4 fl oz) white wine

½ onion, finely chopped

115 g (4 oz) chopped tomatoes

240 ml (8 fl oz) Simple Fish Stock (page 88) or water

Freshly ground black pepper

Salt the fish and set aside for 15 minutes. Pat dry, then dust the fish with flour.

Heat 3 tablespoons of the oil in a frying pan over medium-high heat and fry the fish quickly on both sides, about 4 minutes. Transfer the fish to a cazuela or deep frying pan.

In the same oil, fry the almonds, garlic, parsley and bread until the bread and garlic are crisped, then skim them out.

In a blender or food processor, grind the almonds, garlic, bread and parsley with the saffron and wine to make a paste.

Add the remaining 1 tablespoon oil to the frying pan and sauté the onion over medium heat until softened, about 5 minutes. Add the tomato and sauté for several minutes. Stir in the almond mixture with the stock and cook for 15 minutes.

Season the sauce with salt and pepper and pour over the fish in the cazuela. Simmer very gently (or bake in a 180°C/350°F/gas mark 4 oven) until the fish is done and flakes easily, about 20 minutes. Add some water if sauce seems too thick.

Serve hot, directly out of the cazuela.

SERVES 4

Sardines Baked with Pine Kernels and Clams
Moraga de Sardinas al Horno

When my children were small, we used to spend every Sunday at the beach, sailing a small boat that we launched through the surf. The kids went snorkelling and came back with octopus, which we stored in the freezer and occasionally remembered to thaw and cook (see page 42).

A much-loved beach treat was fresh sardines grilled on a spit over a driftwood fire. Even when the boys were small, they learned to eat the roasted sardines right off the bone.

A beach party, where sardines are grilled at the seaside, is called a *moraga*. It sort of means, 'sardines in a row'. That's why the following dish of 'sardines in a row' has that name. If fresh sardines are not available, use mackerel fillets.

900 g (2 lb) fresh sardines

230 g (8 oz) small hard-shell clams (optional), washed

1 bay leaf

½ teaspoon salt

3 garlic cloves, chopped

4 tablespoons chopped fresh flat-leaf parsley

4 tablespoons pine kernels, toasted

2 tablespoons fine dry breadcrumbs

3 tablespoons olive oil

4 tablespoons white wine

Preheat the oven to 220°C/425°F/gas mark 7.

If the sardines have not been cleaned, proceed as follows: Spread a thick layer of newspapers on the work surface. Use your thumb or a dull knife blade to slide the scales off the sardines on to the paper. Cut off the heads.

Slit the sardines open along the belly and pull out the innards. Wash the sardines and pat dry.

Place the sardines in a single layer in a rectangular oven pan. Place the clams, if using, around the sardines. Break the bay leaf into pieces and tuck them in among the sardines. Sprinkle with the salt.

In a small bowl, combine the garlic, parsley, pine kernels and breadcrumbs. Spread this mixture over the sardines. Dribble the oil over them. Pour the wine into the bottom of the pan.

Bake until the sardines easily separate from the bone if probed with a fork, about 15 minutes.

Serves 4 to 6 as a starter; 8 to 10 as a tapa

Sea Bass with Canary Island Coriander Sauce and 'Wrinkly' Potatoes

Samcocho con Mojo Verde y Papas Arrugadas a lo Canario

This fish dish is from the Canary Islands, a Spanish archipelago off the coast of Morocco.

The potatoes served with the fish are 'wrinkly' from being boiled with salt. They can be served alone as a tapa. Just spear the potatoes on cocktail sticks with the coriander sauce alongside for dipping.

4 whole sea bass or striped bass (each about 340 g/12 oz), gutted and scaled

1 tablespoon salt, plus additional to salt fish

1 tablespoon olive oil

680 g (1½ lb) small new potatoes, scrubbed

Coriander Sauce

2 garlic cloves

1 green chilli, such as jalapeño, or to taste

½ teaspoon ground cumin

1 teaspoon dried oregano

2 tablespoons chopped fresh flat-leaf parsley

8 tablespoons fresh coriander leaves

4 tablespoons olive oil

3 tablespoons white wine vinegar

½ teaspoon salt

Sprinkle the fish with salt and set aside for 15 to 30 minutes. Pat dry.

Preheat the oven to 200°C/400°F/gas mark 6. Place the fish in a baking pan and drizzle with the oil.

Bake the fish until they flake easily, about 20 minutes. (If you are using fillets, cover the pan with aluminium foil and reduce the baking time.)

While the fish are baking, combine the potatoes in a large pan with 450 ml (¾ pint) water and 1 tablespoon salt. Bring to the boil and cook over high heat until all the water has evaporated, about 20 minutes. The potatoes should be tender, coated with white salt, and their skins slightly wrinkled. (They can be reheated by adding a small quantity of water and allowing it to boil off.)

While fish are baking, make the sauce. Combine the garlic, chilli, cumin, oregano, parsley, coriander leaves, oil, vinegar, salt and 4 tablespoons water in a blender and blend until smooth.

Place the baked fish on a serving platter surrounded by the potatoes. Spoon some of the sauce over the fish and potatoes. Serve the remaining sauce separately.

Serves 4

SEA BASS WITH CAPER DRESSING
LUBINA A LA PLANCHA CON ALIÑO DE ALCAPARRAS

The caper bush grows wild in Spain. I found one, improbably, sprouting from a whitewashed wall in the village that had been plastered with political posters. The esteemed caper – which is the tiny bud of the caper flower – is usually preserved in brine or vinegar. Also appreciated in Spain are caper berries, the fatter seed pod of the same plant, which are pickled with their stems still attached. They are usually served with olives on the aperitif tray. (The caper dressing can also be served with the boiled meats of the *cocido*, page 109.)

This fish is 'grilled' on a *plancha* (an iron griddle), a most useful tool in Spanish cooking. My favourite *plancha* is reversible – a ridged grill for meat on one side and a flat one for fish and shellfish on the other.

I like fillets of sea bass for this, but any firm-fleshed fish will do.

4 sea bass fillets (about 680 g/1½ lb total)

Salt

2 teaspoons olive oil

CAPER DRESSING

4 tablespoons chopped fresh flat-leaf parsley

3 garlic cloves, finely chopped

½ teaspoon salt

3 tablespoons extra virgin olive oil

3 tablespoons fresh lemon juice

1 tablespoon capers, drained

Sprinkle the sea bass fillets with salt and set aside for 15 to 30 minutes. Brush an unridged griddle with 1 teaspoon of the oil and heat over a medium heat.

To make the dressing, in a small bowl, combine the parsley, garlic, salt, oil, lemon juice and capers.

Pat the fish dry and brush the flesh side of the fillets with remaining 1 teaspoon oil. Place them, skin side up, on the griddle and cook for 3 minutes (for 12-mm/½-inch fillets).

Turn the fillets skin side down and cook for 3 minutes more.

Transfer the fish to serving plates, flesh side up. Spoon the dressing over and serve immediately.

SERVES 4

SEA BASS IN SAFFRON SAUCE
LUBINA EN AMARILLO

The Spanish love preparing foods that are the colours of the national flag, *roja y gualda* (red and yellow). Red comes most often from pimentón and yellow traditionally came from saffron. Today, the truth is that most home cooks use food colouring, not saffron, in their yellow dishes.

I prefer to make this dish the traditional way, with real saffron lending its distinctive colour and flavour. It's simple, sublime and, yes, yellow.

Any firm-fleshed white fish fillets can be used. Try bream, rockfish or catfish.

4 sea bass fillets (140–170 g/5–6 oz each)

Salt

45 g (1½ oz) plain flour

5 tablespoons olive oil

1 onion, chopped

1 green sweet pepper, cut into 2.5-cm (1-inch) pieces

450 g (1 lb) potatoes, peeled and cut into 2.5-cm (1-inch) dice

½ teaspoon saffron threads, crushed

120 ml (4 fl oz) dry white wine

3 garlic cloves, crushed

1 teaspoon salt

¼ teaspoon freshly ground black pepper

340 ml (12 fl oz) Simple Fish Stock (page 88) or water

Chopped fresh flat-leaf parsley

Cooked peas or broccoli florets

If you are using fresh fish fillets, salt them lightly and set aside for 15 minutes. (This step is not necessary if you are using frozen fish.) Pat fish dry and dust the fillets with flour, reserving any extra.

Heat the oil in a frying pan over medium heat and fry the fish until browned on both sides, about 3 minutes per side. Remove the fish from the pan and set aside.

To the same oil, add the onion, green pepper and potatoes. Sauté over medium heat until the onion is softened, 4 to 5 minutes. Stir in 1 tablespoon of the remaining flour.

Dissolve the saffron in the wine.

Add the garlic, salt and pepper to the potatoes with the fish stock or water. Stir in the saffron and wine. Bring to the boil, then simmer, covered, until the potatoes are tender, about 20 minutes.

Return the fish fillets to the pan to reheat, about 3 minutes. Serve the fish with the potatoes and sauce, with a sprinkling of chopped parsley and a few cooked peas or broccoli florets as a green contrast with the yellow sauce.

SERVES 4

GRILLED SWORDFISH STEAKS
WITH LEMON-PARSLEY DRESSING
PEZ ESPADA A LA PLANCHA

My two sons attended the village school to eighth grade. One year their school sponsored an exchange programme with a group of American students from a Boston suburb. The American teenagers stayed with families in the village and, for two weeks, attended classes at the local school.

I interviewed a number of them and learned that some of the most significant cultural exchanges were happening at dinner tables all over town. Spanish mothers were beside themselves because their young guests ate so little, while the American kids complained that they were supposed to eat too much. They said there was too much bony fish, but they liked fried squid rings. Nobody liked the taste of the milk. Several insisted they couldn't stand olive oil. The Spanish dishes most liked by the Americans were paella and chicken fried with garlic (*pollo al ajillo*). They loved *pipas*, the unshelled sunflower seeds Spanish kids consume by the millions while hanging out. Ice cream kept diplomatic channels open.

Although we were not a Spanish family, we had one of the American students staying with us. After I served this grilled swordfish, I asked him how he liked it. 'Oh, I thought it was a pork chop,' was the reply! Curiously, pork chops are prepared in the identical marinade. And maybe they do taste a little like swordfish.

4 swordfish steaks, 2 cm (¾ inch) thick (each weighing about 170 g/6 oz)

2 garlic cloves, chopped

4 tablespoons chopped fresh flat-leaf parsley

½ teaspoon salt

4 tablespoons fresh lemon juice

2 tablespoons olive oil

Place the steaks in a single layer in a dish. Scatter half of the garlic, parsley, salt and lemon juice over them. Turn the steaks and scatter remaining garlic, parsley, salt and lemon juice over them. Let marinate at room temperature for 30 minutes, turning the steaks once.

Heat the oil in a heavy frying pan until very hot. Add the swordfish and sear them for about 1 minute on each side, until lightly browned and just cooked through.

Serve at once.

SERVES 4

Swordfish in Tomato Sauce, Málaga Style

Pez Espada a la Malagueña

Málaga is a beautiful port city on the Mediterranean. Anything cooked 'Málaga style' usually starts out with a *sofrito*, a fried mixture, containing fresh tomatoes. In this dish, sliced olives add an extra flourish.

1 kg (2¼ lb) swordfish steak, cut about 2 cm (¾ inch) thick

3 tablespoons olive oil

220 g (7½ oz) chopped onion

200 g (7 oz) chopped green sweet pepper

3 garlic cloves, chopped

570 g (1¼ lb) chopped tomato or tomato pulp

120 ml (4 fl oz) white wine

1 tablespoon chopped fresh flat-leaf parsley

1 bay leaf

Pinch ground cloves

Freshly ground black pepper

1 teaspoon salt

4 tablespoons sliced green olives

Cut the swordfish into 6 equal-sized steaks.

In a cazuela or frying pan large enough to hold the swordfish, heat the oil over medium heat and sauté the onion, green pepper and garlic for 5 minutes. Add the tomato, wine, parsley, bay leaf, cloves, black pepper and salt. Cook over high heat for 5 minutes, then simmer for 10 minutes more, until the sauce is somewhat reduced.

Add the swordfish to the tomato sauce. Simmer for 4 minutes and turn the fish steaks. Simmer for 4 minutes more, until the fish is cooked through and flakes easily.

Scatter the olives over the swordfish and serve from the cazuela.

Serves 6

POT-ROASTED TUNA WITH WHITE WINE
ATÚN MECHADO

A good chunk of tuna is delicious pot-roasted, a simple preparation that works equally well with veal or a rump roast. The strips of bacon laced through the tuna both flavour it and keep it juicy. Spanish cooks suggest soaking the tuna in lightly salted water for 30 minutes to whiten the flesh. Personally, I don't think this is necessary.

115 g (4 oz) fatty bacon, thickly sliced (about 4 to 5 slices)

4 tablespoons sliced pimiento-stuffed olives

1 garlic clove, finely chopped

4 tablespoons chopped fresh flat-leaf parsley

1 teaspoon salt

⅛ teaspoon freshly ground black pepper

1 kg (2¼ lb) fresh tuna

2 tablespoons plain flour

3 tablespoons olive oil

1 onion, chopped

1 carrot, sliced

1 celery stalk, diced

240 ml (8 fl oz) white wine

6 peppercorns

3 cloves

2 bay leaves

Cut the bacon into long strips and place them in the freezer for 30 minutes. This stiffens them, making it easier to thread through the tuna.

Combine the olives, garlic, parsley, salt and pepper.

Drain the tuna and pat dry. With a chopstick or finger, poke holes through the tuna. Into each hole insert some of the chopped olive mixture and poke a strip of bacon through it. Continue, using all the bacon strips.

Dust the tuna with flour on all sides. Heat the oil in a deep pan over high heat and brown the tuna on all sides, about 15 minutes. Remove.

Add the onion, carrot and celery to the oil and sauté over medium heat until they are softened, about 5 minutes. Return the tuna to the pan. Add the wine, an equal amount of water, the peppercorns, cloves and bay leaves. Cover and simmer for 1 hour.

Let the tuna rest for 10 minutes before slicing. Serve hot, accompanied by the sauce. Or, refrigerate the tuna without the sauce, slice it and serve it cold.

SERVES 6

BASQUE TUNA AND POTATO STEW
MARMITAKO

The ideal tuna for this dish is *bonito del norte* (light albacore tuna). However, the stew is good with any chunked tuna or even salmon. Wild salmon in Spain is rare and expensive, fished only in the northern Cantabrian rivers, but farm-raised Norwegian salmon is available fresh in markets everywhere in Spain.

3 tablespoons olive oil

1 onion, chopped

4 garlic cloves, chopped

1 green sweet pepper, cut into 2.5-cm (1-inch) pieces

450 g (1 lb) tomatoes, peeled, de-seeded and chopped

2 teaspoons pimentón

Salt and freshly ground black pepper

Crushed red chilli flakes

900 g (2 lb) potatoes, peeled and cut into 4-cm (1½-inch) chunks

240 ml (8 fl oz) white wine

900 g (2 lb) fresh tuna or salmon, cut into 5-cm (2-inch) chunks

Heat the oil in a cazuela or deep frying pan over medium heat and sauté the onion, garlic and green pepper until soft, 4 to 5 minutes. Add the tomatoes, pimentón, salt and black pepper, and red chilli flakes to taste. Cook until the tomatoes are reduced, 10 minutes.

Add the potatoes to the *sofrito*, then the wine, and an equal amount of water. Cover the cazuela and cook over medium heat until the potatoes are nearly tender, 15 to 20 minutes.

Add the fish to the cazuela, cover and cook for another 10 minutes, or until the fish flakes easily.

Let the stew rest, covered, for 5 to 10 minutes before serving.

SERVES 6

MIXED FISH FRY, MÁLAGA STYLE
FRITURA DE PESCADITOS MALAGUEÑA

To eat fried fish at a beach-side restaurant on Málaga's Mediterranean coast is to experience a profound sense of place. Here, close enough to the sea to get your toes wet, where the fishing boats are pulled up on the sand, the fish are fresh. Where olive groves still cover the hills (admittedly, fewer, as resort developments have sprung up), olive oil is on its home ground. This is fried fish at its best.

The fish used are small ones – 10-cm (4-inch) fresh anchovies; sole that measure only 15 cm (6 inches); baby hake, called *pescadilla*; tiny red mullet, arguably the tastiest of Mediterranean fish; rings of squid; sometimes a few peeled prawns. All are dusted with flour, fried golden in bubbling olive oil, and served piping hot, heaped on a platter with nothing more elaborate than lemon to accompany them.

Mixed fish fry is wonderful served with cool, tangy gazpacho. A salt sea breeze is a nice addition.

340–450 g (¾–1 lb) cleaned small fish and squid rings per person (see page 222)

Flour, for dredging

Olive oil, for frying

Salt

Lemon wedges, to serve

Pour oil to a depth of 4 cm (1½ inches) in a deep frying pan. Heat it to 182°C/360°F.

Dredge the fish in the flour, shake off any excess and fry in the hot oil, a few pieces at a time, until they are golden, 3 to 6 minutes. Remove and drain on kitchen towels. Sprinkle with salt.

Serve hot with lemon wedges.

Tips for Preparing a Mixed Fish Fry

To prepare a Mediterranean fish fry, you will need three or four different whole small fish. Some types of fish that can be used include small flounder, plaice, whiting (very much like *pescadilla*), herring, tiny mackerel, smelt and small mullet. In frying, fish on the bone hold together better than fillets, though certainly fillets or crosswise slices of fish can be substituted for whole ones.

Have the fish gutted and heads removed. Sole or flounder are usually skinned. Slice any fish that are more than 20 cm (8 inches) long into 5-cm (2-inch) segments. Squid should be cleaned and cut into rings (see page 9). Peel the prawns, but leave the tails intact. After washing, leave the fish in a colander so it doesn't sit in leaked liquid.

Have a large bowl or tray of flour ready. Dredge several small fish or a handful of squid rings in the flour, then transfer them to a sieve and shake off the excess flour. Spanish cooks use a flat-bottomed coarse sieve with a wooden frame. Removing excess flour prevents it from falling to the bottom of the pan and burning.

The oil is important. Olive oil is a must, of course. Extra virgin produces astonishingly good results, but its high price will probably hold you back from using it for frying. So, choose your favourite brand of pure Spanish olive oil (for more about olive oil, see chapter 3).

A deep-fat fryer is handy because it allows you to fry a larger quantity of fish at one time than you can in a frying pan. The frying basket makes it easy to submerge the fish and then remove it. Plus, electric fryers have thermostatic controls so you can regulate the temperature.

However, you can prepare great fried fish without any special equipment. You will need a deep frying pan or heavy sauté pan with sloping sides. A flat-bottomed wok would work too.

The oil needs to be only deep enough to completely cover the largest pieces of fish. In the case of this fish fry, a depth of 4 cm (1½ inches) is probably sufficient. You will need about a litre (1¾ pints) of oil (more or less, depending on the size of your pan). Don't fill the pan more than one-third full.

Use a deep-frying thermometer if you have one. Heat the olive oil to 179–182°C (355–360°F). Much more than that and your smoke alarm will go off. At this temperature, it takes a cube of bread about 25 seconds to brown. Olive oil is not heated to temperatures as high as other cooking oils (usually 190°C/375°). For this reason, combining two kinds of oil is not recommended. The coating of flour on the fish immediately forms a crust, so the oil doesn't penetrate. The food will fry to a nice gold, not dark brown.

Fry each type or size of fish separately. Fry the larger and thicker ones first.

Use a long-handled skimmer or spatula to carefully place the floured fish in the hot oil. Add the fish in one layer, without crowding. Sometimes moisture escapes from the fish and causes the oil to splutter, so stand well back.

Let the fish fry until golden. Small pieces of fish will be cooked in the time it takes them to turn golden, 3 to 6 minutes. Use the skimmer to remove the fish. Place it on a tray lined with paper towels. Salt it lightly.

When all the fish are fried, serve immediately.

The oil can be cooled, strained and stored in a dark place to be used one or two more times.

SEAFOOD STEWS AND CASSEROLES

Those seafood stews and casseroles are main-course dishes that usually contain several varieties of fish and shellfish.

CATALAN SEAFOOD CASSEROLE WITH RED PEPPER SAUCE
ROMESCO DE PESCADOS Y MARISCOS

The Catalans are renowned for their sauces. These are, depending on how you count, one, two, three, four or five – *sofrito*, *alioli*, *samfaina*, *picada* and *romesco*.

While the Catalans count all five as their very own, in fact, *alioli* (garlic mayonnaise) and *sofrito* (tomato sauce) really are known everywhere in Spain. *Picada*, a sauce of ground nuts, is also made in other regions, where it is known as *salsa de almendra* (almond sauce) or *pepitoria*. So too is *samfaina*, though elsewhere it is called *pisto*.

Romesco, however, is unique to Catalonia, in particular, Tarragona. It is named for a type of dried sweet red pepper called the *romesco*, a plum-shaped pepper with crinkly skin. Traditionally the sauce was confected by grinding the peppers with garlic and nuts in a marble mortar. Now it's quickly made in a blender or food processor.

Romesco sauce can be served alongside grilled shellfish or grilled fish or it can serve as a cooking medium for fish or meat. Thinned, it makes a wonderful dressing for salads and cooked vegetables. In the springtime, the people of Tarragona celebrate the festival of *calçots* – skinny spring onions, grilled over a wood fire. The charred skin is peeled back and the onions dipped into *romesco* sauce. Some grilled Catalan sausages (*butifarra*) complete the outdoor feast.

Here the *romesco* is made with pimentón in place of the dried peppers. The sauce is the cooking medium for a wonderful seafood casserole. A fresh and fruity dry white wine from the Catalan region of Penedés would be perfect with this dish. Use a spoon and serve bread to sop up the sauce.

ROMESCO SAUCE

2 tablespoons pimentón

4 tablespoons red wine

2 tablespoons olive oil

4 tablespoons blanched and skinned
  almonds (see page 6) or skinned
  hazelnuts (see page 8)

1 slice bread

3 garlic cloves

⅛ teaspoon dried mint

1 tablespoon white wine vinegar

Pinch crushed red chilli flakes or ground
  cayenne pepper

Pinch crushed saffron threads (optional)

120 ml (4 fl oz) Simple Fish Stock
  (page 88)

Salt

FISH STEW

3 tablespoons olive oil

680 g (1½ lb) fish fillets, preferably 3 or
  4 different fish

Simple Fish Stock, made from bones and
  trimmings (page 88)

Salt

450 g (1 lb) mussels

King prawns, peeled

230 g (8 oz) small hard-shell clams,
  scrubbed

Chopped fresh flat-leaf parsley

To make the *romesco* sauce, stir the pimentón and red wine together to make a paste.

In a small frying pan, heat the olive oil over medium heat and fry the almonds, bread and garlic until the bread is toasted, about 2 minutes. Transfer to a blender with the pimentón paste, mint, vinegar, red chilli flakes, saffron, if using, the 120 ml (4 fl oz) of fish stock and salt to taste. Purée to make a smooth sauce.

To make the fish stew, in a large cazuela, heat the olive oil over medium heat and add the fillets of fish, flesh side down. Fry for 3 minutes, then turn skin side down and fry 2 minutes longer. They do not need to brown.

Add the *romesco* sauce to the cazuela along with 240 ml (8 fl oz) of the fish liquid. It should just barely cover the pieces of fish. Shake the cazuela to combine the sauce and liquid. Cook over medium heat for 10 minutes.

Place the mussels in a deep pan with 4 tablespoons of water. Cover the pan and bring them to the boil on a high heat. Shake the pan several times, until the mussel shells have opened, 5 to 7 minutes. Discard any mussels that did not open. Discard the half shell that is empty.

Add the mussels, prawns and clams. Cook for 5 minutes more, until the clam shells open.

Let the stew rest for 5 minutes in the cazuela. Sprinkle with parsley and serve the fish and sauce from the casserole into flat soup plates.

SERVES 4

A Fine Kettle of Fish
Caldeirada

✳

Typically, this authentic Galician fisherman's stew was made on board fishing boats by boiling potatoes in seawater with pieces of the day's catch. A simple *ajada*, a sauce of olive oil, garlic, pimentón and a splash of vinegar, enlivens the boiled fish and potatoes.

If possible, use more than one kind of white fish. Turbot or cod is a tasty choice, but take care to poach it gently so the fish doesn't fall apart. Monkfish is good because its firm flesh doesn't disintegrate.

680 g (1½ lb) fish fillets

Salt

680 g (1½ lb) potatoes, peeled and quartered

1 onion, quartered

2 bay leaves

4 tablespoons olive oil

4 garlic cloves, chopped

1 tablespoon pimentón

2 tablespoons white wine vinegar

Cut the fish fillets into chunks. If you are using fresh (not frozen) fish, salt it and set aside for 15 minutes.

Combine the potatoes in a deep pan with 900 ml (1½ pints) water, the onion, bay leaves and 1 tablespoon salt. Bring to the boil and simmer until the potatoes are nearly tender, about 15 minutes. Add the chunks of fish and continue to simmer for 10 minutes more, or until the potatoes are tender.

Meanwhile, in a small frying pan, heat the oil over medium heat and sauté the chopped garlic until golden, about 1 minute. Remove the pan from the heat and stir in the pimentón and vinegar.

When the potatoes are tender and the fish just flakes, pour off most of the liquid and reserve it.

Transfer the fish and potatoes to a serving bowl. Add 240 ml (8 fl oz) of the reserved liquid to the garlic-pimentón sauce. Bring quickly to the boil, stirring, then pour it over the fish and potatoes and serve.

Serves 4

SALT COD

Salt cod – *bacalao* – is a food especially associated with Holy Week, or *Semana Santa*, the solemn days that precede the joyous feast of Easter. This is a time of penance in Catholic Spain, and many people observe the Lenten period by abstaining from meat. On the streets, Holy Week brings massive religious processions and fervent demonstrations of faith.

On Holy Thursdays, I often went to Málaga, to see the processions there, which were much grander in scale than those held in the village. It was a moving spectacle: worshippers carried massive images of Mary, and Christ carrying the cross, on enormous thrones that had been decked with thousands of beautiful flowers. The images were followed by penitents in peaked hoods, rows of faceless spectres.

On Good Friday, I would stay in the village to watch the local processions, which were accompanied only by the sound of muffled drums and a clarion of trumpets. Sombre-faced youths dressed in black suits carried the *pasos*, the floats bearing the images, bedecked with lilies in silver urns.

One float carries the image of Christ crucified, while another carries the Virgin Mary. They depart from different churches, then finally meet in the plaza. Men, women and children follow, faces lighted by the candles they carry. Many women walk barefoot over the rough gravel of the churchyard and down through cobbled streets. They are devout penitents fulfilling a promise.

On signal, the bearers stop to rest their heavy burdens and lower the images, swaying, to the ground. From the street above bursts the piercing wail of a *saeta*, a love song to the Virgin:

From the prettiest flowers
I'm going to make a crown
To put on the Virgin Mary,
Beautiful dove.

In the more than thirty years since I witnessed my first *Semana Santa*, the devotion and passion have, if anything, increased. Now thousands walk in the processions, and the roads leading to the village are clogged with cars for miles. The following days the streets are slippery with candle wax.

Because the Holy Week processions begin after dark and go on until long past midnight, following them through the narrow streets of the city necessitates frequent stops at bars for refuelling. During Holy Week bars serve a wonderful assortment of meatless tapas made with fish, shellfish, vegetables, eggs and, especially, dry salt cod.

How did *bacalao* become so popular? In the days before refrigeration and rapid means of transportation, fresh fish was rarely available to people who lived far inland from fishing ports. So during the Lenten period, when the Catholic Church required abstinence from meat, *bacalao* became an important part of the diet. But, even in my village, where people ate fresh seafood from the nearby coast every day, *bacalao* was brought out during Holy Week. I think it's the mystery of the transformation of *bacalao*, from a texture like cardboard and a smell like dirty socks into a soft, snowy-white fish, that makes it appropriate to the season.

Bacalao once was cheap. The cod banks off Greenland and Newfoundland, fished by Basque and Galician fishermen for centuries, seemed inexhaustible. Now that these banks have been depleted, *bacalao* is as expensive as fresh fish. Nonetheless, it is more popular than ever. The northern Basques and Galicians are real experts in its preparation. In Galicia, where the fresh seafood is fabulous, I have seen shops that sell nothing but *bacalao*, in about 25 different preparations (flakes, chips, cheeks, tails, loins, etc.). In Seville, one popular tapa bar serves only *bacalao* dishes. The most innovative restaurants, even those with Michelin stars, serve *bacalao* dishes.

Bacalao is to fresh fish as ham is to fresh pork. It's different, because the salting process changes both texture and flavour. Perhaps *bacalao* is an acquired taste, but it certainly has inspired some tasty dishes. I strongly recommend that you try it, especially in these outstanding recipes.

See instructions on page 9 for preparing salt cod.

Catalan Salad with Salt Cod, Tuna and Anchovies
Xató

This salad is substantial enough to serve as a luncheon main course, or pair it with one of the tortillas in chapter 5 for a light supper. The dressing for this salad can also be used with cooked vegetables, such as green beans, cauliflower and cabbage.

The salt cod in this salad is not cooked.

DRESSING

115 g (4 oz) peeled and chopped tomato

3 garlic cloves

Crushed red chilli flakes

1½ teaspoons pimentón

3 tablespoons white wine vinegar

4 tablespoons olive oil

Salt (optional)

SALAD

115 g (4 oz) dry salt cod, soaked for 24 hours (see page 9)

Batavia, curly endive or lettuce leaves, cut up

½ (200 g) tin tuna, drained

1 (50 g) tin anchovies, drained

24 stoned green olives

1 tomato, cut up

Chopped spring onion

To make the dressing, in a blender, combine the tomato, garlic, red chilli flakes, pimentón and vinegar. Purée until smooth. With the blender running, pour in the oil. Salt will not be needed if you are using the dressing with this salt fish salad.

Cut the soaked salt cod into julienne strips, discarding any skin and bone.

To serve the salad, place the batavia on a platter. Arrange the strips of cod, chunks of tuna and pieces of anchovy on top with the olives and tomato. Spoon the dressing over the salad and sprinkle some spring onion on top.

SERVES 6 TO 8

'COBBLESTONES' (COD AND BEAN SALAD)

EMPEDRADO

The beans in this satisfying salad supposedly look like a cobbled street – thus the name. Another version of *empedrado* contains beans cooked with rice.

Soak, then precook the salt cod according to the instructions on page 9. You can substitute tinned tuna packed in water for the cod in this salad.

600 g (21 oz) cooked or tinned white beans, such as cannellini, drained

340 g (12 oz) dry salt cod, soaked, cooked and flaked

4 tablespoons chopped fresh flat-leaf parsley

60 g (2 oz) chopped spring onion

230 g (8 oz) chopped fresh tomato

½ teaspoon chopped fennel leaves (optional)

1 garlic clove, crushed

4 tablespoons fresh lemon juice or white wine vinegar

4 tablespoons olive oil

Freshly ground black pepper

Salt (optional)

Lettuce leaves

45 g (1½ oz) stoned black olives, cut in half

2 eggs, hard-boiled and quartered

If you are using tinned beans, rinse them and drain well. Place the beans in a bowl. Add the cod, parsley, spring onion, tomato and fennel, if using.

In a small bowl, whisk together the garlic, lemon juice, oil and pepper. Pour the dressing over the beans and cod. Mix the salad gently. Taste the mixture, then add a pinch of salt if needed (the cod may be salty enough). Let it marinate, covered and refrigerated, for 2 hours.

Arrange the lettuce leaves on a platter. Spread the bean and cod salad on the lettuce. Stud the top with olives and garnish with quartered egg.

SERVES 6 AS A STARTER

COD FRITTERS WITH MOLASSES

TORTILLITAS DE BACALAO CON MIEL DE CAÑA

The Moors introduced the growing and refining of sugar cane to Spain. After the discovery of the New World, Spaniards carried the cultivation of sugar to new continents. In southern Spain, in the coastal areas of Málaga and Granada, sugar refineries, established at the end of the 1500s, thrived for several hundred years, spawning related industries such as rum distilleries. Cane syrup, a sort of light molasses, entered the local culinary tradition.

You could use molasses, runny honey, golden syrup or even maple syrup in this recipe. In fact, you need very little. It is the intriguing contrast of salty and sweet that makes this an outstanding dish, typical of Holy Week in Málaga. Batter-fried aubergine is also served drizzled with honey or molasses.

115 g (4 oz) dry salt cod, soaked for 24 hours (see page 9)

100 g (3½ oz) plain flour

1 teaspoon baking powder

1 tablespoon chopped fresh flat-leaf parsley

1 garlic clove, finely chopped

Pinch crushed saffron thread

2 teaspoons brandy

1 egg, separated

Olive oil, for frying

2 tablespoons molasses or honey

Drain the salt cod, put in a pan with water to cover and bring just to a simmer; then remove from heat. Drain and save the liquid. When the cod is cool enough to handle, remove any bones and skin and flake the fish.

Combine the flour with the baking powder in a small bowl. Combine the parsley, garlic, saffron, brandy and egg yolk in another bowl. Beat in 240 ml (8 fl oz) of the reserved liquid, then the flour mixture. Add the flaked cod. The batter should be the consistency of pancake batter. Let the batter rest for 1 hour, refrigerated.

Beat the egg white until stiff and fold into the batter.

Pour the oil into a large frying pan to a depth of 2.5 cm (1 inch). Heat over medium heat. Drop the batter by the tablespoon into the hot oil, turning to brown on both sides, about 4 minutes.

Drain the fritters on kitchen towels. Serve them hot, drizzled with molasses or honey.

SERVES 10 AS TAPAS

PIQUILLO PEPPERS STUFFED WITH COD

PIMIENTOS DE PIQUILLO RELLENOS

I adore piquillo peppers. They are small (8-cm/3-inch) red peppers that end with a little 'beak', or *pico*. They are roasted, skinned and tinned. Their flavour is both sweet and slightly piquant, quite irresistible. Piquillos are imported from Navarre in the north of Spain and are available at speciality food stores.

In the traditional way, these peppers are stuffed with any seafood mixture in a creamy béchamel sauce. A favourite stuffing is salt cod, but any cooked and flaked fish, prawns or crab could be used. Because these peppers have so much inherent character and flavour, they have become a favourite ingredient for innovative chefs. Once you taste them, you will certainly dream up new ways to use these peppers.

The easiest sauce to make for the peppers is to purée some of them in a food processor with a little olive oil. Another good one is the Biscay red pepper sauce (see the recipe on page 234). A dramatic colour contrast can be created by pairing the bright red peppers with a black sauce (see the recipe for squid in ink sauce, page 198).

For this recipe, you will need about three tins of whole piquillo peppers, each containing 6–8 peppers. The peppers are imported from Spain, and the tins weigh about 230 g each.

If piquillo peppers are not available, try this recipe using very small red sweet peppers, roasted and peeled. One small sweet pepper equals 2–3 piquillos.

In the traditional, home-style preparation, these peppers are first floured, then dipped in beaten egg and finally fried in oil before being sauced and baked. The quick turn in the frying pan forms a sort of skin around the peppers and allows the flesh to soften further. The peppers are not supposed to stay crisp.

A chilled rosé wine from Navarre would be good with the peppers.

Stuffed peppers

2 tablespoons olive oil

2 tablespoons finely chopped onion

1 garlic clove, finely chopped

2 tablespoons plain flour, plus additional
flour, for dredging

1 tablespoon dry Sherry

240 ml (8 fl oz) milk

½ teaspoon anisette liqueur (optional)

340 g (12 oz) flaked salt cod, soaked and
precooked (see page 9)

Salt

12 tinned piquillo peppers, drained

1 egg, beaten

Olive oil, for frying

Sauce

6 piquillo peppers, drained

1 garlic clove

2 tablespoons olive oil

170 ml (6 fl oz) white wine

1 tablespoon plain flour

Salt

4 tablespoons cream or Greek yogurt
(optional)

To make the stuffed peppers, heat the oil in a
saucepan over medium heat and sauté the onion
and garlic, about 4 minutes. Stir in the 2
tablespoons flour and cook for 1 minute, then
whisk in the Sherry and milk. Cook, stirring,
until the sauce thickens, 3 minutes. Remove
from the heat and season with anisette liqueur,

if desired. Stir in the flaked fish. Taste the
mixture and add salt if needed.

Stuff 12 piquillo peppers with the fish
mixture. Place the stuffed peppers on a tray and
chill them in the refrigerator for 2 hours, so the
filling solidifies somewhat.

While the peppers are chilling, prepare the
sauce. Combine 6 piquillo peppers in a blender
with the garlic, oil, white wine, flour and salt to
taste. Process until the peppers are puréed.
Strain the mixture into a small saucepan.

Cook the sauce mixture over medium heat,
stirring constantly, for 5 minutes.

Dip the open end of the stuffed peppers into
flour, then roll them in the flour. Then coat in
the beaten egg. Heat enough oil to cover the
bottom of a frying pan and fry the peppers over
medium heat, a few at a time, turning them until
browned on all sides, 3 to 4 minutes.

Arrange the peppers in a single layer in a
baking dish or in individual ovenproof
casseroles. The peppers can be prepared in
advance up to this point and refrigerated for up
to 24 hours. Bring them to room temperature
before continuing.

Preheat the oven to 180°C/350°F/gas
mark 4.

Spoon the sauce over the stuffed peppers.
Bake for 15 to 20 minutes, or until the sauce is
bubbling. Remove from oven and dribble the
cream, if using, over the top.

Serves 4 to 6 as a starter

COD AND POTATO PURÉE, MULE-DRIVER'S STYLE
BACALAO AL AJO ARRIERO

Long before lorries and trains transported freight from seaports to inland cities, mule drivers made the long overland trek, stopping for food and lodging en route at *ventas* (roadside inns), the truck stops of yore, for food and lodging. Many dishes across Spain are prepared in 'mule-driver's style'. Garlic is almost always one of the ingredients.

This cod and potato purée comes from the picturesque town of Cuenca in La Mancha (east of Madrid), but another cod dish of the same name is made in the Basque country (it has garlic and oil, of course, and tomatoes and peppers, but no potatoes).

I serve this purée with toast or breadsticks as a tapa or, in individual portions, as a starter.

230 g (8 oz) potatoes, peeled and quartered

115 g (4 oz) dry salt cod, soaked (see page 9)

2 slices stale bread (about 60 g/2 oz), crusts removed

3 garlic cloves

3 tablespoons olive oil (preferably extra virgin)

2 eggs, hard-boiled, 1 chopped and 1 sliced

2 tablespoons chopped fresh flat-leaf parsley, plus additional to garnish

⅛ teaspoon freshly ground black pepper

Salt (optional)

Pimentón

In a large pan, cover the potatoes with water. Cook over medium heat until the potatoes are tender, about 20 minutes. Remove them with a slotted spoon. Add the drained salt cod to the water and simmer for 8 minutes more. Drain, reserving the liquid.

In a medium bowl, mash the potatoes with 2 tablespoons of the reserved liquid.

Combine the bread, garlic and oil with 120 ml (4 fl oz) of the reserved liquid in a blender or food processor. Blend until smooth. Stir this mixture into the potatoes.

With your fingers, flake the cod, discarding all the skin and bones. Fold the flakes into the potato mixture with the chopped egg, parsley, pepper and, if necessary, salt. Add additional liquid if necessary; the purée should have the consistency of very thick cream.

Transfer the purée to a serving bowl and smooth the top. Sprinkle with pimentón and garnish with the sliced egg and a little chopped parsley. (This can be made a day in advance and refrigerated.) Serve at room temperature.

SERVES 8 AS A TAPA; SERVES 4 AS A FIRST COURSE

CODFISH IN BISCAY RED PEPPER SAUCE
BACALAO A LA VIZCAINA

This sauce is so good that you will want to try it with fresh fish as well as salt cod, and, for that matter, with chicken, too.

The sauce is made with the bittersweet pulp of red *choricero* peppers. These dry peppers, 15–18 cm (6–7 inches) long, are mild and sweet, not hot like chillies. For this recipe they are soaked in hot water, then ground to a paste. *Choricero* peppers are available from some sources (see page 342), but if you can't get hold of them you could substitute good quality sweet pimentón (Spanish paprika). Make sure your pimentón is fresh (not more than a year old).

3 tablespoons olive oil

60 g (2 oz) serrano ham or bacon, chopped

1 onion, chopped

1 leek, white part only, chopped

2 garlic cloves, chopped

3 tablespoons *choricero* pepper paste or pimentón

1 teaspoon white wine vinegar

Pinch ground cayenne pepper

2 tablespoons chopped fresh flat-leaf parsley

120 ml (4 fl oz) white wine

2 tablespoons fine digestive biscuit crumbs or breadcrumbs

680 g (1½ lb) dry salt cod, cut into 10-cm (4-inch) pieces, soaked (see page 9)

½ teaspoon salt (optional)

Heat the oil in a frying pan over very low heat and add the ham, onion, leek and garlic. Sauté until the onion is very soft, about 30 minutes.

Combine the pimentón, vinegar and 3 tablespoons of water to make a paste. Add a pinch of cayenne. Set aside for 15 minutes.

Stir the *choricero* paste or pimentón mixture into the onions in the frying pan. Add the parsley, wine, crumbs and 240 ml (8 fl oz) of water. Bring to the boil, then simmer, covered, for 30 minutes.

Pour half of the sauce into a cazuela. Arrange the cod pieces on top. Sprinkle with salt, if needed. Pour over the remaining sauce. Cook over medium heat until the fish flakes easily, about 25 minutes. Shake and rock the casserole while the fish is cooking, but do not stir.

NOTE: This recipe makes 340 ml (12 fl oz) of sauce, which can be cooked with other fish or chicken dishes.

SERVES 4

Codfish Topped with Peppers, Bilbao Style

Bacalao a la Bilbaina

This is a delicious variation on the classic Basque recipe for *bacalao al pil pil*, in which salt cod is gently swirled with olive oil and garlic to produce a thick, emulsified sauce. In this version, typical of the city of Bilbao, red and green peppers top the codfish.

680 g (1½ lb) centre-cut dry salt cod, soaked (see page 9)

2 red sweet peppers

2 green sweet peppers

4 tablespoons olive oil

6 garlic cloves

¼ teaspoon salt

1 tablespoon plain flour

Cut the cod into eight pieces, each approximately 10 × 5 cm (4 × 2 inches), removing any bones. Place the cod pieces in a pan of hot water and let soak for an hour. Remove them and pat dry. Save the liquid.

Roast the peppers under the grill until charred on all sides, 25 minutes. Remove them and cover with a cloth. Set aside until they are cool enough to handle. Then remove the skins, stems and seeds. Tear the peppers into strips.

Heat 1 tablespoon of the oil in a frying pan over medium heat. Chop 2 cloves of the garlic and add to the pan with the peppers and their juice. Season with salt. Cover and cook over a low heat for 20 minutes.

Heat the remaining 3 tablespoons oil over medium-high heat in a cazuela. Slice the remaining 4 garlic cloves and add to the oil. Fry until the cloves just begin to turn golden, 2 minutes. Remove the cazuela from the heat and stir in the flour.

Place the pieces of cod, skin side down, in the cazuela in one layer. Return it to medium heat for 2 minutes, shaking the cazuela to mix the flour and oil with the cod.

Place the peppers on top of the cod. Shake and swirl the cazuela to mix. Add 1 tablespoon of the reserved soaking liquid. Shake, rock and swirl the cazuela. Then add another tablespoon of the liquid. Continue, adding a total of 6 tablespoons of liquid.

Cook the cod for 15 minutes over a gentle heat, shaking the cazuela frequently. Serve hot.

SERVES 4 AS A STARTER; SERVES 2 TO 3 AS A MAIN COURSE

9

POULTRY

Roast Chicken (*Pollo Asado*)

Chicken for a Crowd (*Pollo en Lata*)

Chicken Simmered in White Wine (*Pollo al Vino*)

Chicken Sautéed with Fresh Tomato
    (*Pollo con Tomate*)

Sherried Chicken with Mushrooms (*Pollo al Jerez*)

Pan-Fried Chicken Breasts with Sautéed Peppers
    (*Pechugas de Pollo Empanadas con Fritada*)

Maria's Roast Chicken with Meat and Olive Stuffing
    (*Pollo Relleno al Horno al Estilo de María*)

Chicken in Almond-Saffron Sauce
    (*Gallina en Pepitoria*)

Braised Chicken with Vegetables, Catalan Style
    (*Pollo en Samfaina*)

Squab with Mushroom Stuffing
    (*Pichón Relleno de Setas*)

Duck Braised with Olives (*Pato con Aceitunas*)

Roast Stuffed Turkey for Christmas
    (*Pavo Navideño*)

CHICKEN IS FAVOURITE FARE

Among the recipes that I gathered from Spanish cooks more than thirty years ago are several dozen for partridge, turtle dove, rabbit, hare, quail and even pheasant. But surprisingly, I was able to find fewer than a dozen for chicken dishes! At that time, a chicken's purpose was to produce eggs, not dinner, whereas a partridge was free for the shooting. Now, the tables have turned. Chicken can be purchased cheaply, and wild game is scarce.

Some of the best chicken recipes are those intended for the slow cooking of a stewing hen, such as chicken in *pepitoria* (almond sauce) or *cocido* (a meal-in-a-pot) (page 109). Nevertheless, for special occasions, a tender young bird would be plucked from the farmyard. Roasted, sautéed or braised, it was once the centrepiece for holiday meals. Now, of course, chicken is daily fare.

Turkeys, ducks and pigeons were also raised for food in the farmyard not so long ago. Turkey is a bird from the New World, first found in the markets of Mexico and brought back to Spain. It quickly found acceptance and has become a favourite addition to holiday feasts in Spain.

ROAST CHICKEN
POLLO ASADO

For such a simple preparation, it's worth buying a free-range or organically raised chicken for the flavour. You might want to add potatoes, carrots and turnips to roast in the pan with the chicken. In Spain, it's very characteristic to garnish the platter with lettuce leaves and tomato wedges. Sprigs of fresh rosemary look attractive, too.

Salt and freshly ground black pepper

1 whole roasting chicken (about 2.5 kg/ 6 lb)

1 tablespoon brandy

Sprigs fresh rosemary

Sprigs fresh thyme

1 bay leaf

1 tablespoon lard, softened, or 1 tablespoon olive oil

2 garlic cloves, crushed

Vegetables (optional)

120 ml (4 fl oz) white wine

Preheat the oven to 200°C/400°F/gas mark 6.

Sprinkle the salt and pepper in the chicken cavity, then rub the cavity with the brandy. Insert sprigs of rosemary and thyme and the bay leaf into the cavity. Tie the legs together so the chicken keeps its shape.

Combine the lard and garlic. Spread over the chicken. Place the chicken, breast side up, in a flameproof roasting pan (with accompanying vegetables, if desired).

Roast for 30 minutes, then decrease the oven temperature to 180°C/350°F/gas mark 4. Baste with the pan juices and continue roasting, basting from time to time, until the chicken is tender (and the temperature of the thigh meat registers 79°C/175°F), about 2 hours total.

Transfer the chicken to a serving platter and remove the string from the legs. Pour off all the fat that is in the pan. Add the wine and, over medium heat, stir to deglaze the pan. Bring to the boil and strain the pan juices over the chicken. Serve hot.

SERVES 6

CHICKEN FOR A CROWD
POLLO EN LATA

Lata means oven pan. When a gang of relatives or out-of-town friends are getting together at your house, you go to the local bakery and borrow a *lata* – in this case a huge one – fill it with chicken pieces, potatoes and seasoning, and take it back to the bakery to bake for a few hours in the bread oven. It's usually the men who take charge of preparing *lata*. A large roasting pan would work equally well for preparing this dish, which is also made with baby lamb or kid.

4 tablespoons olive oil

1.8 kg (4 lb) potatoes, peeled and sliced 12 mm (½ inch) thick

1 large tomato, sliced

1 green sweet pepper, cut into strips

1 onion, sliced

1 whole head garlic, roasted and peeled (see page 8)

½ tablespoon salt

Freshly ground black pepper

2 tablespoons chopped fresh flat-leaf parsley

1.8 kg (4 lb) chicken pieces (legs, thighs and breasts)

3 bay leaves

1 teaspoon pimentón

½ teaspoon dried thyme

240 ml (8 fl oz) white wine

Preheat the oven to 200°C/400°F/gas mark 6.

Pour 2 tablespoons of the oil into the bottom of a large flameproof roasting pan. Spread a layer of potatoes in the bottom of the pan. Place some of the tomato, green pepper and onion on top. Sprinkle with a few cloves of roasted garlic, salt, pepper and parsley. Continue to layer potatoes and vegetables in the same manner.

Place the chicken pieces on top. Break the bay leaves into pieces and tuck into the potatoes. Sprinkle with pimentón and thyme. Pour the remaining 2 tablespoons oil and the wine over the chicken and vegetables. Place on the hob over medium heat and bring the liquid to the boil. Cover the pan with a lid or with aluminum foil (use oven gloves to protect yourself from burns) and bake for 15 minutes.

Reduce the oven temperature to 160°C/325°F/gas mark 3 and bake for another 60 minutes. Remove the cover or foil and bake for 15 minutes more. Serve hot.

SERVES 8 TO 10

CHICKEN SIMMERED IN WHITE WINE
POLLO AL VINO

Years ago, chicken in Spain was always free-range. Now the birds are battery raised, resulting in chicken that is tender, cheap but incredibly fatty. To reduce some of the fat in this dish, I suggest removing the skin and trimming off all visible fat.

2 tablespoons olive oil

1.1 kg (2½ lb) chicken drumsticks and thighs, skin and all fat removed

1 onion, quartered and sliced

1 whole head garlic, roasted and peeled (see page 8)

240 ml (8 fl oz) dry white wine

½ teaspoon salt

Freshly ground black pepper

2 bay leaves

Pinch dried thyme

A few black olives, sliced

Chopped fresh flat-leaf parsley

Heat the oil in a heavy pan or cazuela over medium heat and brown the chicken pieces very slowly, 10 to 15 minutes. After turning the chicken, add the onion and continue to brown.

Add the garlic, wine, salt, pepper, bay leaves and thyme to the pan. Bring to the boil, then cover and simmer. Cook until the chicken is very tender, 45 to 75 minutes. Remove the bay leaves.

Serve garnished with the olives and a sprinkling of parsley.

SERVES 4

CHICKEN SAUTÉED WITH FRESH TOMATO
POLLO CON TOMATE

The intense flavour of this dish belies the simplicity of its preparation. Be sure to use fresh, vine-ripened tomatoes, which cook down to a thick, flavour-packed jam.

3 tablespoons olive oil

900 g (2 lb) chicken legs and thighs

2 kg (4½ lb) fresh tomatoes

1 garlic clove, chopped

1 teaspoon salt

Freshly ground black pepper

Pinch dried thyme

½ teaspoon pimentón

2 bay leaves

2 tablespoons brandy

Chopped fresh flat-leaf parsley

In a deep frying pan, heat the oil over medium-high heat. Add the chicken pieces and brown on all sides, 10 to 15 minutes. Remove when browned. Pour off all but 2 tablespoons of the fat.

Meanwhile, bring a large pan of water to the boil. Plunge the tomatoes into the boiling water until the skins split, about 45 seconds. Drain, cool, then slip off the skins. Cut the tomatoes in half horizontally and squeeze out the seeds and discard them. Chop the tomatoes coarsely.

Heat the remaining oil in the frying pan over high heat and add the chopped tomatoes, garlic, salt, pepper, thyme, pimentón, bay leaves and brandy. Cook for 5 minutes.

Return the chicken pieces to the pan. Lower the heat to medium and simmer, uncovered, until the chicken is tender, 45 to 75 minutes. Remove the chicken pieces when they are done.

Continue cooking the tomato sauce over medium heat until it is very thick and beginning to brown, about 30 minutes more. Return the chicken to the pan and reheat. Remove the bay leaves.

Serve garnished with parsley.

SERVES 4

SHERRIED CHICKEN WITH MUSHROOMS
POLLO AL JEREZ

※

I once thought cooking with wine was only for very special occasions. That was before I came to live in Spain, where I learned wine was almost as common as water. Added to the cooking pot, wine contributes enormous flavour to the finished dish. Where I first learned Spanish cooking, the wine used in the kitchen was from Montilla (Córdoba), a wine somewhat like dry fino Sherry. So many of my recipes call for Sherry.

But if you do not have a real fino Sherry or Montilla, use a dry white wine. A splash of brandy will fortify the flavour.

1 tablespoon olive oil

900 g (2 lb) chicken legs and thighs

3 spring onions, sliced, or 1 small onion, quartered and sliced

30 g (1 oz) salt pork or pancetta, cut into 6-mm (¼-inch) dice

230 g (8 oz) sliced mushrooms

1 tablespoon plain flour

240 ml (8 fl oz) dry Sherry or Montilla wine

½ teaspoon salt

2 bay leaves

4 tablespoons chopped fresh flat-leaf parsley

Freshly ground black pepper

Spanish Chips (page 162) (optional)

Heat the oil in a frying pan over medium heat and brown the chicken pieces, turning until they are well browned on all sides, about 5 minutes. Transfer the chicken to a cazuela.

Pour off all but 1 tablespoon of the fat in the frying pan. Add the spring onions, salt pork and mushrooms. Sauté over high heat until the onions and mushrooms are slightly browned, about 5 minutes. Stir in the flour. Add the Sherry to the pan and stir to combine the ingredients.

Pour the Sherry mixture over the chicken pieces in the cazuela. Stir in 120 ml (4 fl oz) water, the salt, bay leaves, parsley and pepper. Bring the liquid to the boil, then reduce the heat and simmer the chicken until fork-tender, from 45 to 75 minutes, depending on the size of the pieces.

Serve the chicken in the same cazuela with Spanish chips added, if desired.

SERVES 4

PAN-FRIED CHICKEN BREASTS WITH SAUTÉED PEPPERS
PECHUGAS DE POLLO EMPANADAS CON FRITADA

Fritada is a vegetable mixture somewhere between a *sofrito* – 'fried' tomato sauce – and a *pisto* – stewed peppers, tomatoes, courgettes and aubergine. It can be served hot or cold, as a vegetable side dish or as a sauce in which to cook fish (great with tuna).

4 boneless chicken breast halves (about 900 g/2 lb)

3 tablespoons olive oil, plus additional for pan-frying the chicken

1 onion, chopped

2 green sweet peppers, roasted, peeled (page 7) and cut into 2.5-cm (1-inch) pieces

1 red sweet pepper, roasted, peeled (page 7) and cut into 2.5-cm (1-inch) pieces

4 garlic cloves, chopped

450 g (1 lb) chopped tomatoes (from 900 g/2 lb fresh)

Crushed red chilli flakes (optional)

Salt

Freshly ground black pepper

1 teaspoon dried basil, crumbled

1 egg, beaten with 2 teaspoons of water

70 g (2½ oz) flour

¼ teaspoon hot pimentón

115g (4 oz) fine dry breadcrumbs

Slice each breast half horizontally into three cutlets less than 12 mm (½ inch) thick.

Heat 3 tablespoons of the oil in a deep frying pan over medium heat and sauté the onions for 5 minutes. Add the green and red peppers and garlic and sauté for 5 minutes more. Add the tomatoes, red chilli flakes, if using, 1 teaspoon salt, black pepper and basil. Cook over medium heat, stirring occasionally, until the peppers are soft and all the liquid has cooked away. The vegetables should just begin to stick to the bottom of the pan, about 20 minutes. (If they stick before they are tender, add a little juice from the tomatoes, or water.)

Put the egg in a shallow dish. Combine the flour, ½ teaspoon salt, pimentón and black pepper in another dish. Place the breadcrumbs in another dish.

Dip the chicken cutlets first into the flour, then into the egg, then dredge in breadcrumbs. Pat off the excess and place the cutlets on a tray.

Heat enough oil to cover the bottom of a large frying pan. Fry the chicken pieces over medium-high heat a few at a time until they are golden and crisped. They should cook through in the time it takes to brown them, about 2 minutes per side. Add additional oil to the pan between batches.

Serve the sautéed pepper mixture beside the chicken.

SERVES 6

MARIA'S ROAST CHICKEN
WITH MEAT AND OLIVE STUFFING
POLLO RELLENO AL HORNO AL ESTILO DE MARÍA

I learned to make this festive dish in Maria's kitchen. Maria did the cooking in the tapa bar where I learned the basics of Spanish cooking. She made this stuffing with olives, pine kernels, chopped ham and minced pork to fill a Christmas turkey. Use this stuffing mixture for chicken and turkey, as well as for rolled veal breast.

1 (2.5-kg/6-lb) roasting chicken or small
    turkey

1 tablespoon fresh lemon juice

2½ teaspoons salt

60 g (2 oz) fresh breadcrumbs

70 g (2½ oz) sliced pimiento-stuffed olives

30 g (1 oz) pine kernels

1 egg, hard-boiled and chopped

60 g (2 oz) serrano ham or lean bacon,
    chopped

4 tablespoons chopped fresh flat-leaf
    parsley

1 garlic clove, finely chopped

Freshly ground black pepper

Freshly grated nutmeg

230 g (8 oz) minced pork or beef

2 tablespoons olive oil

2 tablespoons chopped onion

1 chicken liver, chopped

280 ml (½ pint) white wine

Preheat the oven to 180°C/350°F/gas mark 4.

Clean the chicken thoroughly, wash and pat dry. Combine the lemon juice and ½ teaspoon of the salt and rub into the cavity.

In a bowl, combine the breadcrumbs, olives, pine kernels, egg, ham, parsley, garlic, pepper, nutmeg, minced pork and the remaining 2 teaspoons salt.

In a small frying pan, heat 1 tablespoon of the oil over medium heat and sauté the onion and chopped chicken liver until the liver loses its pink colour, about 5 minutes.

Add the liver and onion to the breadcrumb mixture with 4 tablespoons of the wine. Mix well. Stuff the chicken with this mixture. Use a skewer to close the cavity. Place the chicken in a roasting tin. Brush it with the remaining 1 tablespoon oil.

Roast for 45 minutes. Remove the chicken and pour off the excess fat. Brush the chicken with some of the fat, then pour over the remaining wine. Roast for 1 hour more, basting occasionally. (The internal temperature of the stuffing should reach 71°C/160°F.)

Let the chicken rest for 10 minutes before carving. Skim off the excess fat from the liquid in the pan and serve the pan juices separately.

SERVES 6 TO 8

CHICKEN IN ALMOND-SAFFRON SAUCE
GALLINA EN PEPITORIA

Gallina means hen. Indeed, this recipe, with its very Moorish flavours of almonds, saffron and pepper, was once a way to cook a 'mature' barnyard fowl.

1 (2.2 kg/5-lb) chicken or turkey, cut into
    serving pieces

Salt and pepper

Flour

4 tablespoons olive oil

45 g (1½ oz) almonds, blanched and
    skinned (see page 6)

6 garlic cloves

2 slices bread, crusts removed

1 onion, chopped

1 clove

10 peppercorns

½ teaspoon saffron threads

1 tablespoon chopped fresh flat-leaf parsley

140 ml (¼ pint) dry Sherry or white wine

240 ml (8 fl oz) chicken stock, or more
    as needed

1 bay leaf

2 hard-boiled egg yolks

1 tablespoon fresh lemon juice

1 tablespoon slivered almonds, fried in a
    little oil

8-cm (3-inch) triangles of bread, fried crisp
    in oil

Rub the chicken pieces with salt and pepper, then dredge them with flour. Shake off the excess flour.

Heat the oil in a frying pan over medium heat and fry the almonds, 4 garlic cloves and bread slices until they are golden, 2 minutes. Skim them out and reserve.

In the same oil, brown the chicken pieces very slowly on all sides. Transfer the chicken to a cazuela. Add the onion to the remaining oil and sauté until softened, 10 to 15 minutes.

In a mortar, grind the clove, peppercorns and saffron with 1 teaspoon salt. Mix with 1 tablespoon water. In a blender, combine the fried garlic, 2 garlic cloves, almonds, bread, parsley and a few tablespoons of the Sherry. Blend to make a smooth paste. Blend in the spice mixture. Add to the onion with the rest of the wine and stock. Bring to the boil, then pour over the chicken pieces. Put in the bay leaf.

Cook the chicken over low heat until tender, 60 to 90 minutes, stirring occasionally. Add additional stock if the sauce is too thick.

Mash the egg yolks with the lemon juice and a little of the sauce and stir into the cazuela to thicken the sauce.

Serve the chicken garnished with fried slivered almonds and triangles of fried bread.

SERVES 6

BRAISED CHICKEN WITH VEGETABLES, CATALAN STYLE
POLLO EN SAMFAINA

Samfaina is a traditional Catalan sauce, which can also be cooked with rabbit or turkey. It's especially good in the summer when tomatoes and courgettes are at their peak.

1 (1.5 kg/3½-lb) chicken, cut into serving pieces

Salt and freshly ground black pepper

4 tablespoons lard or olive oil

4 tablespoons diced serrano ham or bacon

1 large aubergine (450 g/1 lb), peeled and diced

1 red sweet pepper, cut into 5-cm (2-inch) pieces

1 green sweet pepper, cut into 5-cm (2-inch) pieces

1 large courgette (450 g/1 lb), diced

2 onions, quartered and sliced

3 garlic cloves, chopped

450 g (1 lb) chopped tomatoes

4 tablespoons dry Sherry

1 bay leaf

½ teaspoon dried oregano, crumbled

1 tablespoon chopped fresh flat-leaf parsley

Sprinkle the chicken pieces with salt and black pepper. In a cazuela or flameproof casserole, heat 2 tablespoons of the lard over medium heat. Add the chicken and brown the pieces very slowly on all sides, 10 to 15 minutes. Remove the chicken when browned.

Add the remaining 2 tablespoons fat to the cazuela and sauté the ham, aubergine, both peppers, courgette, onion and garlic for 5 minutes over medium heat. Add the tomatoes, Sherry, salt and pepper to taste, bay leaf, oregano and parsley.

Return the chicken to the cazuela. Cook chicken over medium heat until it is fork-tender, from 45 to 75 minutes, depending on the size of the chicken pieces. The vegetables should release enough liquid to keep the chicken from sticking. If necessary, add a little water to the cazuela.

Remove the bay leaf. Serve the chicken and vegetables.

SERVES 6

SQUAB WITH MUSHROOM STUFFING
PICHÓN RELLENO DE SETAS

I lived for several years in a mill house in the country. Unlike most simple farmhouses, which had only a low loft for sleeping quarters, the mill house had a full second storey. The largest section was the bedroom. A small area had been divided off as a writer's studio. Next to that, accessible through a hatch door, was a dovecote. The pigeons scratched and scrabbled on their side of the partition, sometimes drowning out the clacking of the typewriter. In the evenings, they fluttered out through the high openings of the dovecote to fly over the valley.

The man who farmed the fields below the mill had the rights to haul away the guano, excellent fertilizer. Once or twice a year he came to the house with hessian bags and went in through the hatch door to clean out the droppings. Many farms kept pigeons as a source of guano. The young squabs were a welcome addition to the cooking pot. Here is one way I learned to prepare them.

2 squab or poussin (each 570 g/1¼ lb)

1 tablespoon brandy

Salt and freshly ground black pepper

4 tablespoons olive oil

100 g (3½ oz) chopped Portobello or other mushrooms

60 g (2 oz) chopped chicken liver

30 g (1 oz) chopped serrano ham or bacon

45 g (1½ oz) chopped onion

1 garlic clove, finely chopped

1 tablespoon chopped fresh flat-leaf parsley

Pinch dried thyme

120 ml (4 fl oz) dry Sherry

120 ml (4 fl oz) Simple Stock (page 82) or water

1 bay leaf

Wash the birds and pat dry. Rub their cavities with brandy, salt and pepper. Set aside for 30 minutes.

Heat 2 tablespoons of the oil in a frying pan over medium heat and sauté the mushrooms, liver, ham, onion and garlic until the liver loses its pink colour and the onion is softened, about 5 minutes. Add the parsley, thyme, and salt and pepper to taste.

Stuff the birds with the mushroom mixture and use poultry skewers to close the cavities.

Heat the remaining 2 tablespoons oil in a deep frying pan or flameproof casserole over medium heat. Brown the birds slowly on all sides, 10 to 12 minutes. Add the Sherry, stock and bay leaf. Simmer, covered, until birds are tender, about 45 minutes.

Remove the bay leaf. Split the birds in half to serve.

SERVES 4

DUCK BRAISED WITH OLIVES
PATO CON ACEITUNAS

This slow-braised dish is typical of the *marismas de Guadalquivir*, the wetlands of the lower Guadalquivir River, below Seville, an area incredibly rich in wildlife. The salty, slightly sour olives are a good foil for wild duck. When I make this dish with farm-raised duck, I remove all the skin to reduce the fat.

You can turn this simple hunter's dish into a more sophisticated presentation by substituting boned duck breast (*magret*) grilled rare, sliced and served with the olive sauce.

A fine side dish is a pilaff of long-grain rice – rice that is grown in the Guadalquivir wetlands for export.

1 duck with giblets (about 2 kg/4½ lb), quartered and skin removed

1½ onions

2 cloves

1 celery stalk

1 sprig parsley

¼ teaspoon dried thyme

3 bay leaves

10 black peppercorns

2 strips orange zest

1½ teaspoons salt

2 tablespoons olive oil

2 slices bacon, diced

2 garlic cloves, chopped

170 ml (6 fl oz) dry Sherry

2 carrots, sliced

Freshly ground black pepper

85 g (3 oz) sliced green Spanish olives

Chopped fresh flat-leaf parsley

Combine the giblets, neck and wing tips in a pan with 1.8 litres (about 3 pints) water. Stick the ½ onion with the cloves and add to the pan with the celery, parsley sprig, half of the thyme, 1 bay leaf, peppercorns, 1 strip of the orange zest and 1 teaspoon of the salt. Bring to the boil and simmer until reduced by half. Strain the stock, skim off the fat and reserve the stock.

Cut the remaining onion into quarters and slice them.

In a cazuela or flameproof casserole, heat the oil over medium-high heat and add the bacon, sliced onion, garlic and duck quarters. Brown very slowly, turning the duck, for about 15 minutes.

Add the Sherry and 450 ml (¾ pint) of the reserved stock. Add the carrots, remaining strip of orange zest, remaining thyme, pepper, ½ teaspoon salt and remaining 2 bay leaves. Bring to the boil, then simmer, covered, for 30 minutes. Turn the pieces of duck and simmer another 30 minutes, or until fork-tender.

Skim off any fat from the liquid. Add the olives to the cazuela and cook over low heat for another 20 minutes.

Remove the bay leaves. Serve the duck sprinkled with chopped parsley.

SERVES 4

ROAST STUFFED TURKEY FOR CHRISTMAS
PAVO NAVIDEÑO

✳

This version of stuffed turkey has become my holiday favourite. If turkey is to be served to a crowd, as part of a buffet spread, it is convenient to have the butcher remove the wishbone and breastbone before stuffing and roasting. It is easier to carve.

TURKEY STOCK

Turkey neck and giblets
½ onion
1 celery stalk
1 carrot
1 sprig rosemary
¼ teaspoon dried thyme
1 bay leaf
½ teaspoon salt
4 black peppercorns

TURKEY

1 (4.5–5.5 kg/10–12 lb) oven-ready turkey or capon
Salt and freshly ground black pepper
2 tablespoons Sherry

STUFFING

140 g (5 oz) dried apricots, halved
230 g (8 oz) seedless raisins
115 g (4 oz) pitted prunes, halved
115 g (4 oz) pine kernels
3 tablespoons lard or olive oil
340 g (12 oz) sliced pork loin, julienned
450 g (1 lb) pork sausage, broken up
1 turkey liver, chopped
115 g (4 oz) chopped onion
340 ml (12 fl oz) dry Sherry
1 large apple, chopped
4 tablespoons chopped fresh flat-leaf parsley
2 tablespoons capers
¼ teaspoon pimentón
Freshly grated nutmeg
¼ teaspoon ground cloves
½ teaspoon ground cinnamon
Salt and freshly ground black pepper

To make the stock, combine the turkey neck and giblets (save the liver for the stuffing) in a pan with 900 ml (1½ pints) water. Add the onion, celery, carrot, rosemary, thyme, bay leaf, salt and peppercorns. Bring to the boil and simmer for 45 minutes. Strain the stock and reserve.

Sprinkle the cavity of the turkey with salt and pepper and 2 tablespoons of the Sherry. Let it come to room temperature.

To make the stuffing, combine the apricots, raisins, prunes and pine kernels in a bowl and cover with warm water. Set aside for 1 hour. Drain. (Save the liquid, if desired, for cooking liquid.)

Heat 2 tablespoons of the lard in a frying pan over high heat and sauté the pork loin, sausage meat, turkey liver and onion until the meat loses its pink colour. Add the soaked fruit to the meat with 120 ml (4 fl oz) of the Sherry. Cook for 5 minutes over medium heat, then remove from the heat. Add the apple, parsley, capers, pimentón, nutmeg, cloves, cinnamon and salt and pepper to taste.

Preheat the oven to 180°C/350°F/gas mark 4.

Stuff the turkey with the fruit and meat mixture. Skewer the neck skin to close the crop. Skewer or sew up the body cavity. Truss the turkey, tying the legs and wings close to the body. Rub the turkey with remaining 1 tablespoon lard and place it in a flameproof roasting pan. Cover the turkey with aluminium foil.

Roast for 1 hour. Remove the foil. Pour over the remaining Sherry and the reserved stock. Roast until the turkey is done, 2 to 2½ hours more, basting occasionally with the liquid in the pan.

Remove the turkey to a serving platter. Remove the skewers and string. Skim off the fat from the liquid remaining in the roasting pan. Bring the liquid to the boil and strain it into a sauce bowl. (The sauce is not thickened.) Carve the turkey and serve accompanied by the stuffing and sauce.

SERVES 12 TO 16

Christmas in Spain

Where I live in southern Spain, Christmas is very different from the holidays I remember from my childhood in the Midwest. Here a 'white Christmas' means the blinding white of walls in an Andalusian village on a December morning when the air is so diamond clear you can see the Rif mountains across the sea in North Africa.

The days are usually mild enough to enjoy drinks on the terrace next to a blooming poinsettia tree before Christmas dinner. The nights have a winter chill. Walking through village streets at sundown, you see housewives fanning fires of brush and twigs in round braziers. The brazier fits in the bottom of a round table, covered with a long velvet or felt cloth. The whole family sits around the table on a winter's evening. Each person tucks the cloth around his legs, the feet kept toasty-warm by the coals. This is the 'central heating' of a village home. Although many 'braziers' nowadays are electric, the custom has not disappeared.

And the music. In place of the solemn Christmas carols of northern countries are merry ones: *'Arre, mi burrico,'* Giddyap, little donkey, let's go to Bethlehem, don't kick me now, 'cause I'm going, too.

Spanish-style Christmas carollers make their rounds of the village with drums, tambourines, brass pestle and mortar (a favoured accompaniment to Andalusian songs) and the *zambomba*, a strange rhythm instrument resembling a drum pierced by a stick. The youths rub the stick up and down through the drumhead, and the town echoes with the weird, grunting sound. When you open your door, they come in and sing a few songs. You give them some coins and biscuits and pass the brandy bottle. Then, off they go, streamers flying down the narrow cobbled streets.

More traditional than the Christmas tree in Spanish homes is the nativity scene, lovingly home-made from cork or pieces of wood or shop-bought and elaborately made. Some families use a whole room for the crib, which includes mountains, palm trees, figures of sheep, cows, shepherds, kings, stars and so forth. The one in the village church has a stream with goldfish, live chickens and songbirds. The nativity is kept on display for the twelve days of Christmas, and the three wise men are moved closer to the manger every day until January 6, the holiday of *Los Reyes*, the Three Kings.

Everyone goes visiting to see the neighbours' manger scenes. Children are decked out in their holiday best and constantly admonished to stay out of the dirt. Copper pans and cut-glass goblets gleam on mantle shelves. The table is covered with a hand-made embroidered cloth and adorned with flowers. Winter roses bloom on the patio, and greenery fills every corner.

Brandy and sweet anise are served to accompany the Christmas sweets and the ladies settle back to discuss holiday hairdos (everyone gets a new one), someone's new baby, who's going to the Christmas dance and *abuela's* (granny's) recipe for *roscos* (ring biscuits).

Christmas dinner in a Spanish home takes place on *Noche Buena* (Christmas Eve), an important family occasion. On my first Christmas in Spain, I was invited to share the festive meal with the family that ran the tapa bar where I made my first forays in the kitchen (see chapter 2).

My friend Maria raised a turkey chick in the patio behind the bar. It was a nasty creature that pecked my heels as I went to fetch water from the well at the back of the patio. But finally, the bird's time had come.

I wasn't there for the kill, but I arrived in time to find Maria carefully deboning the turkey under the watchful eye of her *tia-abuela* (great-aunt) whose recipe for truffled turkey this was. The aunt had worked as a cook in the home of well-to-do burghers in Málaga. Such a wealth of ingredients went into that stuffing! Good pork and beef which the butcher minced together with ham; walnuts from the family's small farm; pine kernels, which a small boy brought from the sierra ('Never use packaged pine kernels,' Maria told me. 'They just don't have the same flavour.'); olives; good brandy and a whole array of spices. The aunt's original recipe called for truffles, too, but we skipped those. The turkey simmered all afternoon in its rich stock, then was removed and pressed under a weight.

The dinner was not a formal, sit-down affair. The food was placed on a big round table – sliced serrano ham, sliced sausages, olives, prawns, two or three different salads and, in the centre, the sliced turkey on a big platter, garnished with lettuce, tomatoes, olives and sliced egg.

Family and friends, all dressed in Christmas best, helped themselves to plates of food. The meal's finale was the typical *turrón* (nougat) and marzipan sweets moulded in fanciful shapes. Then it was time for midnight mass and the joyous bells to celebrate the birth of the Christ child.

Christmas is blessedly free of frantic shopping for presents, allowing more attention to feasting! Although *Papa Noël* (Santa Claus) has made his commercial appearance in Spain, traditionally gift-giving is not until January 6, when the *reyes magos* (the three kings) arrive from Bethlehem.

On the eve of the holiday, the kings parade through village streets, costumed and on horseback, tossing sweets to the children. Excited children are up at dawn the following morning to see what the kings have left them. Then it's more biscuits and sweets and family feasting to bring the holidays to a close.

10

MEAT

PORK AND SAUSAGE

Sausage Stuffed Onions

    (*Cebollas Rellenas con Salchicha*)

Sizzling Sausages with Sherry (*Salchichas al Jerez*)

Herb-Marinated Roasted Pork Loin

    (*Lomo en Adobo, Asado con Hierbas*)

Pork Loin Stuffed with Figs and Brandy

    (*Lomo de Cerdo Relleno*)

Roast Pork Shoulder (*Asado de Puerco*)

Orange-Glazed Pork Fillets

    (*Solomillos de Cerdo en Salsa de Naranjas*)

Home-Style Pork Chops in Lemon Marinade

    (*Chuletas a la Casera, con Aliño*)

Pork Chop and Pasta Casserole

    (*Cazuela de Cerdo y Fideos*)

Tripe Stew for St Anthony's Day

    (*Potaje de Callos de San Antón*)

Adobo-Marinated Spare Ribs

    (*Costillas de Cerdo en Adobo*)

Pork Hocks with Greens (*Lacón con Grelos*)

LAMB AND KID

Shepherds'-Style Lamb (*Cordero al Pastor*)

Lamb Stew with Artichokes and Mint

    (*Caldereta de Cordero*)

Moorish Lamb Stew with Prunes

    (*Cordero con Ciruelas Pasas*)

Slow-Braised Lamb Chops with Sherry

    (*Chuletas de Cordero al Jerez*)

Tender Lamb Chops Sautéed with Garlic

    (*Cabrito al Ajo Cabañil*)

BEEF

Braised Oxtails (*Rabo de Toro*)

Bull's Testicles (*Criadillas*)

Andalusian Beef Stew

    (*Estofado de Buey a la Andaluza*)

PORK AND SAUSAGE

One crisp, cold January day in Montecorto, a highland village well known for its hams and sausages, it was pig-butchering day at Concha's house.

Before the sun was up, the men started a big fire to heat an iron cauldron of water in a small yard next to Concha's village house. They were all drinking strong anise brandy, to ward off the chill and, possibly, to prepare themselves for the task at hand. By the time the first rays of sun glistened on the frost-covered hills, the water was boiling. A huge pig was tethered to a post. It took all six of Concha's sons to heave the pig up on to a curved stone, where it hung with legs dangling over. It was Concha herself, the matriarch, who slit the pig's throat. It all happened very fast. She had a bucket ready to catch the blood spurting out, which would be used later for sausage making. She plunged her arms into the bucket up to her shoulders, to stir the blood and keep it moving so it would not coagulate as it cooled. Steam and mist swirled around her.

The pig was butchered the following day, when it had cooled and aired. The fatty belly meat was chopped to mix with spices for chorizo sausage. The two hams were hung in preparation for salting. The prized fillet was cut free. The whole loin was boned and marinated in vinegar with spices to preserve it. Spare ribs were separated, some to be barbecued fresh, the remainder salt-cured.

And immense quantities of fat! Concha's six sons slung slabs of fat over their shoulders and carried them away to be salted down in wooden troughs. Salt pork is a valuable item in the larder, to be cooked with bean dishes. Other fat would be rendered down to white lard. Some of it goes to bakeries, which make tender-crumbed biscuits with it. Some lard, flavoured with red pimentón, is used to pack pieces of cooked meat in clay jars, to be kept in conserve. Once the fat solidifies, it protects the meat from the air, a sort of confit. Later, in the kitchen, the red lard, *manteca colorada*, and bits of meat are spread on bread in place of butter and used in frying in place of olive oil.

Once the meat was cut up, the women, under Concha's direction, started the sausage making. The blood was gradually combined with a mixture of cooked rice, onions, spices and chopped pork fat. Using a big sausage funnel, they stuffed the casings with the mixture. Once stuffed and tied off in links, the sausage was boiled in cauldrons, then drained and hung from poles to dry for a week.

The minced meat for chorizo was allowed to marinate in a huge bowl for two days before being stuffed into casings. Chorizo is not precooked, but hung to dry for a week, after which it can be stewed, fried or grilled.

Another mixture was prepared consisting of finely chopped pieces of meat and fat, which would become *salchichón*, a cured sausage somewhat like salami, which is air-dried and eventually served as a cold sliced meat. None of these sausages is smoked, although in regions of high humidity, such as in northern Spain, smoking is used in the drying process.

The winter hog slaughtering has always been a very communal occasion, with families gathering to help each other out and making a party of it at the same time.

My friend Juncal told me that when she was growing up in a small village near Seville, in November, the *matarife* (butcher) made the rounds of villages, spending a week in each one, and going from house to house slaughtering hogs.

Her family didn't raise its own pig, so her older brother and sister were sent to market to buy one. Leading it home by a rope, they were not supposed to pull on the rope or the pig would baulk, and its muscles would seize up, causing the meat to toughen. So they raced home behind the pig.

Each family took it in turns to help the others, with the men doing the cutting up and the women the chopping and stuffing. The very public act of slaughtering a pig may well derive from the days of the Spanish Inquisition, when *converso* Jews, those who had converted to Christianity, might be accused of secretly observing Jewish law if they did not publicly display their pig. Butchering a hog could save one from being burned at the stake.

Sausage Sampler

These are some of the most important Spanish sausages. While some can be difficult to find in the UK, most are available through the sources listed at the end of the book (see page 342).

Butifarra blanca. A Catalan smooth-textured white sausage made of minced pork and spices, which is cooked before curing. Good for barbecuing, it can be sliced and fried or simmered in soups. (Bratwurst is a possible substitute.)

Chorizo. Chorizo is made from chopped or minced pork meat and fat, and sometimes beef as well, which has been macerated with sweet and hot pimentón or the pulp from sweet choricero peppers, plus pepper, garlic and oregano. Spanish chorizo is not spicy-hot as is Mexican chorizo. After stuffing in casings, the sausages are air-dried. Chorizo tied off into short links, *en ristra*, usually is 'soft', with a higher fat content and only semi-cured. It is stewed, grilled or fried. Thick rolls (*cular*) or thinner 'candle' ones (*vela*) are cured longer; they are solid and are sliced and eaten as cold sandwich meats or just on their own. Pamplona chorizo is a cured version. Chorizo can also be made from *jabalí* (wild boar). Although there is no close substitute for chorizo, garlic-pork sausage can be used.

Lomo embuchado. Cured pork loin, stuffed in wide casings.

Longaniza. A long, skinny sausage, either flavoured as for chorizo or as for salami. Cured and eaten raw.

Morcilla. Blood sausage. It is boiled, then dried. Spiced with cinnamon, cloves, nutmeg and anise and containing onion, rice and pine kernels. Morcilla is usually stewed, but it can also be grilled or sliced and eaten cold. Asturian morcilla is also smoked. There is no true substitute for morcilla, but, in cooking, you could use black pudding or any pork sausage and add a pinch of cloves and cinnamon to the stew.

Morcón. A thick sausage made of diced pieces of meat.

Salchicha. Fresh, raw pork link sausage, made of fresh pork and fat and spices. These must be cooked.

Salchichón. A hard cured sausage, somewhat like salami.

Sobreasada. A soft, spreadable sausage from Majorca, flavoured similarly to chorizo. Spread it on slabs of hot toasted bread.

SAUSAGE STUFFED ONIONS
CEBOLLAS RELLENAS CON SALCHICHA

In Extremadura, where folks gather for the traditional pig butchering, this stuffed onion dish is traditional. The inner parts of the onion are finely chopped to use in the mixture for morcilla, while the onion shells are stuffed with minced pork or sausage meat and roasted.

6 to 8 medium onions (7 cm/2½ inches diameter), left unpeeled

2 teaspoons salt

230 g (8 oz) minced pork or loose pork sausage meat

1 garlic clove, crushed

⅛ teaspoon ground cinnamon

Pinch freshly grated nutmeg

¼ teaspoon coarsely ground black pepper

½ teaspoon pimentón

½ teaspoon dried oregano

Pinch ground cloves

Pinch ground aniseed

2 tablespoons olive oil

1 tablespoon pine kernels

2 tablespoons white wine

1 tablespoon plain flour

45 g (1½ oz) grated cheese, such as Manchego or semi-cured goats' milk cheese

Wash the onions and trim off the tops. Place the unpeeled onions in a pan with water to cover plus 1 teaspoon of the salt. Bring to the boil and cook for 10 minutes. Drain, saving the cooking liquid.

Remove and discard the skins. Trim the bottom root ends. When the onions are cool enough to handle, use a spoon to hollow out the centre of the onion, leaving about three outer layers intact. (Save the centres for another use.)

Meanwhile, combine the minced pork with the garlic, remaining salt, cinnamon, nutmeg, pepper, pimentón, oregano, cloves and aniseed. Let the meat marinate in the refrigerator for 1 hour.

Heat 1 tablespoon of the oil in a frying pan over low heat. Brown the marinated meat mixture, using a wooden spoon to break it up into small pieces, until the meat loses its pink colour, about 5 minutes. Stir in the pine kernels and the wine. Simmer for 5 minutes more.

Use a spoon to stuff the onion cavities with the meat mixture. Place the onions in a cazuela or casserole dish. Combine the flour with 240 ml (8 fl oz) of the reserved onion liquid and pour over the stuffed onions. Sprinkle them with the grated cheese.

Preheat oven to 180°C/350°F/gas mark 4.

Bake the onions, covered with aluminium foil, until very tender, about 45 minutes.

Serve hot.

SERVES 6 AS A STARTER OR SIDE DISH

Sizzling Sausages with Sherry

Salchichas al Jerez

This is a tasty dish for a tapa party, but I also like it served with greens alongside warm lentils for lunch. Spanish fresh pork sausage is flavoured with garlic and oregano, but any sweet pork link sausage can be used for this recipe.

450 g (1 lb) fresh pork link sausage
1½ teaspoons olive oil
5 tablespoons dry Sherry
Chopped fresh flat-leaf parsley

Use kitchen scissors to cut the links into 4-cm (1½-inch) pieces. Heat the oil in a frying pan over medium heat and brown the sausage pieces on all sides, about 5 minutes. Add the Sherry and cook over medium heat for 3 minutes.

Serve sprinkled with parsley. If the sausage pieces are to be served as a tapa, spear them with cocktail sticks.

Serves 10 to 12 as a tapa; serves 4 to 6 as part of a meal

Herb-Marinated Roasted Pork Loin
Lomo en Adobo, Asado con Hierbas

An *adobo* marinade traditionally was used for preserving uncooked meat or fish. It almost always contains vinegar, oregano, garlic and pimentón. A whole pork loin, submerged in its vinegar marinade, would keep for a week or two in cold weather. Then it could be sliced and fried in oil to make a quick and satisfying meal.

This recipe is an adaptation – the marinade is more of a rub for the meat, with only enough vinegar to give flavour, not preserve the meat.

I serve this roast pork loin, sliced and garnished with sprigs of fresh rosemary, thyme and bay, for a buffet supper, accompanied by Chard with Raisins and Pine Kernels (page 157) and Cauliflower, Mule-Driver's Style (page 149).

4 garlic cloves

1 tablespoon pimentón (if available, use part sweet, part bittersweet)

1 tablespoon dried oregano

½ teaspoon coarsely ground black pepper

Pinch dried thyme, or ½ teaspoon chopped fresh

Pinch dried rosemary, or ¼ teaspoon finely chopped fresh

1 teaspoon salt

1 tablespoon olive oil

120 ml (4 fl oz) Sherry vinegar or white wine vinegar

1.4 kg (3 lb) boned pork loin

Combine the garlic, pimentón, oregano, pepper, thyme, rosemary, salt, oil and vinegar in a blender and process until smooth. Place the meat in a nonreactive bowl and rub the marinade into it. Cover and refrigerate for 24 to 48 hours, turning the meat several times.

Preheat the oven to 180°C/350°F/gas mark 4. Drain the meat and place it in a roasting pan. If you are using a meat thermometer, insert it horizontally.

Roast the meat, uncovered, to an internal temperature of 74°C (165°F). It will take about 1 hour, depending on the thickness of the meat. If you are not using a thermometer, test the meat for doneness after 1 hour – cut into the centre of the piece of meat. The meat should be juicy and only slightly pink in the centre. If it is still red, roast for another 15 to 20 minutes.

Allow the meat to rest for 10 minutes before slicing and serving.

SERVES 8 TO 10

PORK LOIN STUFFED WITH FIGS AND BRANDY
LOMO DE CERDO RELLENO

This is the sort of dish reserved for special occasions – perhaps the *almuerzo* (luncheon) following a wedding or christening.

900 g (2 lb) boneless and rindless pork loin

Salt and freshly ground black pepper

2 slices bread, soaked in water for 15 minutes

60 g (2 oz) chopped ham

1 tablespoon chopped pork fat

5 tablespoons chopped fresh flat-leaf parsley

60 g (2 oz) chopped dry figs

1 tablespoon brandy

2 garlic cloves, finely chopped

⅛ teaspoon crumbled dried rosemary

3 tablespoons olive oil

1 small onion, chopped

1 carrot, sliced

240 ml (8 fl oz) dry Sherry

Open up the piece of meat by first making a lengthwise cut almost through it. Open like a book. Starting from the inside 'spine' of the book, slice horizontally to the left, through the middle of the left-hand 'pages', cutting completely through the tops and bottoms of the 'pages' but leaving the left end still connected, so that you've created another flap of meat which will fold out to your left, doubling the surface of the meat on which to lay your stuffing. Repeat on the right-hand side. Opened out, the meat should make a rectangle of four

sections, about 4 cm (1½ inches) thick. Sprinkle with salt and pepper.

Squeeze out the bread and mash it in a bowl. Add the ham, pork fat and parsley. Soak the figs in the brandy for 10 minutes. Add the figs to the ham mixture with the garlic, rosemary, ¼ teaspoon salt and freshly ground black pepper. Mix well.

Spread the stuffing mixture on the meat. Starting at the narrowest end, roll the meat up. Secure with a skewer, then tie it at intervals with butcher's string.

Heat the oil over medium-high heat in a pan large enough to hold the piece of meat. Brown the meat on all sides, 12 to 15 minutes, adding the onion and carrot when meat is nearly browned.

Add the Sherry and the same volume of water. Bring to the boil, then simmer, covered, until the meat is tender, about 1 hour.

Remove the meat to a chopping board and allow it to rest for 10 minutes before slicing crosswise. Skim the fat from the pan juices and purée the juices and cooked vegetables in a blender. Arrange the sliced meat on a platter and drizzle with some of the puréed sauce. Pass the remaining sauce at the table.

SERVES 6 TO 8

ROAST PORK SHOULDER
ASADO DE PUERCO

Accustomed to the titbit-sized tapas of Andalusia, I was amazed to discover the gargantuan portions of tapas in Galicia in the top northwest corner of Spain. At one tapa bar, a van pulled up at the kerb and a baker's boy got out carrying a huge tray, squeezing past us to deliver it to the bar. The tray held a whole leg of roast pork. The barman sliced the pork, layered some of it on a split bread roll, crossed it with strips of roasted peppers and then drizzled some of the meat juices over the top. He served us a free sample, which was very good indeed.

Serve this roast as an impressive centrepiece for a supper buffet. The pork must be marinated for 24 hours, so be sure to plan ahead.

3 tablespoons flat-leaf parsley

1 teaspoon fresh rosemary, chopped, or
    ¼ teaspoon dried and powdered

1 teaspoon fresh thyme, chopped, or
    ¼ teaspoon dried and crumbled

2 bay leaves

1 tablespoon dried oregano, crushed

8 garlic cloves

4 tablespoons olive oil

1 teaspoon salt, plus more if needed

½ teaspoon coarsely ground black pepper

1 bone-in pork shoulder (or leg)
    (about 2 kg/4–5 lb), trimmed of fat

240 ml (8 fl oz) dry Sherry or white wine

240 ml (8 fl oz) beef or chicken stock (see
    page 82)

2 teaspoons cornflour

Roasted peppers (optional)

Bread

ONE DAY BEFORE COOKING

Combine the parsley, rosemary, thyme, bay leaves and oregano in a food processor and process until finely chopped. Add the garlic and process. Then add the oil, 1 teaspoon salt and the pepper. Prick the meat all over with a skewer. Rub it on all sides with the herb-garlic mixture. Cover and marinate, refrigerated, for 24 hours.

Bring the meat to room temperature before roasting.

TO COOK

Preheat the oven to 230°C/450°F/gas mark 8.

Place the pork in a flameproof roasting pan. Roast for 20 minutes, then reduce the oven temperature to 180°C/350°F/gas mark 4 and continue roasting, allowing about 25 minutes per 450g (1 lb). Turn the meat occasionally and baste with any juices.

About 30 minutes before the meat is done, pour the Sherry over the meat.

When the meat is done (cooked to an internal-temperature reading of 145°F on an instant-read thermometer), remove to a platter. Allow it to rest for at least 15 minutes before carving. Add the stock to the pan with the juices and heat, stirring.

Mix the cornflour with 3 tablespoons of water, stir until smooth and whisk it into the pan. Stir over medium heat until the liquid thickens slightly.

To serve as a tapa, put slices of pork on bread, drizzle with a little of the sauce and top with roasted peppers, if using.

SERVES 25 TO 30 AS A TAPA; SERVES 10 TO 15 AS A MAIN COURSE

ORANGE-GLAZED PORK FILLETS
SOLOMILLOS DE CERDO EN SALSA DE NARANJAS

Serve this at a festive dinner party. Chard with Raisins and Pine Kernels (page 157) would be a good side dish. Cook pork chops in the same manner.

3–4 pork fillets (about 1.5 kg/3½ lb total)

3 tablespoons olive oil

1 small onion, finely chopped

3 garlic cloves, chopped

240 ml (8 fl oz) medium-dry Sherry (such as *oloroso seco***)**

240 ml (8 fl oz) orange juice

½ teaspoon dried thyme

½ teaspoon salt

Freshly ground black pepper

Orange slices, to garnish

In a frying pan large enough to hold the fillets, heat the oil over medium-high heat and brown the fillets on all sides, 8 to 10 minutes. Add the onion and garlic.

When the meat is well browned, add the Sherry, orange juice, thyme, salt and pepper. Cover the pan and simmer, turning the fillets once, until they are just cooked through, 15 to 20 minutes.

Remove the meat and keep warm. Turn up the heat and reduce the remaining sauce until it is thick and syrupy.

Slice the fillets, arrange on a serving plate garnished with orange slices and spoon over the sauce.

SERVES 8

HOME-STYLE PORK CHOPS IN LEMON MARINADE
CHULETAS A LA CASERA, CON ALIÑO

This is a favourite way to prepare pork chops at home. Tangy lemon juice complements the flavour of fresh pork. A heap of Spanish chips (page 162) is the perfect accompaniment.

In tapa bars, thin slices of pork loin are marinated in the same manner as these pork chops. They are fried very quickly on both sides and served on a slice of toasted baguette. These open-faced sandwiches are called *montaditos*, which translates roughly as 'up in the saddle'.

4 centre-cut pork loin chops, each 2 cm (¾ inch) thick (about 680 g/1½ lb)

1 teaspoon salt

2 garlic cloves, coarsely chopped

2 tablespoons chopped fresh flat-leaf parsley

Pinch dried thyme

¼ teaspoon pimentón

4 tablespoons fresh lemon juice

2 tablespoons olive oil

Sprinkle the chops with salt on both sides. Place them in a shallow dish and sprinkle with the garlic, parsley, thyme, pimentón and lemon juice. Set aside to marinate for 15 minutes. Turn the chops and marinate for another 15 minutes.

In a large frying pan, heat the oil over medium heat. Lift the chops out of the marinade and brown them for about 4 minutes on each side. They should be cooked through and slightly pink near the bone.

Pour any remaining marinade into the pan and raise the heat slightly. Cook for another 2 minutes until the chops are slightly glazed. Serve immediately, spooning pan sauce over the chops.

SERVES 4

PORK CHOP AND PASTA CASSEROLE
CAZUELA DE CERDO Y FIDEOS

This is a popular dish in Valencia, where it is called *fideuá*, the local lingo for *fideos*, a kind of vermicelli noodle. Despite the name, this recipe is most often made with tiny (12-mm/½-inch) elbows that have a pinhole through them. The pasta doubles in size during slow cooking. You could use spaghetti broken into 12-mm (½-inch) pieces. Meaty spare ribs, cut into pieces, may be used in place of the pork chops. This casserole needs only a salad to make a full meal.

4–6 pork chops (about 680 g/1½ lb)

Salt and freshly ground black pepper

3 tablespoons olive oil

2 onions, chopped

1 green sweet pepper, cut into 2.5-cm (1-inch) pieces

3 garlic cloves, chopped

Crushed red chilli flakes

2 tomatoes, peeled, de-seeded and chopped (about 340 g/12 oz)

2 teaspoons pimentón

¼ teaspoon dried thyme, crumbled

115 g (4 oz) shelled green peas, frozen or fresh

2 bay leaves

340 g (12 oz) vermicelli or spaghetti, broken into 12-mm (½-inch) pieces

Season the chops with salt and black pepper. Heat the oil in a 30-cm (12-inch) cazuela or flameproof casserole over medium-high heat. Brown the chops on both sides, 5 to 6 minutes, and remove them, reserving the oil in the cazuela.

Add the onions, pepper and garlic to the cazuela and sauté until the onions begin to brown. Add the red chilli flakes and tomatoes and continue cooking until the tomatoes are reduced, about 15 minutes.

In a small bowl, stir the pimentón into 4 tablespoons water until smooth. Add to the cazuela with 1 litre (about 2 pints) water, the thyme, peas, bay leaves and ½ teaspoon salt. Return the pork chops to the cazuela.

Cook over high heat until the liquid is boiling. Stir in the pasta and continue to cook over high heat for 5 minutes. Reduce the heat to medium-low and cook for 20 minutes more. Don't stir after the first 10 minutes of cooking. The pork and pasta should be very tender. Some liquid will remain, so the pasta is 'juicy', but not soupy.

Let the casserole rest for 5 to 10 minutes before serving.

SERVES 4 TO 6

TRIPE STEW FOR ST ANTHONY'S DAY

POTAJE DE CALLOS DE SAN ANTÓN

A few miles outside the village where I live there is a small shrine in the countryside dedicated to San Antón Abad, St Anthony Abbot, the patron saint of pigs and other farm animals. The saint's special day falls in mid-January. When the weather is fine, locals make a day's pilgrimage, or *romería*, to the chapel, to attend a late morning mass, then picnic on the rocks of the bluff that overlooks the coast. In bygone times it was an occasion for the blessing of farm stock. Now, in some locales, people bring their household pets to receive the priest's benediction.

It's customary to raffle off a baby pig during the San Antón festivities. One year, when nobody claimed the prize, the local brotherhood that maintains the shrine raised up the pig themselves. The following year, they cooked up all the parts of the pig – tripe, ears, trotters, tail and fat – in this traditional stew that is always served on *el dia de San Antón*.

I have omitted the ear, trotter and tail from this preparation. These days, you should be able to find ready-to-cook tripe at your butcher's. However, if you are starting from scratch, scrub the tripe under running water. Put it in a basin with water to cover with 2 tablespoons of salt and 4 tablespoons of vinegar. Let it soak for 2 hours, then drain the tripe and wash again in running water. Bring a large pan of water to the boil, add the tripe and bring the water to the boil again. Boil for 5 minutes and drain. Bring a large pan of fresh salted water to the boil. Add the tripe and bring again to the boil. Reduce heat to a simmer and cook for 1 hour. Drain, saving the liquid. Use the cooking liquid in place of water in the following recipe.

450 g (1 lb) cooked pig's tripe, cut into 2.5-cm (1-inch) squares

450 g (1 lb) fresh pancetta or lean pork belly, cut into 12-mm (½-inch) dice

450 g (1 lb) chickpeas, soaked overnight and drained

1 whole head garlic, roasted and peeled (see page 8)

3 bay leaves

2 sprigs parsley

1 teaspoon crushed red chilli flakes

1 onion, coarsely chopped

1 tomato, quartered

¼ teaspoon freshly ground black pepper

¼ teaspoon ground cloves

1½ teaspoons pimentón

Pinch saffron threads, crushed

1½ teaspoons salt

¼ teaspoon ground cumin

2 garlic cloves, crushed

115 g (4 oz) chorizo sausage

230 g (8 oz) morcilla (blood) sausage, black pudding or pork sausages

Combine the tripe and pancetta in a large deep pan with fresh water to cover. Bring to the boil and skim off any foam. Add the chickpeas, roasted garlic, bay leaves, parsley, chilli flakes, onion and tomato. Bring again to the boil. Cover and simmer for 1 hour.

Combine the pepper, cloves, pimentón, saffron, salt, cumin and crushed garlic in a small bowl. Add some of the liquid from the cooking pan and stir to dissolve. Stir the spices into the pan. Cook slowly for 1 hour more. If necessary, add additional boiling water to keep the stew a little soupy.

Add the chorizo and morcilla. Cook for 30 minutes longer. Remove the links of chorizo and morcilla from the stew. Use scissors to cut the sausages into small pieces, then return the pieces to the pan.

Let the stew rest for 10 minutes before serving. (The stew can be prepared in advance and reheated.)

SERVES 6 TO 8 AS A MAIN DISH; SERVES 16 AS A TAPA

ADOBO-MARINATED SPARE RIBS
COSTILLAS DE CERDO EN ADOBO

These marinated ribs are pan-cooked, but you can also cook them on the barbecue, using a griddle with a domed lid. Place the rack of ribs in the centre of the griddle, with coals banked on either side of the griddle. Don't place the ribs directly over the coals, because the pimentón in the marinade will burn. Cover the griddle and roast the ribs, turning occasionally, until they are done (about 45 minutes). Then position them over direct heat just until nicely browned on both sides.

Serve these ribs with baked potatoes and with a side dish of Cauliflower Salad with Lemon Dressing (page 140).

1.2 kg (2¾ lb) meaty spare ribs

3 garlic cloves

4 tablespoons white wine vinegar

1 tablespoon chopped fresh flat-leaf parsley

1 teaspoon dried oregano, crumbled

¼ teaspoon chopped fresh rosemary

1 tablespoon sweet pimentón

1 teaspoon hot pimentón

1 teaspoon salt

Freshly ground black pepper

2 tablespoons olive oil

120 ml (4 fl oz) dry Sherry

Split the slab of ribs in half across the bones. Then cut them into two-rib pieces, about 8 cm (3 inches) across. (If the ribs are to be barbecued, they can be left in a large slab.)

In a blender, combine the garlic, vinegar, parsley, oregano, rosemary, both kinds of pimentón, salt, pepper and 1 tablespoon water. Blend until smooth.

Rub the pieces of rib with the spice mixture. Place them in a nonreactive container, cover, and marinate, refrigerated, for at least 6 hours or up to 24 hours.

Heat the oil in a deep pan or large frying pan over medium heat. Add the ribs and brown them on both sides, 8 to 10 minutes, taking care that they don't burn.

Stir 240 ml (8 fl oz) water into any remaining marinade and pour it into the pan along with the Sherry. Cover and simmer over medium-low heat, turning occasionally, until the ribs are tender and most of the liquid has cooked away, about 30 minutes.

Serve hot.

SERVES 4

PORK HOCKS WITH GREENS
LACÓN CON GRELOS

From one end of the country to the other, pork – and its by-products, ham and sausages – is the favoured meat. Sometimes it turns up in unexpected places, for instance, the Jewish quarter of the Galician town of Ribadavia.

In medieval days, Ribadavia was an important wine-trading centre and grew to have an important Jewish community. After Spain's unification and the order of expulsion against the Jews, many converted to Christianity, thus preserving their positions of high rank. Converts ate pork – forbidden by Jewish dietary laws – to prove their Christianity.

The *barrio judío* (Jewish quarter), which makes up the centre of Ribadavia, preserves much of its medieval character, with buildings of granite blocks and thick pillars supporting heavy balconies and arcaded façades. Under the balconies or arcades, craftsmen – shoemakers, tailors, weavers, silversmiths – could carry on their work out-of-doors, protected from rain.

Strolling through the quarter, I came upon a butcher's shop, Carnecería La Hebraica, under the sign of the Jewish six-pointed star. The butcher was standing in the doorway and greeted us with a smile.

I asked him if he had kosher meat – that is, meat prepared according to Jewish dietary laws. It seemed that a butcher with a Hebrew name, with the Jewish star on his signboard, might have some.

'No, no,' he said. 'No demand for it in Ribadavia these days. But I know what it is – I used to work on cruise ships, and we always had Jewish people who ate kosher food.'

We walked into the Hebraica shop – he had several kinds of ham, cured pork shoulder, every cut of fresh pork, pigs' ears, snouts, tails, ribs. Everything but the squeal. As far as I could tell, no joke was intended. The shop's name was inspired only by its location in the Jewish quarter.

This Galician dish is made with *lacón*, salt-cured pork hocks. The *lacón* is soaked for 24 hours to remove some of the salt, then boiled. Fresh pork or cooked ham can be substituted. The most typical greens are *grelos*, the stems and leaves of a type of turnip. Cabbage or chard can be substituted.

1.8 kg (4 lb) pork hocks or ham on the
   bone

1 slice onion

1 bay leaf

Salt

1.4 kg (3 lb) greens, washed and chopped

450 g (1 lb) chorizo sausage

900 g (2 lb) medium potatoes, peeled

Freshly ground black pepper

Combine the meat in a large saucepan with the
onion, bay leaf and water to cover. If you are not
using salt-cured meat, add salt to the water.
Bring to the boil, skim off any foam, then
simmer for 2 hours.

Add the chopped greens and simmer for
30 minutes more. Then add the chorizo and
potatoes. Cook until the potatoes are tender,
about 25 minutes more.

Serve the sliced pork, greens, sausages and
potatoes on a platter. If desired, the stock can
be served as a first course, with the addition of
soup noodles. Or use it to make Galician Soup
with Beans and Greens (page 101).

SERVES 6 TO 8

LAMB AND KID

Some of the best meat dishes in Spain are made with lamb or kid. In spite of this, I have included only a few recipes for its preparation. That's because most lamb (and kid) dishes in Spain are prepared with tiny, baby lamb, not spring lamb. Baby lamb and kid are very pale in colour and have almost no fat. They are roasted in big bread ovens, in the Castillian style, or slowly braised in shepherds' stews.

Unfortunately, baby lamb and kid are not easily found in British butchers' shops. These dishes, in my opinion, do not translate if made with spring lamb. I love spring lamb roasted medium, still pink. But when it is cooked in a slow braise, it just becomes lamb stew, lacking the pale and delicate texture of baby lamb. You will find my very favourite recipe for baby kid, baked in a deep casserole, made with chicken (see page 241).

Baby lamb should be milk-fed, between 4 and 7 weeks old, and weigh, after butchering and dressing-out, from about 5.5 to 7 kg (12–15 lb). Spring lamb, which has begun to graze, can be anywhere from 4 months to 1 year old. The meat is pink to red and has a layer of fat.

Besides lamb roasts and braises using the leg and shoulder, many traditional dishes make use of other parts of the lamb. Roasted lamb's head is a much-appreciated dish. Tails, ribs, shanks, feet, livers, testicles and tripe are also popular. In some Madrid tapa bars, you can order *zarajos*, a La Mancha speciality of marinated lamb's tripe, wrapped around grapevine twigs and roasted. I enjoy eating these preparations in bars and restaurants, but I rarely cook them in my kitchen. Therefore, I have not included recipes for their preparation.

What do shepherds eat? Don Quixote and Sancho share a meal with goatherds on one of their first forays. The meal consists of stewed goat, dry acorns, hard cheese and wine from a wineskin.

Shepherds who are out in the hills for many days at a time depend on small game, sometimes brought down with a slingshot. Rabbit, partridge and sausage might all be cooked together in a cauldron and, in the case of one such stew, served on top of flat unleavened bread, which in former times was baked on a hot stone (see Hunters' Stew, page 297).

Migas, a savoury concoction of breadcrumbs fried with garlic (see page 61), is also shepherds' fare. Cured meats – sausages, ham and beef jerky (*cecina*) – which need no refrigeration, and, of course, cheese, are also part of the shepherds' stores.

SHEPHERDS'-STYLE LAMB
CORDERO AL PASTOR

When new lambs are born, the flock is culled of baby males (which are of no use for milk). In older times, the shepherds might use the baby lamb in this *caldereta*. The meat of the suckling lamb is cut into small pieces, bones and all.

If you are using spring lamb, which is larger, use boneless meat from the shoulder or leg, cut up as for stew.

5 peppercorns

1 clove

3 garlic cloves

Salt

1 teaspoon pimentón

2 tablespoons white wine vinegar

4 tablespoons dry white wine

1–1.4 kg (2¼–3 lb) baby lamb, cut into small pieces, or about 800 g (1¾ lb) boneless lamb, cut into 5-cm (2-inch) cubes

4 tablespoons olive oil

1 tablespoon plain flour

Sprig fresh thyme or pinch dried

Sprig fresh rosemary or pinch dried

1 bay leaf

Sprig fresh mint

3 sprigs parsley

680 g (1½ lb) small potatoes, peeled

240 ml (8 fl oz) milk

Freshly ground black pepper

Chopped fresh flat-leaf parsley

The day before cooking, in a mortar, combine the peppercorns, clove, garlic and ½ teaspoon salt, and crush. Mix with the pimentón, vinegar and wine, and rub the meat with this mixture. Marinate overnight, covered and refrigerated.

Pour the oil into a flameproof casserole or cazuela and heat it over medium-high heat. Turn the meat in the oil, just to seal it, without letting it brown, about 2 minutes. Stir in the flour and blend well, then add the herbs and 450 ml (¾ pint) water. Add the potatoes. Cover and simmer until the liquid is reduced, about 1 hour.

Add the milk, salt and pepper to taste, and cook until the sauce is smooth, about 15 minutes more.

Serve sprinkled with chopped parsley.

SERVES 6

LAMB STEW WITH ARTICHOKES AND MINT
CALDERETA DE CORDERO

Every year a picture appears in the newspapers of flocks of sheep being driven through the Puerta del Sol in the centre of Madrid. In times past, when the wool of Merino sheep was a source of wealth, the Mesta, a sheep owners' guild, controlled migratory routes. Vast herds of sheep were moved from northern Spain to southwestern Spain and back again, with the change of seasons, in the *trashumancia* (transhumance) from summer to winter pastures. The routes guaranteeing access for migrating herds are protected by royal decree. With the decline in the wool business, fewer herds cross the country, and most of them are transported by lorry or train. In fact, many of the routes have been closed off by fences – or paved over as national highways.

This shepherds' stew appears in the cooking from the northern regions of Aragon, Navarre and La Rioja to the southern regions of Andalusia and Extremadura, at both extremes of the migratory routes.

The shepherd in the field has no fresh vegetables, but he may add wild artichokes, wild thistles and herbs.

As baby lamb is not widely available, I have adapted this dish to use chunks of boneless spring lamb, preferably cut from the shoulder or leg. This recipe makes a stew with a lot of thick gravy, so serve it with a spoon. If you don't want to use lamb's liver to thicken and flavour the sauce, add 2 tablespoons of flour instead.

900 g (2 lb) boneless lamb, cut from leg
    or shoulder

5 tablespoons olive oil

1 slice bread, crust removed

3 garlic cloves

230 g (8 oz) lamb's liver, cut into 4 pieces

1 onion, chopped

1 teaspoon salt

¼ teaspoon dried thyme

Freshly ground black pepper

2 globe artichokes, quartered, or 115 g
    (4 oz) tinned or bottled artichoke
    hearts

240 ml (8 fl oz) white wine

1 teaspoon pimentón

450 g (1 lb) potatoes, peeled and cut into
    chunks

Chopped fresh mint

Cut the meat into chunks. They don't have to be of equal size.

In a flameproof casserole, heat half of the oil over medium-high heat. Add the bread, 2 cloves of the garlic and the liver, and brown, about 4 minutes. Remove with a slotted spoon, transfer to a plate and set aside.

Add the remaining oil to the pan and heat over medium heat. Add the lamb and sauté, turning the meat a few times. Add the onion. Continue turning the meat over medium heat for 5 minutes. It needn't be browned. Add the salt, thyme, pepper, artichokes and the wine. (If you are using tinned or bottled artichoke hearts, add them later, with the potatoes.)

In a blender, combine the fried bread, fried garlic, pieces of liver, the remaining clove of raw garlic and pimentón with 240 ml (8 fl oz) of water. Blend to make a smooth paste. Stir into the meat with another 240 ml (8 fl oz) water.

Simmer the stew for 30 minutes. Then add the potatoes (and tinned or bottled artichoke hearts, if using). Simmer for 20 minutes more, until the meat and potatoes are tender.

Serve sprinkled with mint.

SERVES 4 TO 6

Moorish Lamb Stew with Prunes
Cordero con Ciruelas Pasas

This dish, with Moorish or Sephardic roots, is also prepared with beef or chicken. I like to serve the stew with plenty of rice to soak up the flavourful sauce.

If you don't have sweet wine, substitute a tablespoonful of honey. Rosemary or thyme honey adds a subtle herbal flavour.

900 g (2 lb) boneless lamb, cut into 4-cm (1½-inch) cubes

Salt and freshly ground black pepper

4 tablespoons fresh lemon juice

3 tablespoons olive oil

1 onion, chopped

2 garlic cloves, chopped

2.5-cm (1-inch) piece of lemon zest, finely chopped

Pinch ground cloves

⅛ teaspoon ground cinnamon

¼ teaspoon saffron threads, crushed

4 tablespoons sweet wine, such as Málaga muscatel

130 g (4½ oz) pitted prunes

In a bowl, season the lamb with salt and pepper, then pour in the lemon juice. Marinate the meat for a few hours or overnight, refrigerated, turning it occasionally.

Heat the oil in a cazuela or deep frying pan over medium heat. Sauté the onion and garlic until the onion is lightly browned, 5 minutes. Drain the meat and pat it dry, reserving the marinade. Add the meat to the pan and brown it for a few minutes.

Add the lemon zest, cloves and cinnamon. Dissolve the saffron in a spoonful of water and add to the pan with the remaining marinade, 120 ml (4 fl oz) water and the wine. Cover and simmer for 45 minutes.

If prunes are very dry, plump them in a little wine or water while the meat is cooking. Drain. Add the prunes to the pan and cook for 15 minutes, or until the meat is very tender.

Serve hot.

SERVES 4

Slow-Braised Lamb Chops with Sherry
Chuletas de Cordero al Jerez

I like to make this slow-braised dish with meaty 'chops' cut from the leg. It's also a good way to cook lamb shanks or neck. Double-Mashed Potatoes (page 163) would be good served with the lamb chops.

2 tablespoons olive oil

1 kg (2¼ lb) lamb chops

1 onion, chopped

1 carrot, diced

1 garlic clove, chopped

240 ml (8 fl oz) dry Sherry

⅛ teaspoon ground cloves

2 bay leaves

¼ teaspoon salt

Freshly ground black pepper

Heat the oil in a large frying pan over high heat and brown the chops on both sides, about 6 minutes. Transfer them to a large saucepan.

Sauté the onion, carrot and garlic in the fat remaining in the frying pan over medium heat for 5 minutes. Add them to the saucepan with the lamb chops. Stir in the Sherry, cloves, bay leaves, salt, pepper and 170 ml (6 fl oz) of water. Cover and simmer until the lamb is very tender, about 45 minutes.

Remove the lamb chops and cover to keep warm. Remove and discard bay leaves. Place the vegetables and liquid in a blender and purée to make a smooth sauce. Return the sauce and the lamb chops to the saucepan until both are heated through.

Serve hot.

Serves 4

TENDER LAMB CHOPS SAUTÉED WITH GARLIC
CABRITO AL AJO CABAÑIL

Although it may seem strange to take up skiing in southern Spain, in fact the high mountains of the Sierra Nevada, visible from the city of Granada, have Europe's southernmost ski resort. I used to spend a few days there every winter, enjoying the drive up with a stop for lunch at one of the many roadside *ventas*. All of them featured a local speciality – baby kid fried up with lots of garlic.

As neither baby kid nor baby lamb is easy to find in Britain, I've created a variation of the dish using lamb chops. Make sure they are well trimmed of excess fat. You really only need the nugget of tender meat.

3 tablespoons olive oil

1 kg (2¼ lb) lamb chops, trimmed of all fat

1 tablespoon pimentón

2 slices bread, crusts removed

240 ml (8 fl oz) white wine

4 garlic cloves

½ teaspoon ground cumin

1 teaspoon dried oregano, crumbled

Salt and freshly ground black pepper

Heat the oil in a frying pan over high heat and quickly fry the lamb chops until browned on both sides, about 6 minutes. Remove the pan from heat. Drain off the excess fat. Stir the pimentón into the pan.

Combine the bread, wine, garlic, cumin and oregano in a blender. Allow the bread to soften for 5 minutes, then process until smooth. Pour this mixture into the frying pan with the lamb chops. Add 240 ml (8 fl oz) water and salt and pepper. Bring to the boil, then simmer the lamb chops for 10 minutes.

Serve hot.

SERVES 4

BEEF

One of the most quintessential Spanish experiences I have had was spending a day on a ranch where fighting bulls were raised for the *corrida* (the bullfight). I was writing a magazine article about one of Spain's first female bullfighters. Mari, the *torera*, who has now long since retired from the bullring, invited me to come along to the ranch where bulls for an upcoming bullfight were to be selected.

The ranch owner, José, himself a former bullfighter, raised the special breed of *toro bravo* (brave fighting bull), magnificent animals destined for the bullring. His ranch in southwestern Spain comprised acres of scrubby hills cut by ravines. A strong wind soughed through the cork trees and clouds of dust filtered the brilliant sunshine. After the spring rains, wildflowers bloomed everywhere and the pastures were green with new grass. Many of the cows had calves at their sides and tiny baby pigs ran underfoot.

We had breakfast in the low-ceilinged kitchen of the whitewashed *cortijo* (country house). As with many Andalusian country houses, the kitchen was in a separate building, across the walled courtyard from the main house. The enclosed courtyard had a gate tall enough and wide enough for a carriage with three pairs of horses to drive through.

After a country breakfast of boiled coffee with milk, *migas* (breadcrumbs crisped in oil, see page 61) and a *copa* (glass) of anise brandy,

the group returned to the bulls. *Vaqueros* on horseback herded the bulls into corrals. After sorting and selecting, three bulls were chosen and loaded on to a waiting truck. The remaining herd, which included everything from yearlings – tiny creatures not long separated from their mothers – to a massive, black stud bull, was escorted back to the fields.

Then young cows were herded in. From these, several were selected to be tested for their 'bravery', the fierce instinct to charge that distinguishes this breed. Mari and José took turns working with them, passing them with the big, colourful capes and the smaller red *muleta*, then sighting along a make-believe sword and thrusting the sword-hand down along the animal's back as the horns passed by. The cows that charged would be saved for breeding bulls for the bullfight. Otherwise, they became like any other beef cattle, raised for meat.

Another day, two hours before the trumpets would announce the beginning of the bullfight, I joined Mari in the hotel room where she was dressing for the *corrida*. A woman friend – a *bruja* (witch) – arrived to do Mari's hair and mutter a few incantations for good luck. This witch was a plump and friendly sort who had a pouch of herbal potions. She gave Mari some juniper berries to chew for a nervous stomach while she waited for Manolo, her sword handler, who would help her dress.

When Manolo arrived, Mari first pulled on white tights, then bright pink stockings, a heavy white shirt and high-waisted trousers encrusted in embroidery. Manolo helped her with the braces, tie and waistband and hooked the tiny buttons up the legs. She put on the short jacket, and he held her by the seams and gave her a stiff, hard shake to settle her body into the tight-fitting suit.

Her thick, long curls were plaited and the plait twisted into a bun above the nape of her neck. The triangular hat was set flatly above. She was ready. It was time to go.

WHERE'S THE BEEF?

Although bullfighting has a long legacy in Spain's culture, raising beef cattle for eating does not. The reason is that much of the land is too arid to provide good pasturage. Only in Spain's green north and parts of central Castile were cattle traditionally raised, both for meat and dairy. For this reason, there are fewer recipes for beef than for pork and lamb. Most of the beef recipes I learned were for slow-braised dishes, for the tougher and more economical cuts.

Cattle were slaughtered young because it wasn't profitable to feed them longer. Called *ternera*, meaning veal, the meat was usually yearling beef, having neither the succulence of baby veal nor the juicy, red-meat flavour of a full-grown steer.

Today, modern feeds have made the raising of fine beef cattle possible in every area of the country. In fact, the best steak I've ever eaten in my life was in – not Chicago or Kansas City – but Madrid, in a Basque restaurant serving Galician beef. It was a *chuletón*, a massive rib 'chop', grilled over a wood fire, then carved off the bone.

BRAISED OXTAILS
RABO DE TORO

Bullfighting is not a 'fight' in Spanish, but a *corrida* or 'bull run'. The newspaper reports of the previous day's *corrida* appear, not on the sports page, but on the culture page, with the reviews of books, ballet and paintings. The bullfighter is awarded 'trophies', not for 'winning', but for his display of artistry in the ring. One ear, two ears, then the tail are cut for the most profound perfomance. On great occasions, *se abre la puerta grande*, the *torero* is carried out on the shoulders of his fans through the main gates of the plaza. After it is all over, the bulls' carcasses are butchered to be sold. So rarely is the tail awarded to a *torero*, that usually it is part of the meat on sale. Of course, you don't need the tail of a bull to make this deeply satisfying braised dish. Oxtail from the butcher's is perfect. Accompany the meat with fried potatoes. A full-bodied red wine from Ribera del Duero would go nicely with the braised oxtail.

1 whole oxtail, cut crosswise into 8-cm (3-inch) segments

3 tablespoons olive oil

1 onion, chopped

1 leek, white part only, chopped

3 carrots, diced

2 garlic cloves, chopped

4 rashers bacon, chopped

5 tablespoons brandy

120 ml (4 fl oz) red wine

1 tomato, peeled, de-seeded and chopped

1 bay leaf

1 sprig parsley

1 sprig thyme

Salt and freshly ground black pepper

Crushed red chilli flakes

Pinch ground cloves

Chopped fresh flat-leaf parsley

Wash the oxtail very well, then blanch the pieces in boiling water for 5 minutes and drain.

In a large saucepan or flameproof casserole, heat the oil over medium heat and add the onion, leek, carrots, garlic and bacon. Sauté until the onion is soft, about 5 minutes.

Add the oxtail and brown over medium-high heat, about 8 minutes. Add the brandy, carefully set it alight and stir until the flames die down. Then add 120 ml (4 fl oz) of water, wine, tomato, bay leaf, parsley, thyme, salt, pepper, red chilli flakes and cloves. Cover and simmer until the meat is very tender, about 2 hours. Add additional water or wine as needed. The sauce should be fairly reduced. (This can be made in advance, refrigerated, skimmed of fat and reheated before serving.)

Remove the bay leaf. Serve sprinkled with chopped parsley.

SERVES 4

BULL'S TESTICLES
CRIADILLAS

The testicles of the *toro bravo* (brave fighting bull) killed in the *plaza de toros* are especially prized, because they are said to confer the essence of *machismo*. But, in fact, in Spain, this offal can be found in ordinary butcher's shops, of ordinary young beef cattle. When I take my cooking students on a market tour, we usually find *criadillas* in the butchers' stalls. I tell them eating *criadillas* is really a lot like eating brains.

However, as you probably will not find this item in your local supermarket, I suggest trying this recipe with calves' sweetbreads or brains.

1 pair *criadillas* (about 450 g/1 lb) or
    450 g (1 lb) sweetbreads

2 teaspoons white wine vinegar

1 teaspoon salt

1 slice onion

1 bay leaf

1 egg, beaten with 1 teaspoon water

60 g (2 oz) fine dry breadcrumbs

½ teaspoon salt

Pinch ground cayenne pepper

Pinch dried thyme

Olive oil

Lemon wedges, to serve

Have the butcher remove the membrane from the *criadillas*.

Bring a pan of water to the boil with the vinegar, salt, onion and bay leaf. Add the *criadillas* and simmer for 10 minutes. Remove and pat dry. The *criadillas* will not be cooked through. Slice them 6 mm (¼ inch) thick.

Put the beaten egg in a shallow dish. Combine the breadcrumbs, salt, cayenne and thyme in another. Dip the slices first in egg, then in breadcrumbs.

Heat enough oil in a heavy frying pan to cover the bottom to a depth of 6 mm (¼ inch). Fry the slices over medium-high heat until they are well browned and crisp on both sides.

Serve hot with lemon wedges.

SERVES 6 AS A TAPA; SERVES 2 AS A MAIN COURSE

Andalusian Beef Stew

Estofado de Buey a la Andaluza

This tasty preparation with tomato and green pepper works well with pot roast or whole beef tongue, as well as stewing beef. Served with crusty bread and a hearty red wine, it is a complete meal. This stew is somewhat soupy, as the cooking liquid is not thickened, so serve it in soup plates.

900 g (2 lb) stewing beef, cut into 2.5-cm (1-inch) cubes

1 green sweet pepper, cut into strips

1 onion, sliced

230 g (8 oz) chopped tomato

2 tablespoons olive oil

120 ml (4 fl oz) dry Sherry

2 bay leaves

Pinch cloves

¼ teaspoon ground cinnamon

Pinch saffron threads, crushed (optional)

1 teaspoon salt

1 whole head garlic, roasted and peeled (see page 8)

2 carrots, sliced

2 large potatoes, peeled and diced

In a flameproof casserole, combine the beef, green pepper, onion, tomato, oil, Sherry and 240 ml (8 fl oz) of water. Bring to the boil and add the bay leaves, cloves, cinnamon, saffron, if using, and salt. Add roasted garlic. Cover and simmer very slowly until the meat is almost tender, about 1 hour.

Add the sliced carrots and the potatoes. Cover and simmer for another 30 minutes, adding more water if necessary, until the meat and potatoes are very tender.

Remove the bay leaves. Serve in soup plates.

SERVES 4 TO 6

11

GAME

Partridge Stuffed with Pork and Spices
(*Perdiz Rellena*)

Quail Simmered with Fresh-Podded Beans
(*Codornices con Pochas*)

Quail in a Sherry Vinegar Marinade
(*Codornices en Escabeche*)

Pasta with Rabbit and White Beans
(*Gurullos con Conejo*)

Rabbit in Almond Sauce
(*Conejo en Salsa de Almendras*)

Rabbit Cooked with Herbs in the Sierra Style
(*Conejo a la Serrana*)

Hare Stew with Pasta (*Liebre con Andrajos*)

Hunters' Stew (*Gazpachos de Cazadores*)

A Partridge for Six

Below my house, in the *arroyo* where wild oleanders bloom, I can hear the chuckling sounds of wild partridges. Higher up I hear the cooing of turtledoves nesting in the tall canebrake. Rabbits zip about through the stubble of weeds on the hills. Occasionally I glimpse wild mountain goats that inhabit the higher sierras. Every autumn, with the opening of the hunting season for small game, I worry that the following spring my small game preserve will be bereft of these creatures. So far, however, I have been lucky.

Many years ago, in this very same *arroyo*, Paco shot a partridge, which was cooked by Maria (the same Paco and Maria of the Bar Estéban in chapter 2) and eaten by six of us.

Paco set off from the village by scooter with my funny shaggy dog following close behind his big setter. My dog had never retrieved anything bigger than Champagne corks.

Paco had permission to shoot on a friend's *finca* (property), dry, rolling unirrigated lands cut by canyon-like *arroyos*. Paco, who knew the land and the birds, said he would put up the partridge at the bottom of the first *arroyo* beyond the big rocks. And he did. And he missed. He said he would find the same band in another *arroyo* where the nest was. My *arroyo*.

He hunted in that direction for another three hours and found the partridges right where he had predicted. He shot and got one. The setter, perhaps offended by another dog's presence, wouldn't retrieve.

He returned to the house with panting dogs. Paco removed the bird from the thong on his belt and handed it to me. A big, old male, tough to eat but beautiful to look at. He insisted I have the bird. I insisted it was his. We finally agreed that he would take it, but I would come to town later to help Maria prepare it and share the feast.

Maria cleaned and plucked the bird. She bought pork and ham and instructed me to chop them finely. Then she grated breadcrumbs into the meat, seasoned it with garlic, nutmeg and salt, and stuffed the partridge. It was browned in oil, then braised with Montilla wine (similar to dry Sherry) until very tender.

Meanwhile, she also bought pork steaks and made fried potatoes and an enormous salad.

When we sat down to supper – there were six of us – everyone had a tiny piece of the stuffed partridge as well as some pork, potatoes and salad. It was a very festive meal and we still like to tell about how six of us dined on one partridge.

Partridge Stuffed with Pork and Spices

Perdiz Rellena

This dish can be made with any small bird – poussin, chicken, squab. Partridge is darker fleshed, gamier and leaner than domestic fowl. Allow one bird weighing 450–680 g (1–1½ lb) per person as a main course. Split in half, each bird serves two as a starter.

Pumpkin Sauté (page 155) would enhance the autumnal flavour of the stuffed partridges, if you are serving them as a main course.

4 partridges (about 450 g/1 lb each)

Salt

2 tablespoons fresh lemon juice

450 g (1 lb) minced pork

85 g (3 oz) chopped lean bacon

1 garlic clove, finely chopped

45 g (1½ oz) grated fresh breadcrumbs

4 tablespoons chopped fresh flat-leaf
    parsley

Pinch dried oregano

Freshly grated nutmeg

Pinch ground cloves

Freshly ground black pepper

1 egg, beaten

4 tablespoons olive oil

240 ml (8 fl oz) dry Sherry or Montilla
    wine

1 bay leaf

1 carrot, sliced

½ onion, sliced

Clean the birds of all viscera. Wash them and pat dry. Rub the cavities with a little salt and 1 tablespoon of the lemon juice.

In a bowl, combine the minced pork, bacon, garlic, breadcrumbs, parsley, oregano, nutmeg, cloves, pepper and ½ teaspoon salt. Add the egg and mix well. Divide this mixture into four portions and stuff each partridge with it. Skewer the cavities closed. Use kitchen string to tie the legs and wings close to the body.

Heat the oil over medium-high heat in a cazuela or flameproof casserole large enough to hold the birds in one layer. Brown them in the oil slowly, turning so they brown on all sides, 6 to 8 minutes.

Add the Sherry, 450 ml (¾ pint) water, bay leaf, carrot and onion. Bring the liquid to the boil, then cover the cazuela and simmer the partridges, turning them occasionally, until fork-tender, about 1 hour.

Remove the skewers and string. If the partridges are to be served halved, serving 8, split them in the kitchen. Spoon a little of the cooking liquid over the partridges and serve the rest of the pan juices and vegetables separately.

Serves 8 as a starter; serves 4 as a main course

QUAIL SIMMERED WITH FRESH-PODDED BEANS
CODORNICES CON POCHAS

At the weekly farmers' market in the Basque town of Guernica, I met a man selling *pochas* (fresh-podded white beans). These are mature white beans still in their shells, before they have been dried. I asked to buy 230 g (8 oz), just to take home a tiny sample. He refused to sell them to me. He swore that his beans were so good that when I tasted them, I would kill myself for not having purchased more.

They were, indeed, remarkably good. Thankfully, I had purchased a sufficient quantity that suicide was not contemplated.

If shell beans are not available, use any dry white beans, or even black-eyed beans, soaked overnight. If possible, purchase quail that has been partly boned (breastbone and backbone removed).

A robust red wine from the La Rioja region goes well with this dish.

6 quail

450 g (1 lb) shelled fresh-podded beans (about 680 g/1½ lb unshelled)

2 bay leaves

3 pinches dried thyme

1 onion slice

3 tablespoons olive oil

30 g (1 oz) bacon, diced

½ onion, chopped

1 small carrot, chopped

½ green sweet pepper, chopped

4 garlic cloves, chopped

230 g (8 oz) chopped tomato

Coarse salt and freshly ground black pepper

240 ml (8 fl oz) white wine

Chopped fresh flat-leaf parsley

Mild pickled green chillies, to serve

Using a small, sharp knife, remove the boneless breast fillets and reserve them. Cut off the legs and split the remaining carcass.

In a medium saucepan, combine the beans with water to cover (about 900 ml/1½ pints). Add the bay leaves, 1 pinch of thyme and the onion slice. Bring to the boil, skim off any foam, then cover and simmer for 30 minutes. Add 120 ml (4 fl oz) cold water and continue to simmer. Fresh-podded beans should cook in less than an hour; dried beans may take up to 2 hours.

Heat 2 tablespoons of the oil in a frying pan over high heat. Sauté the quail legs and carcasses until browned, 8 to 10 minutes. Add the bacon, chopped onion, carrot, green pepper and garlic, and sauté until lightly browned. Add the tomato, salt and pepper, 1 pinch of the thyme, wine and 450 ml (¾ pint) water. Bring to the boil, then simmer for 45 minutes.

Remove the quail legs and reserve. Discard the carcasses. Add all of the remaining cooking liquid to the beans. Cook for another 30 minutes. Add the quail legs to the beans.

Shortly before serving, season the reserved quail breasts with the remaining 1 pinch of thyme, salt and freshly ground black pepper. Heat the remaining 1 tablespoon oil in a frying pan over medium-high heat and sauté the breasts for about 2 minutes on each side.

Serve the beans with the quail legs in deep plates and place a sautéed breast on top of each serving. Sprinkle with chopped parsley. Serve green chillies as a side dish to accompany the beans.

SERVES 6

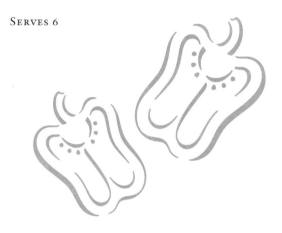

QUAIL IN A SHERRY VINEGAR MARINADE
CODORNICES EN ESCABECHE

Quail are farm-raised, so they are becoming more available in butchers' shops. They weigh about 140 g (5 oz) each, so you need to allow two or three per person.

Escabeche, a vinegar marinade, was once used to conserve game. With freezers now available to most hunters, this is no longer necessary. However, marinated birds (partridges are also prepared this way) are so tasty that this dish is still very popular. It is usually served at room temperature, garnished with lettuce.

5 tablespoons olive oil

12 quail

1 onion, cut into thin wedges

6 garlic cloves, slivered lengthwise

1 carrot, sliced

¼ teaspoon peppercorns

3 cloves

½ teaspoon dried thyme, crumbled

2 bay leaves

1 sprig parsley

450 ml (¾ pint) white wine

240 ml (8 fl oz) Sherry vinegar

1 teaspoon salt

Heat the oil in a frying pan over medium heat and brown the quail on all sides, 5 to 6 minutes. It may be necessary to do this in two batches. Remove them as they are browned and place them in a large saucepan.

In the oil remaining in the frying pan, sauté the onion, garlic and carrot over medium-high heat until the onion begins to brown, about 5 minutes. Pour the contents of the frying pan over the quail in the large saucepan.

Add the peppercorns, cloves, thyme, bay leaves, parsley, wine, vinegar, salt and 670 ml (1¼ pints) water to the quail. Bring to the boil, then simmer, uncovered, until the quail are tender, 20 to 25 minutes. Remove and discard bay leaves and parsley.

Allow the quail to cool. Pack them into a nonreactive bowl or wide-mouthed jar and pour the cooking liquid over them. Cover tightly and refrigerate for 48 hours.

Serve the quail at room temperature or reheated in their marinade. To serve as a tapa, quarter the quail and serve accompanied by paper napkins.

SERVES 4 AS A MAIN COURSE; SERVES 6 TO 12 AS A STARTER; SERVES 12 TO 24 AS A TAPA

PASTA WITH RABBIT AND WHITE BEANS
GURULLOS CON CONEJO

Made with wild rabbit or hare, this is a very good dish typical of Almería in eastern Andalusia. Farm-raised rabbit can be substituted, or even chicken or turkey.

The simple pasta is made by rolling thin ropes of dough, then twisting off short lengths. The pasta is not cooked separately, but added right to the stock. If you don't want to make the pasta, substitute shop-bought orzo.

An autumn salad, such as the Garlic Coleslaw with Pomegranate Seeds (page 139), is a good complement to the rabbit.

PASTA

140 g (5 oz) strong flour wheat

½ teaspoon salt

1 tablespoon olive oil

A few drops yellow food colouring (optional)

STEW

115 g (4 oz) white beans, such as cannellini beans, soaked overnight

4 tablespoons olive oil

4 garlic cloves

1 *ñora* (dried sweet red pepper), stem and seeds removed, or 2 teaspoons pimentón

1 rabbit (about 1 kg/2¼ lb), cut into serving pieces

1 onion, chopped

1 red sweet pepper, chopped

1 large tomato, peeled, de-seeded and chopped

120 ml (4 fl oz) dry Sherry

Salt and freshly ground black pepper

Pinch dried thyme

Pinch fennel seeds

To prepare the pasta, combine the flour and salt in a bowl or on a pastry board. Make a well in the centre and add the oil, 5 tablespoons water and some food colouring, if using. Mix the flour into the liquid until combined. Turn the dough out on to a lightly floured board and knead the dough until smooth and elastic, about 5 minutes. Cover it and let it rest for 1 hour at room temperature.

Take small balls of dough and roll them on a board into 3-mm (⅛-inch) thick ropes. Twist off 12-mm (½-inch) pieces (or cut the ropes into 12-mm/½-inch lengths). Spread on a clean cloth to dry until you are ready to cook them. The pasta can be thoroughly dried and stored or used fresh.

To make the stew, drain the soaked beans, place in a saucepan and add water to cover, bring to the boil, skim off any foam, cover and simmer until tender, 30 to 90 minutes, depending on beans. Drain and reserve the liquid.

While the beans are cooking, heat the oil in a cazuela or flameproof casserole over medium-high heat and fry the garlic and *ñora* (dried pepper), about 2 minutes. (If you are substituting pimentón, do not add it yet.) Remove the garlic and *ñora* from the cazuela and set aside.

In the same oil, brown the rabbit over medium-high heat, adding the chopped onion and red pepper. Then add the tomato, Sherry, 450 ml (¾ pint) water or reserved bean cooking liquid, salt and pepper, thyme and fennel seeds.

In a mortar with a pestle, grind together the fried garlic and *ñora* (or pimentón, if using) and add to the rabbit with the beans. Cover and cook over low heat until the meat is nearly tender, about 40 minutes. Add the pasta to the cazuela and cook until it is tender, about 5 minutes for freshly made pasta, or 8 to 10 minutes for dried pasta.

Serve in soup bowls.

SERVES 4

Rabbit in Almond Sauce
Conejo en Salsa de Almendras

Although this dish was originally made with wild rabbit, I prepare it with the farm-raised rabbit that my local butcher always has available. It is young and tender and cooks very quickly (and, it's worth knowing, is low in fat and cholesterol). If you are using a larger animal (wild or domestic rabbit, hare, squirrel or, even, chicken), you will need to allow a longer cooking time and additional liquid.

While there are many versions of this dish, I especially love this Catalan one, which has a mysterious touch of chocolate added to the basic ground almond mixture. The sauce traditionally would be slightly thickened with *galleta,* a not-too-sweet plain biscuit, or dry crumbs from sponge fingers. Digestive biscuits make an acceptable substitute.

1 rabbit (about 900 g/2 lb), cut into 6 to 8 pieces

Salt and freshly ground black pepper

4 tablespoons olive oil

30 g (1 oz) almonds, blanched and skinned (see page 6)

4 garlic cloves

1 onion, chopped

¼ teaspoon ground cinnamon

⅛ teaspoon ground cloves

¼ teaspoon freshly ground black pepper

1 teaspoon salt

1 tablespoon digestive biscuit crumbs or fine breadcrumbs

240 ml (8 fl oz) dry white wine

1 teaspoon unsweetened cocoa powder

Season the rabbit with salt and pepper. In a pan, heat the oil over medium-high heat and fry the almonds with 3 garlic cloves, about 2 minutes. When the almonds and garlic are golden, remove from the pan.

Combine the almonds, fried garlic, the remaining 1 clove of raw garlic, cinnamon, cloves, pepper, salt, crumbs and wine in a blender and process until smooth.

In the oil remaining in the pan, fry the rabbit over medium heat until browned on both sides, 5 to 10 minutes. Add the mixture from the blender. Simmer the rabbit for 15 minutes.

Stir the cocoa into 4 tablespoons water. Add to the rabbit. Simmer for another 20 minutes or until the rabbit is fork-tender.

Serve hot.

Serves 4

Rabbit Cooked with Herbs in the Sierra Style
Conejo a la Serrana

The sierra where wild rabbit and hare abound is perfumed with thyme and rosemary. These herbs are perfect for seasoning game dishes.

45 g (1½ oz) plain flour

¼ teaspoon coarsely ground black pepper

½ teaspoon salt

1 teaspoon crumbled oregano

¼ teaspoon crumbled dried thyme

Pinch chopped fresh rosemary

1 rabbit (about 900 g/2 lb), cut into 8 pieces

4 tablespoons olive oil

60 g (2 oz) bacon, diced

230 g (8 oz) mushrooms, preferably wild mushrooms, sliced

70 g (2½ oz) chopped onion

4 garlic cloves, chopped

2 tablespoons brandy

120 ml (4 fl oz) white wine

Combine the flour with the pepper, salt, oregano, thyme and rosemary. Dredge the rabbit in the flour, patting off the excess. Reserve 1½ teaspoons of the flour mixture.

Heat 3 tablespoons of the oil in a deep frying pan over medium-high heat and brown the rabbit on all sides, 6 to 8 minutes. Remove the pieces as they are browned.

Add the remaining 1 tablespoon oil to the pan. Add the bacon, mushrooms, onion and garlic and sauté over medium-high heat until the onions are softened, about 4 minutes.

Return the rabbit to the pan. Stir in the reserved flour mixture. Add the brandy, wine and 240 ml (8 fl oz) water. Stir to mix, then simmer, covered, until rabbit is very tender, about 45 minutes.

Serve hot.

Serves 4

HARE STEW WITH PASTA
LIEBRE CON ANDRAJOS

The meat of wild hare is much darker and richer than rabbit. My friend Antonia's brother hunts hare and freezes them, so I always know where I can obtain this unusual meat. For the hare you could substitute the dark meat of chicken or turkey.

Andrajos means 'rags' – tattered pieces of home-made pasta. Use lasagne noodles broken into irregular pieces.

1.4 kg (3 lb) hare, chicken or turkey pieces

½ onion

1 sprig parsley

1 sprig mint

1 sprig thyme

Salt and freshly ground black pepper

4 tablespoons olive oil

1 green sweet pepper, chopped

1 onion, chopped

4 garlic cloves, chopped

115 g (4 oz) mushrooms, sliced

230 g (8 oz) chopped tomato

½ teaspoon ground cumin

2 teaspoons pimentón

115 g (4 oz) lasagne noodles, broken into irregular pieces

1 tablespoon chopped fresh flat-leaf parsley or fresh mint

In a large saucepan, combine the hare, 1.8 litres (about 3 pints) water, ½ onion, parsley, mint, thyme, and salt and pepper. Bring to the boil, then cover and simmer until the meat is tender, about 1 hour. Strain and reserve the stock.

When the meat is cool enough to handle, remove and discard the skin and bones. In a cazuela or flameproof casserole, heat the oil over medium-high heat and sauté the pepper, chopped onion, garlic and mushrooms until the onion is soft, about 5 minutes.

Add the tomato and cook until reduced, about 15 minutes. Stir in the cumin, pimentón, and salt and pepper to taste. Add 900 ml (1½ pints) of the reserved stock, and the boned meat.

When the liquid is boiling, add the noodles. Continue to boil until they are tender, about 12 minutes.

Serve in soup bowls, garnished with chopped parsley.

SERVES 6

Hunters' Stew
Gazpachos de Cazadores

Hunters' stew is not a gazpacho in the same sense as Andalusian cold soup, but it does derive from the same root, as it contains pieces of bread. In this case, the bread is an unleavened one, once cooked on a hot stone on the campfire but now produced commercially. This bread, *torta ázima*, is virtually identical to unleavened Jewish matzoh, although the *torta* is baked in 40-cm (15-inch) rounds. The *torta* is broken into bits and added to the stew near the end of cooking time, making a sort of 'instant' pasta. You can use water biscuits in place of matzoh.

If game is not available, the dish can be made using domestic rabbit and the dark meat of chicken or turkey. A red wine from Valdepeñas or La Mancha would be a good match.

2–3 kg (4½–6½ lb) meat (rabbit, partridge, hare, chicken, turkey)

5 tablespoons olive oil

1 whole head garlic, cloves peeled

450 g (16 oz) peeled and chopped tomato, fresh or tinned

60 g (2 oz) salt pork or bacon, in one piece

4 tablespoons brandy (optional)

3 bay leaves

1 sprig fresh thyme, or ½ teaspoon dried

1 sprig fresh rosemary, or ¼ teaspoon dried

115 g (4 oz) sliced Portobello mushrooms (optional)

Salt and freshly ground black pepper

1 teaspoon pimentón

140 g (5 oz) water biscuits

Cut all of the meat into small pieces of similar size. Heat the oil in a deep frying pan over high heat and brown the meat a few pieces at a time, 5 to 10 minutes. When browned, transfer the pieces to a large deep saucepan.

Add the peeled garlic cloves to the oil in the frying pan and sauté them for a few minutes. Then add the tomatoes and cook until they release some of their juice. Stir the tomatoes and garlic into the saucepan with the meat. Add the salt pork, brandy, if using, and 2.25 litres (4 pints) of water. Add the bay leaves, thyme, rosemary, mushrooms, if using, salt and pepper and pimentón. Bring to the boil, then simmer slowly until the meats are very tender, about 1½ hours.

Strain the liquid into another large saucepan. When the meats are cool enough to handle, remove and discard the skin and bones. Cut the salt pork into pieces. Add the meat to the liquid in the saucepan, along with salt pork, bits of tomato, garlic and mushrooms.

Bring to the boil and add the water biscuits. Simmer for 15 minutes. Serve the meats, strained liquid and water biscuits in deep plates.

Serves 6 to 8

12

PUDDINGS
AND
SWEETS

CAKES, BISCUITS AND PIES

Sponge Cake (*Pan de Bizcocho*)

Drunken Cakes (*Borrachos*)

Sponge Biscuits (*Mostachones*)

Crisp Oil Biscuits (*Tortas de Aceite*)

'Bisquettes' (*Perrunillas*)

Cinnamon Christmas Cookies (*Mantecados*)

Wine-Scented Ring Biscuits (*Roscos de Vino*)

Nun's Sighs (*Suspiros de Monja*)

Almond Sugar Biscuits (*Almendrados*)

Almond Torte from Santiago de Compostela
    (*Torta de Almendras de Santiago*)

Grape Tarts (*Tortas de Uvas*)

'Gypsy's Arm' (Rolled Cake with Custard Filling)
    (*Brazo de Gitano*)

Custard Cream (*Cremadina*)

Pumpkin Bars (*Cortadillos de Cidra*)

DEEP-FRIED PASTRIES

Dough for Fried Pastries
    (*Masa para Empanadillas y Pestiños*)

Little Empanadas with Pumpkin Jam
    (*Empanadillas con Dulce de Calabaza*)

Fried Twists (*Pestiños*)

SWEETS AND CONFECTIONS

Fig and Almond Rolls (*Pan de Higos*)

Quince Sweet (*Dulce de Membrillo*)

Pumpkin Jam (*Dulce de Calabaza*)

Poached Fruits in Wine Syrup (*Arrope*)

Crunchy Caramel Almonds (*Garrapiñadas*)

Almond-Honey Nougat (*Alajú*)

Angel's Kisses (*Yemas*)

PUDDINGS

Rice Pudding with Cinnamon (*Arroz con Leche*)

Catalan Custards with Burnt Sugar Topping
    (*Crema Catalana*)

Rich Custard with Caramel (*Flan con Caramelo*)

Lemony Cheese Custard Squares (*Quesada*)

Sherry Jelly (*Gelatina de Vino de Jerez*)

FROZEN DESSERTS

Meringue Milk Ice (*Leche Merengada*)

Sweet Almond Milk (*Horchata*)

Almond Nougat Ice Cream
    (*Helado de Turrón de Jijona*)

Frozen Fig Terrine (*Tarta Helada de Higos*)

Chocolate Sauce (*Salsa de Chocolate*)

FIESTA SWEETS

Hot Chocolate (*Chocolate a la Taza*)

Doughnuts (*Buñuelos*)

HEAVENLY SWEETS

'*Bizcocho, hecho con huevos*' (sponge cake, made with eggs), said Paca, as she presented me with a going-away gift of heavenly sweet sponge cake. Indeed, her *bizcocho* was made with freshly laid eggs from the hens she kept on the back patio. In those days, she carried her eggs to a nearby *tienda* (a tiny food shop), weighed them and purchased the same weight of sugar (minus a tablespoon for the shells) and half their weight of flour. A very simple recipe.

It is a cake that is also made by nuns who sell their selection of sweets to the public. When I was collecting recipes from the Clarisa nuns of the Santa Isabel convent in Córdoba, I sampled this same sponge cake, plus *almendrados* (almond biscuits), *buñuelos* (doughnuts), *bollos* (buns) and *roscos* (rings).

I was fascinated to find every one of these recipes in Sephardic cookery books. The Sephardim were Spanish Jews who lived, more or less in harmony, with the Arabs, or Moors, who ruled much of Spain between the 8th and 15th centuries. Sephardic cooking, of course, was influenced by the Moors.

When King Ferdinand and Queen Isabella ordered the expulsion of the Jews in 1492 (the same Catholic monarchs who, in the same year, conquered the last Moorish kingdom of Granada and dispatched Columbus on his voyage), many chose to convert to Christianity rather than flee their homeland. These *conversos* (converts) continued to cook their traditional foods.

The Cordóban Clarisa nuns also have a convent in the nearby town of Lucena. Lucena in medieval times was an all-Jewish town. It looks to me like a straight line of descent from medieval Arabic and Sephardic delicacies – those sponge cakes, almond biscuits and many other sweets in the Spanish repertoire – which have been preserved by nuns. Many are named for 'heavenly' delights – angel's hair, heavenly bacon, nun's sighs, saints' bones, glorias.

Many of Spain's best-loved sweets and pastries still are made in convents and sold to the public. Where the nuns are cloistered, meaning they don't have contact with the outside world, you place your order through a *torno* (a revolving window). A voice on the other side of the wall asks you what you want. The turnstile turns and the package, prettily wrapped, is delivered. You place your money in the turnstile and it turns back.

Fried sweets are another category of treats. At Christmastime, instead of a holiday 'bake-up', several women get together for a 'fry-up', producing heaps of sugary, anise-flavoured rings, little turnovers filled with pumpkin jam and fritters bathed in honey.

Usually these biscuits, cakes and pastries are not served as dessert. In Spanish homes, dessert is usually fresh fruit in season. The sweets, so beloved by all, are served on fiesta days, or any day, with mid-morning coffee, afternoon tea, and any time a friend comes visiting.

CAKES, BISCUITS AND PIES

SPONGE CAKE
PAN DE BIZCOCHO

This same recipe appears in Sephardic (Spanish Jewish) cookery books, where it is called *pan de España*, or Spanish cake.

Today bakeries make *bizcocho* with fewer eggs and added shortening. Many recipes call for baking powder. But here is the original sponge cake, as I learned to make it, and as village women still make it.

The cake can be split and filled with fruit jam or pastry cream and topped with whipped cream. It makes a fine base for fresh fruits. The batter can also be baked in flat, rectangular pans and then cut into squares (see Drunken Cakes, opposite).

8 large eggs, separated
1 teaspoon fresh lemon juice
450 g (1 lb) sugar
1 teaspoon grated lemon zest
300 g (10½ oz) plain flour, sifted

Preheat the oven to 180°C/350°F/gas mark 4. Grease a 25-cm (10-inch) springform tin or two 24 x 33-cm (9 x 13-inch) cake tins.

In a large mixing bowl with an electric mixer, whisk the egg whites on high speed until they hold stiff peaks. Whisk in the lemon juice.

At medium speed, add the egg yolks a little at a time, whisking until they are incorporated. Then beat in the sugar and lemon zest.

Fold the flour into the egg mixture in three batches. Combine well.

Pour the batter into the prepared tin. Bake for 45 to 55 minutes, or until a thin skewer inserted in the centre comes out clean. (Shallow rectangular tins will need less baking time.)

Let the cake cool in the tin for 10 minutes. Then, loosen sides with a knife. Release the spring and remove the sides. Set the cake on a rack to cool completely. If baked in rectangular tins, remove from tins and cool on a rack.

SERVES 16

DRUNKEN CAKES
BORRACHOS

✳

The Sherry syrup is also delicious poured over sliced oranges.

1 450-g (1-lb) Sponge Cake (half the recipe, page 302)

170 g (6 oz) sugar

1 strip orange zest

170 ml (6 fl oz) medium-sweet Sherry

2 tablespoons slivered almonds

½ teaspoon ground cinnamon (optional)

If you are making a fresh cake, prepare it according to the direction on the previous page, baking the cake in a flat, rectangular tin. If you are using leftover cake, cut it into layers about 4 cm (1½ inches) thick. Place the layers in a tin. Prick the crust all over with a skewer.

In a saucepan, boil the sugar with 170 ml (6 fl oz) water and the orange zest for 3 minutes. Remove from the heat and add the Sherry. Spoon this syrup over the cake and set aside for 30 minutes.

Cut the cake into 4-cm (1½-inch) squares. Sprinkle with slivered almonds and cinnamon, if desired. Place the squares in 4-cm (1½-inch) fluted paper cases.

MAKES ABOUT 24 CAKES

SPONGE BISCUITS

MOSTACHONES

This soft biscuit is baked on sheets of rough brown paper and, when cool, wrapped in the same paper. It's the sort of sweet that Spaniards like to dunk into breakfast coffee, but it's especially good topped with a heap of sliced strawberries and a dollop of whipped cream.

4 eggs, separated

140 g (5 oz) sugar

Drop of fresh lemon juice

85 g (3 oz) plain flour

½ teaspoon ground cinnamon

Preheat the oven to 180°C/350°F/gas mark 4. Line 2 baking sheets with nonstick baking parchment.

In a large mixing bowl with an electric mixer, whisk the egg whites at high speed until stiff. Reduce the speed to medium and gradually whisk in the yolks, sugar and lemon juice. Reduce the speed to low, then add the flour and cinnamon.

Use a big spoon to ladle the batter on to the baking sheets. Leave at least 5 cm (2 inches) between spoonfuls, as the batter will spread slightly. Bake until the tops are golden, 10 to 12 minutes.

Cool the biscuits on racks and store them in airtight tins.

MAKES 15 BISCUITS

CRISP OIL BISCUITS
TORTAS DE ACEITE

I serve these spicy cookies for breakfast with coffee or tea, for dessert with cheese and fruit compotes, or to accompany a mellow *oloroso* Sherry on a rainy afternoon with classical guitar music playing on the stereo.

120 ml (4 fl oz) olive oil

1 strip lemon zest

1½ teaspoons aniseed

1 tablespoon sesame seeds

120 ml (4 fl oz) dry white wine

340 g (12 oz) plain flour

½ teaspoon salt

½ teaspoon baking powder

5 tablespoons honey

2 tablespoons sugar, for sprinkling

Heat the oil in a saucepan over high heat with the strip of lemon zest until hot but not smoking, about 2 minutes. Remove from the heat and add the aniseed and sesame seeds. Discard the lemon zest and cool the oil.

Pour the cooled oil and spices into a mixing bowl and add the wine. Combine the flour, salt and baking powder in another bowl. Stir the dry ingredients into the oil and wine.

Turn the dough out on to a board (it will not be necessary to flour the board) and give the dough four or five turns, kneading only enough to incorporate all the flour. Cover and let the dough rest at room temperature for 30 minutes.

Preheat oven to 180°C/350°F/gas mark 4.

Divide the dough in half. Roll half out between two sheets of clingfilm to a thickness of 3 mm (⅛ inch). Remove the clingfilm, then use a pastry cutter to cut into 13-cm (5-inch) rounds. Place them 2.5 cm (1 inch) apart on an ungreased baking sheet. Gather up the scraps and reserve. Roll out and cut the remaining dough in the same way. Then press the scraps together, roll them out and cut into rounds.

Bake the biscuits until golden-brown and crisped, about 20 minutes.

While the biscuits are baking, in a small saucepan, boil the honey with 3 tablespoons water for 8 minutes. Remove and keep warm.

Remove the biscuits when done and immediately use a brush to paint the tops with the warm honey. Sprinkle the tops of the biscuits generously with sugar. Transfer to wire racks and let cool completely.

MAKES 12 BISCUITS

'BISQUETTES'

PERRUNILLAS

I was served these biscuits accompanied by strong anise brandy for a mid-morning snack at an olive oil mill in Extremadura. I asked one of the women for the recipe, and she began to explain how to cream the lard and sugar, then work in flour. Another woman interrupted. *Perrunillas*, she said, were made with olive oil, not lard. We were, after all, at an olive mill.

These biscuits date back to Moorish times, when indeed they would have been made with oil, as neither Muslims nor Jews consumed pig fat. Olive oil gives a biscuit a little crunch, while the version made with lard is more crumbly.

400 g (14 oz) plain flour

¼ teaspoon bicarbonate of soda

1 teaspoon ground cinnamon

⅛ teaspoon salt

2 eggs, separated

255 g (9 oz) sugar

240 ml (8 fl oz) olive oil

1 tablespoon grated lemon zest

⅛ teaspoon aniseed, crushed (optional)

Beaten egg or egg white

30 g (1 oz) almond halves

Sift together the flour, bicarbonate of soda, cinnamon and salt.

In a mixing bowl, whisk the egg whites at high speed until they are stiff. Set aside 1 tablespoon of the sugar. Whisk the remaining sugar into the whites.

Whisk the yolks, olive oil, lemon zest and aniseed, if using.

Stir in the dry ingredients until well mixed, making a soft dough. Chill the dough for 30 minutes or up to 24 hours.

Preheat the oven to 180°C/350°F/gas mark 4.

Roll the dough into 4-cm (1½-inch) balls and flatten them slightly to a thickness of 2 cm (¾ inch). Place 2.5 cm (1 inch) apart on an ungreased baking sheet.

Brush the tops with the beaten egg, sprinkle with reserved 1 tablespoon sugar and press an almond half in the centre of each.

Bake until biscuits are lightly golden, about 15 minutes.

Remove them to a wire rack to cool completely. Store in an airtight container.

MAKES 30 BISCUITS

Cinnamon Christmas Cookies
Mantecados

This is the first of the trinity of Spanish Christmas cookies – *mantecados*, cinnamon biscuits made with lard; *polverones*, 'powder' biscuits, and *roscos de vino*, tiny, wine-scented doughnuts.

The winter hog-butchering season coincides with the Christmas holidays. A by-product of butchering is lard, which is used in these melt-in-the-mouth biscuits. As the name is derived from *manteca*, which means lard, I suggest no substitutions here. In any case, lard is no less healthful than butter.

Polvorones are made with virtually the same dough, but with less cinnamon and without the sesame seed. After baking, they are dusted heavily with icing sugar to 'powder' them.

270 g (9½ oz) plain flour

30 g (1 oz) ground almonds

170 g (6 oz) lard

130 (4½ oz) icing sugar

1 egg yolk

⅛ teaspoon lemon extract

2 tablespoons ground cinnamon

Pinch salt

1 tablespoon sesame seeds

Preheat the oven to 190°C/375°F/gas mark 5. Place the flour and almonds in separate shallow oven tins and toast in the oven until lightly coloured. The almonds need about 3 minutes and flour needs 10, stirring every 4 minutes. Remove from the tin immediately when done and cool, then mix together. Reduce the oven temperature to 180°C/350°/gas mark 4.

In a mixing bowl, beat the lard on medium speed until fluffy. Gradually add the sugar, then the egg yolk, lemon extract, cinnamon, salt and 2 teaspoons water.

Stir the toasted flour and almond mixture into the lard. Turn out on a board or marble work surface. Combine the dough by kneading it with a few squeezes. Gather together in a ball and let it rest, at room temperature, for 1 hour.

Roll or pat the dough on an unfloured surface to a thickness of 2 cm (¾ inch). Use a 5-cm (2-inch) pastry cutter to cut rounds of the dough. Place them 2.5 cm (1 inch) apart on an ungreased baking sheet. (Use a knife to lift them from the board.) Gather the remaining dough, roll it out and cut again.

Sprinkle the biscuits with a few sesame seeds and press them gently into the dough.

Bake the biscuits for 10 minutes. Transfer to wire racks to cool. The texture of the biscuits is soft and crumbly.

Once they are cool, wrap each biscuit individually in an 18-cm (7-inch) square of tissue paper, twisting the ends to enclose.

MAKES ABOUT 20 COOKIES

WINE-SCENTED RING BISCUITS
ROSCOS DE VINO

If possible, purchase almonds already blanched, skinned and ground for this recipe, then toast them to bring out the flavour. If ground almonds are not available, first toast the skinned almonds in the oven until golden, then grind them in a food processor.

300 g (10½ oz) plain flour

45 g (1½ oz) ground almonds

230 g (8 oz) lard, vegetable shortening or butter

120 ml (4 fl oz) Málaga muscatel wine or sweet Sherry

1 teaspoon ground cinnamon

¼ teaspoon ground cloves

70 g (2½ oz) icing sugar

Preheat the oven to 190°C/375°F/gas mark 5. Line 2 baking sheets with nonstick baking parchment.

Spread the flour in a shallow baking tin. Place the almonds in another tin. Toast the flour and almonds in the oven, stirring occasionally, until they are lightly toasted. The almonds will take about 3 minutes. Flour needs 10 minutes. Remove and cool completely. Combine the flour and almonds.

In a mixing bowl, cream the lard on medium speed. Beat in the wine, cinnamon and cloves. Add the flour-almond mixture in three additions, beating at low speed just until combined to make a soft dough. Refrigerate the dough for at least 45 minutes or up to 24 hours.

Divide the dough in half. Roll or pat out one half on a very lightly floured board or marble work surface to a thickness of 12 mm (½ inch). Use a 5-cm (2-inch) doughnut cutter to cut into rings (if you don't have one, use a pastry cutter and cut out the middle with a thimble). Place them 2.5 cm (1 inch) apart on the baking sheet. Gather up scraps of dough and chill.

Roll out and cut the remaining dough in the same manner.

When all the dough has been cut, bake the rings until lightly browned, 10 to 14 minutes.

Place the sugar in a shallow tin. While they are still warm, roll the baked rings in the sugar. Transfer to wire racks and let them cool.

Once cool, wrap each biscuit individually in an 18 cm (7-inch) square of tissue paper, twisting the ends to enclose.

MAKES 30 BISCUITS

NUN'S SIGHS
SUSPIROS DE MONJA

These delicate, cloud-like puffs are among the sweets confected in convents. They are as sweet and light as a sigh.

280 g (10 oz) sliced almonds

2 large egg whites

170 g (6 oz) sugar

½ teaspoon fresh lemon juice

Preheat the oven to 180°C/350°F/gas mark 4. Line 2 baking sheets with nonstick baking parchment or, alternatively, have ready about 30 small (5-cm/2-inch) fluted paper cases on a baking sheet.

Spread the sliced almonds in a shallow oven tin and toast them in the oven, stirring once or twice, until they are very lightly toasted, about 5 minutes. Set aside to cool.

Reduce the oven temperature to 120°C/250°/gas mark ½.

In a mixing bowl, whisk the egg whites on high speed until stiff. Whisk in the sugar and the lemon juice. Fold the almonds into the egg whites.

Drop mounds of batter by the tablespoon on to baking sheets 5 cm (2 inches) apart, or into the paper cases, mounding it.

Bake for 45 minutes. Turn off the oven and let the puffs cool in the oven. Store them in an airtight container.

MAKES ABOUT 30 PUFFS

ALMOND SUGAR BISCUITS
ALMENDRADOS

Here's a nicely flavoured biscuit that's found at every bakery. It should become a favourite for filling your biscuit tin.

170 g (6 oz) sugar

140 g (5 oz) ground almonds

1 teaspoon grated lemon zest

2 large eggs, separated

30 g (1 oz) sliced almonds

Preheat the oven to 180°C/350°F/gas mark 4. Line 2 baking sheets with nonstick baking parchment.

In a mixing bowl, combine the sugar, ground almonds and lemon zest.

In another bowl, whisk the egg whites at high speed until stiff. On medium speed, whisk in the yolks. Fold the egg mixture into the almond mixture.

Drop the batter by the tablespoon on to the baking sheets. The batter will spread, so leave 5 cm (2 inches) between biscuits. Sprinkle the tops of the biscuits with sliced almonds.

Bake the biscuits until lightly browned around the edges, 10 to 12 minutes.

Remove from the oven and let the biscuits cool on the baking sheets. Store them in an airtight container.

MAKES 24 BISCUITS

Almond Torte from Santiago de Compostela
Torta de Almendras de Santiago

Santiago de Compostela is a town in verdant northwest Spain, where the pilgrimage site of the shrine of St James is located. This torte is usually decorated with an image of the ornate cross of St James, made by laying a pattern of the cross on the cake, then covering the rest of the surface with icing sugar.

It is a bit of a mystery why this almond torte originated in northwest Spain where almonds do not grow. Perhaps it was confected originally with chestnuts, which abound in this region. If you can find skinned and ground almonds, use them for this recipe.

I like to serve the torte in thin wedges accompanied by a tart purée of apricot or raspberries. The fruit sets off the flavour of the almonds very nicely.

450 g (1 lb) ground almonds

155 g (5½ oz) butter

520 g (18½ oz) granulated sugar

7 eggs

170 g (6 oz) plain flour

1 tablespoon grated lemon zest

3 tablespoons fresh lemon juice

Icing sugar

Preheat the oven to 180°C/350°F/gas mark 4. Butter a 25-cm (10-inch) springform tin.

Spread the almonds in a baking tin and toast them in the oven, stirring them frequently, until lightly coloured, 3 to 5 minutes. Allow the almonds to cool.

In a mixing bowl, cream the butter and sugar until light and fluffy. Beat in the eggs, one at a time. Stir in the flour, the ground almonds and lemon zest.

Pour the batter into the springform tin and bake until a skewer inserted in the centre comes out clean, about 45 minutes.

Cool the torte for 10 minutes, then remove from the tin and cool on a rack. Prick the surface of the torte with a skewer and drizzle the lemon juice over the top. Dust the surface with icing sugar. (If desired, place a template of the St James Cross on the torte, sprinkle with icing sugar, brushing off the excess, and remove the template.) Place on a serving plate.

Serves 10

Grape Tarts
Tortas de Uvas

I discovered these tarts in northern Spain, during the autumn season of the *vendimia* (grape harvest), near the wine region of La Rioja. They were made with tiny black wine grapes. You can use Champagne grapes or blueberries.

PASTRY DOUGH

470 g (17 oz) plain flour

2 teaspoons baking powder

½ teaspoon salt

½ teaspoon aniseed

115 g (4 oz) lard, margarine or butter

120 ml (4 fl oz) vegetable oil

1 egg yolk

FILLING

230 g (8 oz) tiny grapes or blueberries

85 g (3 oz) sugar

1 egg yolk, beaten, to finish

1½ tablespoons icing sugar, to finish

To make the pastry dough, combine the flour, baking powder, salt and aniseed.

In a mixing bowl, cream the lard at medium speed. Beat in the oil. Beat in the egg yolk and 120 ml (4 fl oz) cold water. Stir in the dry ingredients and pat into a soft dough.

On a floured board, roll out the dough into a rough rectangle. Fold the top third down to the centre. Then fold it down to the bottom. Turn the dough and roll again into a rectangle.

Repeat the folding and rolling twice more. Gather the dough into a ball, wrap in clingfilm and refrigerate for 2 hours.

Preheat the oven to 180°C/350°F/gas mark 4.

To make the filling, combine the grapes and sugar.

Roll out the chilled pastry dough 6 mm (¼ inch) thick. Cut it into five or six 20-cm (8-inch) rounds. Place spoonfuls of grapes on each round. Fold the dough in half, enclosing the filling. Moisten the edges and roll the edges together to seal. Place the tarts 2.5 cm (1 inch) apart on a greased baking sheet. Prick the tops with a fork. Brush them with beaten egg yolk.

Bake the tarts until the crusts are golden, about 25 minutes.

Remove the tarts from the oven and sift icing sugar over them.

Transfer to a wire rack and cool.

SERVES 5 TO 6

'GYPSY'S ARM' (ROLLED CAKE WITH CUSTARD FILLING)
BRAZO DE GITANO

Nobody seems to know how this cake came to be called 'the arm of a gypsy'. Perhaps, the phrase has a double meaning.

140 g (5 oz) plain flour, sifted

½ teaspoon baking powder

4 eggs, separated

155 g (5½ oz) granulated sugar

Grated zest of 1 lemon

2 tablespoons icing sugar

Custard Cream filling (recipe follows)

1 teaspoon unsweetened cocoa powder

Preheat the oven to 160°C/325°F/gas mark 3. Prepare a 28 x 43-cm (11 x 17-inch) Swiss roll tin by brushing it with oil, then placing a sheet of greaseproof paper on the bottom. Grease the paper. (If you have nonstick baking parchment, it is not necessary to grease the paper.)

Combine the flour and baking powder. Set aside.

In a mixing bowl, whisk the egg whites at high speed until stiff.

In another bowl, combine the yolks, granulated sugar and lemon zest. Whisk on medium speed until thick and pale. Whisk in a quarter of the egg whites. Then fold in the remaining whites. Stir in the flour mixture until combined. Spread the batter evenly in the baking tin. It will be very thin.

Bake the cake until the top springs back when pressed in the centre, about 15 minutes.

Sprinkle a sheet of greaseproof paper or nonstick baking parchment, large enough to hold the cake, with 1 tablespoon of the icing sugar. Invert the cake on to the paper. Peel off the paper. Trim off the crisp edges of the cake.

Spread the cake with the Custard Cream filling. Starting at a narrow end, roll up the cake, enclosing the filling. Sift the remaining 1 tablespoon icing sugar over the top. Sift the cocoa over the sugar. Slide the cake from the sheet of paper on to a serving dish.

Keep the cake refrigerated until you are ready to serve it, and use it within 2 days.

SERVES 10

CUSTARD CREAM
CREMADINA

The custard, which is used as a filling in the rolled cake in the previous recipe, can also be served as a pudding or spooned over fresh fruit. Full cream milk makes a richer version, but semi-skimmed milk will work as well.

450 ml (¾ pint) milk

5 tablespoons cornflour

155 g (5½ oz) sugar

3 egg yolks

1 teaspoon vanilla extract

In a medium bowl, combine a quarter of the milk with the cornflour. Stir until it is very smooth. Add the sugar and egg yolks to the cornflour mixture and beat until smooth.

Scald the remaining milk. Pour it through a sieve into a heatproof jug. While beating the egg mixture with a whisk, slowly pour the hot milk into the eggs.

Pour the custard mixture into a clean saucepan. Cook over medium heat, beating constantly, until it thickens. Cook, stirring, on a low heat for 5 minutes more. Remove from the heat and stir in the vanilla. Beat the custard well. Let the custard cool before spreading it on the cake or using it for another dessert.

MAKES 450 ML (¾ PINT)

PUMPKIN BARS
CORTADILLOS DE CIDRA

In Spain, these bars are filled with 'angel's hair', golden, crystallized threads made from *cidra* or Malabar gourd. This beautiful green and white striped gourd, which I grow as 'sculpture', is not commonly found in Britain, but the filled bars are equally good made with pumpkin jam. A perfect autumn treat.

450 g (1 lb) lard or soft vegetable lard
540 g (19 oz) plain flour
200 g (7 oz) plus 1 tablespoon icing sugar
¼ teaspoon salt
1 teaspoon lemon extract
340 g (12 oz) Pumpkin Jam (page 323)

Cream the lard until light and fluffy.

Sift together the flour, 200 g (7 oz) of the icing sugar and salt. Add to the creamed lard with the lemon extract. Combine thoroughly.

Preheat the oven to 160°C/325°F/gas mark 3.

Divide the dough in half. Spread half the dough in a 30 x 17-cm (12 x 7-inch) tin and pat it down to 12 mm (½ inch). Spread the pumpkin jam over the dough. Pat the remaining dough in a second layer over the jam.

Bake until lightly golden, about 50 minutes.

Remove from the oven. Cut the pastry into bars about 6 x 4 cm (2½ x 1½ inches). Sift the remaining icing sugar over them.
Let cool in the baking tin.

Once cool, wrap the bars individually in tissue paper or set them on a serving plate.

MAKES ABOUT 30 BARS

DEEP-FRIED PASTRIES

In the great land of olive oil exists a whole class of pastries that are called *frutas del sarten*, 'fruits of the frying pan'. They come in all shapes and sizes – ears, puffs, leaves, rosettes, rings, twists and tarts – and are tantalizingly crisp and sweet at the same time.

Most are made from a simple dough that contains no sugar but is spiced with aniseed and cinnamon. After shaping, the pastries are fried, drained briefly, then dipped in honey or sugar syrup. They aren't greasy at all, because the dough quickly forms a crust in the bubbling oil so that the fat doesn't penetrate.

Olive oil is best for frying, though other vegetable oils can be used. Olive oil has a lower smoking temperature than other vegetable fats, so heat it just to 182°C/360°F. At that temperature, the oil is shimmering-hot. Use a deep-fat fryer if you have one. Otherwise fry the pastries in a deep frying pan or a heavy sauté pan with sloping sides. The oil needs to be only deep enough so that the pieces of dough are fully immersed.

Usually 4 to 5 cm (1½ to 2 inches) is sufficient. Don't crowd the pieces in the frying pan. Use a skimmer to remove them and drain on kitchen towels.

DOUGH FOR FRIED PASTRIES
MASA PARA EMPANADILLAS Y PESTIÑOS

Use this basic dough for fried tarts, strips, twists, etc. For savoury pasties, omit the cinnamon, cloves and orange juice from the dough and increase the salt to ½ teaspoon. The dough can be prepared ahead and refrigerated or frozen. Bring it to room temperature before rolling it out.

170 ml (6 fl oz) olive oil

1 strip orange zest

1 tablespoon sesame seeds

1 tablespoon aniseed

1½ teaspoons ground cinnamon

⅛ teaspoon ground cloves

120 ml (4 fl oz) white wine

1 tablespoon brandy or anise brandy

2 tablespoons orange juice

¼ teaspoon salt

500 g (18 oz) plain flour

Heat the oil over high heat in a small frying pan with the orange zest until the zest begins to brown, about 1 minute. Remove from the heat, cool for 1 minute. Remove and discard the orange zest. Then stir in the sesame seeds and aniseed. Pour into a mixing bowl and allow to cool.

Add the cinnamon, cloves, wine, brandy, orange juice and salt to the oil. Using a large wooden spoon, stir in the flour to make a soft dough. Turn out on to an unfloured board and knead very briefly, just to combine well.

Let the dough rest, covered, for at least 1 hour. The dough can be prepared in advance and refrigerated. Allow it to come to room temperature before proceeding with the recipe.

Roll out very thinly (less than 3 mm/⅛ inch) and shape and fry as directed in the recipe.

MAKES ENOUGH DOUGH FOR 28 SMALL TARTS (OR PASTIES) OR 50 FRIED TWISTS

LITTLE EMPANADAS WITH PUMPKIN JAM
EMPANADILLAS CON DULCE DE CALABAZA

These tiny fried pies, which are especially popular at Christmas time, can be filled with thick jam made of pumpkin or sweet potato, or 'angel's hair', a jam made from a kind of Spanish gourd. In a pinch, you can substitute any sort of fruit jam.

Dough for Fried Pastries (page 317)
340 g (12 oz) Pumpkin Jam (page 323)
Olive oil, for frying (see page 316)
255 g (9 oz) honey
2 tablespoons sugar

Roll out the dough very thinly on a lightly floured board. Prick the dough all over with a fork. Use an 11-cm (4½-inch) pastry cutter to cut out rounds.

Working with one disc of dough at a time, place a spoonful of jam on one half. Moisten the edges of the dough with water, then fold the round in half, enclosing the filling. With your fingers or the tines of a fork, crimp the edges together firmly to seal the tart. Place on a tray. Continue filling and shaping the remainder of the dough.

Pour the oil into a deep frying pan to a depth of at least 4 cm (1½ inches). Heat the oil to 182°C/360°F. Fry the tarts, four or five at a time, until they are golden-brown on both sides, about 5 minutes. Remove and drain on kitchen towels. Let the tarts cool completely.

Make a dipping syrup. Bring the honey and 3 tablespoons water to the boil in a small saucepan. Let it bubble for 8 minutes. Remove from the heat.

While syrup is hot, dip the tarts into it, one by one. Place them on a rack positioned over a pan to catch the drips. Sprinkle them with the sugar. Let them dry for 1 hour. (They will still be a little sticky.) Alternatively, the hot honey dip can be omitted and the tarts can simply be dredged in sugar while they are still hot.

Allow the tarts to cool, then arrange them on a platter.

MAKES ABOUT 28 SMALL TARTS

FRIED TWISTS
PESTIÑOS

Some fried pastries, in the shape of flowers, leaves and cylinders, require special moulds, irons or tubes to shape them. This one is just strips of dough, twisted, pinched and fried, then bathed in honey syrup. I make them with the scraps and trimmings of dough after cutting rounds for the tarts in the previous recipe. One version is called *borrachuelos* (inebriated) because the dough is made with wine and brandy.

Spanish cooks drop the pinched dough directly into the hot oil. I prefer to shape them all and place them on a tray. Then I hook the *pestiños* on to the handle of a wooden spoon and lower them into the oil.

Dough for Fried Pastries (page 317)

Olive oil, for frying (see page 316)

255 g (9 oz) honey

45 g (1½ oz) ground toasted almonds (optional)

Roll out the dough thinly (less than 3 mm/ ⅛ inch). Prick it all over with a fork. Cut it into strips approximately 10 × 5 cm (4 × 2 inches). Moisten your fingers, join opposite corners of each strip and pinch them together in the centre, making a sort of skewed tube. Set the shaped dough on a tray.

Heat the oil in a deep frying pan to 182°C/360°F. Fry the pieces a few at a time until golden-brown, about 5 minutes. Remove and drain on kitchen towels. Allow to cool.

Prepare the syrup by combining the honey and 3 tablespoons water in a small saucepan. Bring to the boil, then let it bubble for 8 minutes. Remove from the heat.

While the syrup is still hot, dip the fried pastries into the honey, then into ground almonds, if using. Place them on a rack over a pan to dry for 1 hour.

MAKES ABOUT 50 TWISTS

Sweets and Confections

Fig and Almond Rolls
Pan de Higos

Fig trees grow everywhere in my village, even springing up wild in rock crevices. In former times, the fruit was far more important than it is today, providing a source of sweetener in place of honey or sugar. What wasn't consumed by humans was used as animal fodder. While figs are used less extensively today, they are still much appreciated in both their fresh and dried forms.

Ripe figs, picked in late summer, are spread to dry on a ground cloth in the sun. When fully dried, they are packed into a *serete* (a woven straw basket) and cinched tightly closed. The baskets are placed in a special wooden fig press and winched down. Once pressed, the figs are impervious to insect infestation and will keep for months.

I used to help a neighbour make dozens of these fig rolls, which are a Christmas season favourite. She would grind the spices in a mortar and add a little melted chocolate to the mixture. The fig rolls sold in local shops today are very heavily flavoured with anise liqueur – too much so for my taste. These rolls have a more delicate flavour, rather like fig rolls without the biscuit. The rolls, which keep for months, make a thoughtful home-made gift.

900 g (2 lb) dried figs, stems removed

4 tablespoons icing sugar

115 g (4 oz) blanched and skinned almonds (see page 6)

1 teaspoon ground cinnamon

¼ teaspoon aniseed, ground

¼ teaspoon freshly ground black pepper

¼ teaspoon ground ginger

Grated lemon zest

85 g (3 oz) plain chocolate, melted (optional)

4 tablespoons anise brandy, brandy or sweet wine

3 tablespoons sesame seeds, toasted

Sprinkle the figs with 2 tablespoons of the icing sugar. Put the figs through a mincer (or chop them in batches in a food processor). Place the pulp in a bowl.

Set aside 16 almonds. Chop the rest and add to the figs.

Mix the remaining 2 tablespoons icing sugar with the cinnamon, aniseed, pepper, ginger and lemon zest. Sprinkle it over the fig mixture and mix it in.

Add the chocolate, if using, and the anise brandy. With your hands, knead the mixture to blend well.

Divide the fig mixture into four equal portions. Roll each into a log, about 15 cm (6 inches) long and 4 cm (1½ inches) thick.

Spread the sesame seeds on a sheet of greaseproof paper or nonstick baking parchment. Roll the fig logs in the sesame, patting to flatten the logs slightly. Press 4 reserved almonds into the top of each of the fig rolls.

Let the rolls dry for 12 hours, then wrap them tightly in clingfilm.

To serve, cut the rolls crosswise into 12-mm (½-inch) thick discs and place on a sweets tray.

MAKES FOUR 6-INCH ROLLS

QUINCE SWEET
DULCE DE MEMBRILLO

On a trip through the sierra of Ronda in Andalusia, on the way to the beautiful town of Arcos de la Frontera, we stopped at a mountain village for lunch. It was autumn, and clouds swirled around pine-clad peaks. Rain fell steadily in the village, and no one was in the streets. We finally found a small inn where meals were served. We were the only guests.

The food was stupendous. We were served a wild rabbit – brought in that morning from traps – cooked in a wine sauce, and two pork tongues served whole, braised tender in a slightly sweet sauce. For dessert, there was *dulce de membrillo,* still slightly warm and quivery. The young man who served us said his mother had made the rose-coloured jelly that morning.

Quince jelly is increasingly easy to find in British food shops. Serve it for breakfast with toast, for dessert with a few walnuts and fresh white cheese, or paired with a mature cheese as a starter.

I include the recipe for *membrillo* in case you should happen to have a prolific quince tree or find a bounty of this fragrant fruit in the market. It is a wonderfully old-fashioned fruit and full of flavour. Quince is also naturally high in pectin, which causes this jam to set into a dense, solid form. You can even add a little quince to orange marmalades and other preserves to help them set.

2.2 kg (5 lb) quinces (5–6 large fruits)
1.4 kg (3 lb) sugar

Wash the quinces and combine them in a large deep saucepan with water to cover. Bring to the boil and cook them, until they are tender if pierced with a skewer, about 45 minutes. Remove the quinces from the liquid and cool them. Reserve the liquid.

Peel and core the quinces. Purée the fruit in batches in a blender or food processor with 240 ml (8 fl oz) of the reserved cooking liquid. You should have about 1.5 litres (2½–2¾ pints) of purée.

Combine the quince purée in a large, heavy pan with the sugar and let sit for 30 minutes.

Bring the fruit and sugar mixture to the boil, stirring constantly, then reduce the heat so it gently simmers. Simmer the quince purée until it is reduced to a thick jam. As it cooks down, you will have to stir constantly so that it doesn't scorch. The jam is done when it becomes glossy and translucent and begins to stick to the bottom of the pan – about 30 minutes. A test spoonful on a cold plate solidifies immediately.

While the purée is cooking, line a 10 x 30 x 8-cm (4 x 12 x 3-inch) terrine mould or loaf tin with clingfilm, making sure the clingfilm extends past the edges.

When the purée is thickened, spoon it into the prepared mould. Tap the mould to settle the mixture. Let it cool, uncovered, then cover and refrigerate overnight.

Unmould the solidified jelly. If desired, it can be cut into 5-cm (2-inch) thick crosswise slabs and each slab individually wrapped in clingfilm. The quince jelly keeps refrigerated for up to 3 months.

To serve as a tapa, cut the jelly into 12-mm (½-inch) cubes and spear them on cocktail sticks with cubes of mature Manchego cheese.

PUMPKIN JAM

DULCE DE CALABAZA

In the village market where I shop, the pumpkins are enormous – 60 cm (2 feet) across, green-skinned but wonderfully orange-fleshed. They are sold in slices. In addition to making an unusual filling for pastries, this jam is something different to spread on breakfast toast. It can also be made using orange-fleshed sweet potato or any other variety of winter squash.

1 small pumpkin or winter squash (1.1–1.4 kg/2½–3 lb) or 450 g (1 lb) purée

450 g (1 lb) sugar

1 teaspoon finely chopped lemon zest

⅛ teaspoon ground cloves

8-cm (3-inch) cinnamon stick

If you are using fresh pumpkin or winter squash, remove the skin and cut the flesh into chunks. Place in a large saucepan with 140 ml (¼ pint) of water, bring to the boil, and cook until fork-tender, 15 minutes. Drain the pumpkin in a colander for 2 hours. Then mash it or purée it in a food processor.

Combine the purée, sugar, lemon zest, cloves and cinnamon in a heavy pan. Place the pan, partially covered to prevent splattering, over high heat, until the mixture is bubbling. Reduce the heat and cook, stirring frequently, until the purée is thickened to jam consistency, 20 to 25 minutes.

Place in clean jars and seal. Cool completely, then refrigerate. Use within 2 weeks.

MAKES ABOUT 570 ML (I PINT)

POACHED FRUITS IN WINE SYRUP
ARROPE

Before commercially tinned goods became commonplace, fruits were primarily consumed fresh, in their season, or dried. Some fruits kept better than others, of course. Apples could be stored for several months in cool weather; oranges were left unpicked on the trees so they would last a bit longer; and melons would keep if suspended in mesh bags from beams.

Another very ancient way to preserve fruit was in grape must (the juice extracted from grapes in the first step of wine making, before fermentation takes place). The must was reduced to a thick syrup to concentrate the sugar. Then fruits – as well as some vegetables such as aubergine, winter squash and sweet potato – were slaked in quicklime and cooked in the syrup. It was a delicious way to ensure that fruit could be enjoyed all year round. The following is an adaptation. It is not a preserve, so refrigerate and use within a few days.

Be as adventuresome as you like with this dessert. Pumpkin, sweet potato and aubergine really do absorb the sweet syrup, but, if you prefer, use only fruits. This compote would be good with ice cream and Crisp Oil Biscuits (page 305).

1.8 litres (about 3 pints) white grape juice or muscatel wine

115 g (4 oz) sugar

Zest of 1 orange, slivered

Zest of 1 lemon, slivered

5-cm (2-inch) cinnamon stick

4 cloves

230 g (8 oz) dried figs

230 g (8 oz) raisins

about 1 kg (2¼ lb) various fruits and vegetables, such as firm pears, apples, firm melon, pumpkin, winter squash, aubergine, sweet potato, peeled and cut into 4-cm (1½-inch) chunks

Slivered almonds

2 tablespoons brandy (optional)

Combine the juice in a large saucepan with the sugar, orange and lemon zest, cinnamon and cloves. Bring to the boil, then cook at a slow boil over medium heat until reduced by half, about 35 minutes.

Add the figs, raisins, and fruit and vegetables to the juice. Simmer all together until the fruits are tender, about 30 minutes. Remove the cloves and the cinnamon stick. Add the slivered almonds and brandy, if desired.

Serve at room temperature or cold.

The fruits keep, covered, in the refrigerator for up to 4 days.

SERVES 12

CRUNCHY CARAMEL ALMONDS

GARRAPIÑADAS

Fran was a school friend of one of my sons. After finishing school, he joined an uncle in business, making caramelized almonds at a street stall in the village. Passing tourists are offered a free sample, and they usually end up buying a whole bag. I don't blame them – these crunchy-sweet almonds are totally addictive.

Fran uses a round-bottomed copper pan, for good heat conduction. He adds a sprinkling of vanilla, which creates a tantalizing aroma that wafts up and down the street and lures in the customers. And, the important secret – he adds the sugar in three stages, so it caramelizes in layers, creating a thick and crunchy covering. He stirs almost constantly with a wooden paddle. In my kitchen I use a round-bottomed steel (not stainless) wok. The round bottom keeps the caramel from getting stuck in the corners.

200 g (7 oz) sugar

½ teaspoon vanilla extract

200 g (7 oz) almonds (not skinned)

Combine a third of the sugar, the vanilla extract and 120 ml (4 fl oz) water in a heavy pan, preferably round-bottomed. Bring to the boil over high heat, stirring to dissolve the sugar. Add the almonds. Cook, stirring constantly, until the syrup thickens and begins to adhere to the almonds, 4 to 5 minutes.

Sprinkle with another third of the sugar. Stir the almonds constantly until the sugar begins to liquefy and adhere to the almonds.

Sprinkle with the remaining sugar. Continue stirring, just until the sugar melts and coats the almonds. Remove from heat and turn the almonds out on to a baking sheet. The whole process takes 10 to 12 minutes.

When they are cool enough to handle, separate the almonds that are stuck together.

MAKES ABOUT 340 G (12 OZ)

ALMOND-HONEY NOUGAT
ALAJÚ

These sweets comes from Cuenca, a picturesque town in La Mancha in central Spain. When I made them in my kitchen, the aroma attracted hundreds of bees, which swarmed around my screen door.

Naturally, I use local honey that comes from hives set in the hills immediately above my house. There the bees feed on the rosemary and thyme flowers that bloom on the steep slopes and produce a wonderfully aromatic honey. This honey, however, is stronger in flavour than the mild lavender and flower honey I had sampled in Cuenca, and thus resulted in a slightly different-tasting sweet. I recommend that you use any mild-flavoured honey for this recipe.

The sticky almond mixture is sandwiched between edible wafers of rice paper.

450 ml (¾ pint) honey
270 g (9½ oz) blanched and skinned
   almonds (see page 6)
170 g (6 oz) fine dry breadcrumbs
2 teaspoons grated lemon zest
12 (15-cm/6-inch) rounds of rice paper or
   wheat wafers

Cook the honey to the soft-ball stage (112°C/234°F). If a small spoonful is dropped into iced water it will form a soft ball. Stir in the almonds, breadcrumbs and lemon zest. Cook, stirring, for another 5 minutes, until the mixture pulls away from the sides of the pan.

Have ready 6 rounds of rice paper or wafers on a marble work surface, or each on a dinner plate. Spread the almond mixture on the rounds. Press another round of rice paper on top of each circle, sandwiching the almond paste.

When completely cooled, trim off any excess rice paper. Wrap the sweets in clingfilm. Cut into thin slices to serve.

MAKES SIX 13-CM (5-INCH) DISCS

ANGEL'S KISSES
YEMAS

At one time, Spanish vintners used large quantities of egg white to clarify the new wine. The yolks were often donated to convents, where nuns made them into sweets. These candied egg yolks are so delectable that one poet declared that eating *yemas* was like nibbling the lips of an angel. The sweet is traditionally made in several shapes, depending on the convent. Place the sweets in fluted paper sweet cases or wrap them individually in tissue paper. Store them in the refrigerator.

12 egg yolks
200 g (7 oz) granulated sugar
1 teaspoon grated orange zest
60 g (2 oz) icing sugar

Warm a conical metal sieve (a chinois) by pouring boiling water through it. Sieve the egg yolks into a heavy saucepan.

In another saucepan, combine the granulated sugar with 240 ml (8 fl oz) water and the orange zest. Bring to the boil, cover the pan and boil for 3 minutes. Then uncover and cook, without stirring, until the syrup reaches the soft-ball stage (112°C/234°F).

Using a wooden spoon, beat the sugar syrup little by little into the strained egg yolks.

Simmer the yolks and syrup, stirring constantly. Lift the pan from the heat while stirring to prevent the yolks from cooking too rapidly. Cook until the mixture forms a thick custard and leaves the sides of the pan (88°C/190°F). Remove from the heat and continue beating as the mixture cools.

Sprinkle some of the icing sugar on a marble slab or on a plate. Spread the egg paste in a 2.5-cm (1-inch) layer on it. Leave to cool completely.

Dust your hands with additional icing sugar and form small balls of the paste (about 4 cm/1½ inches in diameter). Shape them into little cones or cylinders. Roll them in icing sugar and place on a tray. Chill.

Place the sweets in fluted paper cases or wrap in tissue.

MAKES ABOUT 18

PUDDINGS

Simple to make and rich with eggs and milk, these puddings are favourites in home and farmhouse kitchens. Since eggs and milk are most plentiful in the springtime, these recipes are often prepared for Lenten meals, lending a touch of sweetness to the meatless days before Easter.

The most common pudding flavourings are cinnamon and lemon zest, but you can substitute a vanilla pod for the cinnamon stick if you like.

RICE PUDDING WITH CINNAMON
ARROZ CON LECHE

When my friend Rosa decides to make this pudding, she takes her pail to her neighbour's yard and milks one of the goats. Goats' milk, Rosa declares, is the very best for making this rice pudding. If you don't have access to goats' milk, or neighbours kind enough to share theirs, it's delicious with cows' milk, too.

230 g (8 oz) medium-short-grain rice
    (e.g. risotto rice)

⅛ teaspoon salt

5-cm (2-inch) cinnamon stick

Strip of lemon zest

1.15 litres (2 pints) milk

100 g (3½ oz) plus 1 tablespoon sugar

1 tablespoon ground cinnamon (optional)

In a medium saucepan, combine the rice with the salt, cinnamon, lemon zest and 450 ml (¾ pint) of water. Bring to the boil, then cover and cook over low heat until the water is absorbed, about 5 minutes. Stand for another 5 minutes. Then rinse the rice under running water, reserving the lemon zest and cinnamon stick.

Rinse out the pan. Combine the cinnamon stick, lemon zest, milk and 100 g (3½ oz) of the sugar in the pan and bring to the boil. Add the rice to the milk and return to the boil. Reduce the heat, cover the pan and cook the rice until it is very soft, about 12 minutes more. (A heat diffuser is useful to keep the rice from scorching.) The pudding should still be somewhat soupy, the rice very tender.

Pour the pudding into a serving bowl or ladle into six individual pudding dishes. Sprinkle the tops with remaining 1 tablespoon of sugar and ground cinnamon, if using. Rather than using the cinnamon, you can caramelize the sugar topping under the grill, if so desired. The pudding thickens as it cools. It is usually served chilled.

SERVES 6

CATALAN CUSTARDS WITH BURNT SUGAR TOPPING
CREMA CATALANA

I was delighted to find the traditional tool for caramelizing the tops of these custards in a local hardware shop. It is simply an iron disc mounted on a rod. The disc is heated until it is red-hot and held over the sugar to melt it. If you are using the iron (sometimes called a salamander), be sure to wipe it clean with a wet rag after caramelizing each pudding, and before reheating again. You can also melt the sugar with a small gas blowtorch, now sold in many kitchenware and camping shops. A grill does not work very well for caramelizing the sugar topping unless you are able to place the pudding dishes very close to the heat source.

6 egg yolks

200 g (7 oz) sugar

900 ml (1½ pints) milk

Zest of 1 lemon

5-cm (2-inch) cinnamon stick

3 tablespoons cornflour

In a large bowl, beat the egg yolks with three-quarters of the sugar. Combine three-quarters of the milk in a pan with the lemon zest and cinnamon stick. Bring to the boil, then remove from the heat. Strain the milk and whisk it into the beaten yolks.

Stir the remaining milk and cornflour together in a small bowl until smooth. Stir it into the custard mixture.

Pour the custard into a clean saucepan and cook over low heat, stirring constantly, until it just begins to bubble. Remove from the heat and divide between 6 shallow pudding dishes or ramekins. Cool the custard. The puddings can be made up to 24 hours in advance and refrigerated, but bring them to room temperature before continuing with the recipe.

Shortly before serving, sprinkle the tops of the custards with the remaining sugar. Caramelize the tops with a heated iron (salamander) or kitchen blowtorch.

SERVES 6

RICH CUSTARD WITH CARAMEL
FLAN CON CARAMELO

If you use a metal pudding mould for this recipe, you can make the caramel right in the mould. However, if you are using the individual ramekins or custard cups, make the caramel in a saucepan and pour it into the cups. Classic flan is flavoured with cinnamon and lemon zest, but it is easy to vary the recipe by using in their place a strip of orange zest or a vanilla pod.

400 g (14 oz) sugar
5 eggs, lightly beaten
900 ml (1½ pints) milk
**Cinnamon stick or vanilla pod or strip of
orange zest or strip of lemon zest**

Preheat the oven to 160°C/325°F/gas mark 3. Have ready eight 240-ml (8-fl oz) custard cups (preferably metal ones).

Combine 100 g (3½ oz) of the sugar in a small heavy saucepan with 3 tablespoons water. Cook over medium-high heat for 3 to 4 minutes until the sugar melts and turns a dark gold. Quickly pour the syrup into the custard cups, tilting them to cover the bottoms.

Combine the remaining sugar with the eggs.

Pour the milk into a saucepan, add one of the flavourings and heat to scalding point. Pour the hot milk through a sieve into a heatproof jug. Pour it slowly into the beaten eggs, beating as you pour.

Divide the custard mixture between the custard cups, filling each about two-thirds full. Set the custards in a baking tin or dish large enough to fit them, and pour boiling water into the tin until it is halfway up the sides of the custard cups.

Bake the custards until set (a thin skewer comes out clean), about 1 hour. Cool, then refrigerate.

Immediately before serving, loosen the custards with a knife and invert each on to an individual dessert plate.

SERVES 8

LEMONY CHEESE CUSTARD SQUARES
QUESADA

This dessert, which is more like a custard than like cheesecake, comes from Cantabria, a small region on the northern coast of Spain, which produces several extraordinary cheeses (see chapter 5). It is made with soft, fresh cheese, before the curds have been pressed or salted. You can use unsalted cottage cheese, beaten smooth, or fromage frais or yoghurt that has been drained for 1 hour in a colander lined with muslin.

The smooth, lemony squares are especially good served with sliced strawberries.

4–5 slices stale bread, crusts removed

240 ml (8 fl oz) milk

1 teaspoon grated lemon zest

2.5-cm (1-inch) piece of cinnamon stick

3 tablespoons butter

155 g (5½ oz) sugar

3 eggs

450 ml (¾ pint) fromage frais or other unsalted fresh cheese

Break the bread into pieces and pulse in a food processor until the bread is reduced to fine crumbs. The crumbs should more than fill a 280-ml (½-pint) glass. Remove 3 tablespoons of the crumbs and reserve them in a small bowl.

Combine the milk, lemon zest and cinnamon stick in a small saucepan. Bring to the boil and remove from the heat. Let cool until lukewarm, then remove and discard the cinnamon.

Preheat the oven to 190°C/375°F/gas mark 5.

Pour the milk over the breadcrumbs in the food processor. Process until smooth.

Using an electric mixer, cream the butter in a mixing bowl at medium speed. Gradually beat in the sugar, then the eggs, one by one. Add the fromage frais and combine well.

Stir in the bread and milk mixture from the food processor.

Butter a 23 × 33-cm (9 × 13-inch) rectangular baking tin and sprinkle with the reserved 3 tablespoons of breadcrumbs. Pour the batter into the tin. Bake until the custard is set and a skewer comes out clean, about 35 minutes.

Allow to cool in the tin. Loosen the edges and turn out on to a work surface. Cut the custard into pieces that measure approximately 7 × 5 cm (3 × 2 inches). Arrange them on a serving platter.

MAKES 18 SQUARES

SHERRY JELLY

GELATINA DE VINO DE JEREZ

This unusual gelatine dessert is dominated by the sophisticated flavour of Sherry. A grown-up dessert indeed. Serve it with sliced oranges or strawberries, a crisp biscuit on the side and, perhaps, a touch of whipped cream or custard on top. Use a medium-dry Sherry, such as *oloroso seco*, or a sweet cream Sherry.

1 tablespoon unflavoured gelatine

450 ml (¾ pint) medium-dry Sherry

Grated zest of 1 orange

3 tablespoons sugar

Sliced oranges or other fruit

Whipped cream (optional)

In a small bowl, sprinkle the gelatine over 120 ml (4 fl oz) of water and let sit for 5 minutes. In a small saucepan, combine the gelatine mixture with 240 ml (8 fl oz) water and stir over low heat until the gelatine is completely dissolved.

In another small saucepan, heat the Sherry, orange zest and sugar until the sugar is dissolved. Do not boil. Stir the hot Sherry into the gelatine mixture.

Pour the mixture into a 1-litre (1¾-pint) mould or bowl. Cool to room temperature, then refrigerate overnight, until the jelly is set.

Serve the jelly spooned over sliced oranges or other fruit. Accompany with whipped cream, if desired.

SERVES 6

Frozen Desserts

Meringue Milk Ice
Leche Merengada

Meringue milk is a sort of Spanish milkshake – sweetened egg whites are folded into a cinnamon-milk mixture to make a foamy drink. Now it is usually served soft-frozen. It is particularly popular in the eastern coastal region of Valencia. I have tasted rich versions of this dessert, in which the milk is slowly reduced by half, then enriched with cream. But it's quite delightful without the enrichments.

900 ml (1½ pints) milk

200 g (7 oz) sugar

Zest from 2 lemons

5-cm (2-inch) cinnamon stick

1 clove

3 egg whites

½ teaspoon fresh lemon juice

1 teaspoon ground cinnamon

Combine the milk, sugar, lemon zest, cinnamon stick and clove in a pan. Simmer, stirring frequently, for 10 minutes. Strain the milk into a metal bowl and discard the solids. Chill the milk. When the milk is quite cold, place in the freezer until it is soft-frozen. Stir it occasionally to mix the frozen and liquid milk.

Beat the egg whites on high speed until they hold stiff peaks. Beat in the lemon juice.

Remove from the freezer the soft-frozen milk and beat at high speed until smooth. On low speed, beat in half of the egg whites. Fold in remaining egg whites by hand, mixing thoroughly.

Serve the meringue milk ice immediately or return it to the freezer to freeze slightly longer. It should be the consistency of soft-freeze ice cream. If it is allowed to hard-freeze, remove it from the freezer about 40 minutes before serving, so it begins to thaw. Spoon the milk ice into goblets and sprinkle each with cinnamon.

Serves 6

Note: When making meringue milk ice, which contains uncooked egg whites, or any other dish including raw egg, you need to make quite sure that your eggs come from a safe source.

Sweet Almond Milk
Horchata

If you visit Valencia, you must try *horchata de chufas*, a sweet, refreshing summer drink or ice made with ground *chufas*. These are tiger nuts or earth almonds, small tubers of a cultivated sedge (*Cyperus esculentus*). If you can't get to Valencia, make it at home with ground almonds instead of tiger nuts. *Horchata* derives from the orgeat of the Moors, who once inhabited Valencia and made the drink with ground almonds, other seeds and nuts, as well as *chufas*.

Fresh *chufas*, sometimes sold by street vendors, are about the size of almonds, have a crisp texture and a taste reminiscent of coconut.

The *horchata* is creamier and smoother if blanched and skinned almonds are pounded in a mortar. However, this is a laborious process. It is still enchanting made with finely ground almonds.

The *horchata* can be served as a drink or soft-frozen. In Spain it is not likely to be served as a dessert but rather, just as you might treat yourself to an ice cream, as a mid-afternoon stop at an *horchatería*.

400 g (14 oz) finely ground almonds

200 g (7 oz) sugar

450 ml (¾ pint) milk

5-cm (2-inch) cinnamon stick

2 tablespoons fresh lemon juice

Combine the almonds and sugar in a heatproof bowl. Combine the milk, cinnamon and 450 ml (¾ pint) water in a pan. Bring to the boil and pour over the almonds. Stir to dissolve the sugar. Set aside for 3 hours.

Strain the mixture through a fine sieve lined with muslin into a jug or bowl, pressing on the solids. Discard the ground almonds (or save for another use). Stir the lemon juice into the drink. Chill.

Serve very cold in tall glasses or freeze the mixture. To freeze, place the mixture in a container and freeze until partially frozen. Remove and whip in a food processor to make *granizado de horchata* (almond milk granita).

Serves 4

Almond Nougat Ice Cream
Helado de Turrón de Jijona

In Spain, the traditional Christmas meal is not complete without a selection of *turrón* (almond nougat sweets) and *mazapán* (marzipan), which is sweetened almond paste coloured and moulded in the shape of fruits, fish and flowers. Both sweets have Moorish origins but, over the centuries, they have become the sweetmeats of choice for Christian festivities.

Turrón is made of toasted almonds, honey and egg whites. Alicante-style *turrón* is white nougat, very crunchy, with chunks of almonds. Jijona-style *turrón* is made from the same mixture, but it is ground into a creamy, fudgy paste. The soft *turrón* is used to make this delectable ice cream.

You should be able to get *turrón* at good delicatessens, but if you have trouble finding it, try the Sources listing at the end of this book (see page 342). Best-quality *turrón* has a high quantity of almond oil. Keep it cool or refrigerated.

6 egg yolks
130 g (4½ oz) sugar
570 ml (1 pint) milk
170 ml (6 fl oz) double cream
1 vanilla pod
185 g (6½ oz) Jijona (soft) *turrón*
Grated bittersweet chocolate (optional)

In a mixing bowl, beat the egg yolks and sugar with a handheld mixer at medium speed until combined.

Pour the milk and half of the cream into a saucepan, add the vanilla pod and heat to scalding point. Strain it into a heatproof jug or bowl. At medium speed, beat the hot milk into the yolk mixture.

Return the milk-yolk mixture to the pan. Cook, stirring constantly, over medium heat for 2 minutes. Remove and beat again for 5 minutes as the custard cools. Beat in the remaining cream. Chill the custard.

Put the *turrón* in the freezer for 5 minutes. Then chop coarsely in a food processor. When the custard is cold, fold the chopped *turrón* into the custard. Pour into a 1-litre ice cream-maker and freeze according to manufacturer's directions. Freeze until hard.

Allow the ice cream to soften for 15 minutes before serving. Serve sprinkled with grated chocolate, if desired.

Serves 8

FROZEN FIG TERRINE
TARTA HELADA DE HIGOS

Made with alternating layers of digestive biscuits, sweet custard and fig purée, this beautiful dessert presents a lively contrast of textures and flavours. Prepare the terrine at least one day before serving, so it has time to freeze.

340 g (12 oz) dried figs

670 ml (1¼ pints) milk

4 egg yolks

155 g (5½ oz) sugar

Pinch salt

240 ml (8 fl oz) single cream

1 teaspoon vanilla extract

45 g (1½ oz) chopped walnuts

120 ml (4 fl oz) sweet wine, such as Málaga muscatel, Pedro Ximenez or oloroso Sherry

155 g (5½ oz) digestive biscuits

120 ml (4 fl oz) whipping cream

2 teaspoons icing sugar

Chocolate Sauce (recipe follows)

Remove the stems from the figs and cut the figs in half. Combine in a bowl with two-thirds of the milk. Soak the figs for at least 6 hours, or overnight, in the refrigerator.

Pour the milk through a sieve into a saucepan and set aside. Pulse the figs in a food processor until they are chopped to a pulp. Set aside.

In a mixing bowl, beat the egg yolks, sugar and salt at medium speed.

Add the remaining milk and the single cream to the saucepan with the strained milk. Bring to the boil and remove from the heat. Pour the milk and cream through a sieve into a heatproof jug or bowl. Pour the hot milk into the yolks and beat.

Return this custard mixture to the pan and cook over medium-low heat, stirring constantly, until slightly thickened, about 2 minutes. Remove from the heat and stir in the vanilla. Beat with a wire whisk for 5 minutes as the custard cools.

Stir 120 ml (4 fl oz) of the custard and the walnuts into the chopped figs. Refrigerate the fig mixture. Place the rest of the custard in a metal bowl and freeze it until it has the consistency of soft ice cream.

Lightly butter a loaf tin that measures 26 × 8 cm (10½ × 3¼ inches) and is at least 5 cm (2 inches) deep.

Pour the sweet wine into a shallow bowl. Dip a digestive biscuit into the wine on both sides. Place it in the bottom of the loaf tin. Continue dipping digestives and cover the bottom of the tin.

Spread half of the soft-frozen custard on top of the digestive layer. (Return the remaining custard to the freezer.) Continue dipping digestives to make a layer covering the custard. Split the biscuits, as needed, to fill in the cracks. Spread the chilled fig mixture on top. Cover with another layer of dipped digestives. Spread the remaining custard over it. Finish with a layer of dipped biscuits.

Cover the tin with aluminium foil and place it in the freezer until it is frozen solid.

Loosen the edges of the terrine with a knife and unmould it on to a tray or platter. Return it to the freezer.

Whip the cream and beat in the icing sugar. Ice the frozen terrine with the cream. Return it to the freezer, uncovered, until the cream is frozen. The terrine can then be wrapped in foil and kept frozen until serving time.

To serve, have dessert plates ready, each with a pool of Chocolate Sauce. Remove the ice-cream cake from the freezer 15 minutes before serving time. Use a knife dipped in hot water to slice the terrine. Place the slices on the plates, drizzle with additional Chocolate Sauce, if desired, and serve immediately.

SERVES 12

CHOCOLATE SAUCE
SALSA DE CHOCOLATE

I keep leftover chocolate sauce in the freezer. It's a great last-minute addition to cakes, ice cream and other desserts.

340 g (12 oz) dark- chocolate
60 g (2 oz) unsalted butter
240 ml (8 fl oz) milk

Combine the chocolate, butter and milk in a saucepan. Melt the chocolate, stirring constantly, until the sauce is very smooth.

Cool the sauce, beating occasionally. Serve the sauce at room temperature. The sauce can be frozen and reheated in the microwave.

MAKES 450 ML (¾ PINT)

FIESTA SWEETS

Each town honours its patron saint with an annual *feria* (town fair). Some have very ancient origins in pagan rites, which later took on saints' names to keep them compatible with the Catholic Church. Others grew up around important livestock fairs. A village *feria* is a party on a grand scale, usually accompanied by carnival rides, sports competitions, cultural exhibitions, feasting and round-the-clock partying.

A group of us used to go to the August *feria* in Málaga every year to attend several of the afternoon bullfights and stay on for nighttime *feria* festivities. In those days the *feria real* (main promenade) spread out under the wonderful trees of the broad avenue of the Alameda. (It has long since moved to fairgrounds outside the city.) The avenue was lined with *casetas* ('little houses'). Some of these pavilions were private, mounted by *peñas* (clubs and associations). Most – sponsored by civic groups, political parties and winemakers – were open to all. The *casetas,* besides selling food and drink, offered live music and dancing.

A short stroll from the bullring was the *caseta* of one of the makers of *cava*, which is what sparkling wine is called in Spain. There we would install ourselves after the bullfight, with bottles of bubbly and plates of grilled prawns, watching the show of fancy horses and riders parade by us, until finally it was dark and the twinkling *feria* lights came on. The party went on all night, with eating and drinking, clapping, dancing and singing.

In my village, the *feria* takes place early in September, in honour of the *Virgen de la Peña* (the Virgin of the Rock), so-called because the image of Mary was discovered in a stone grotto on the edge of town. Baby girls are often named in honour of the patron, so lots of girls in town are called Peña – Rock. If I had had a daughter, I might have named her Rock, too.

On the night honouring the Virgin, her image – in the form of a tiny doll – is carried through the village streets, accompanied by multitudes of townspeople, who light the way with candles. On the return to her shrine, there is a spectacular fireworks display.

When the village was poor, people saved all year to be able to splurge on special treats during *feria* – a night out with bottles of *fino* Sherry, grilled prawns and roast chickens, bars of sweet almond nougat, dancing till dawn, flamenco shows and rides for the kids. Now people have money, but they still do it all – for a whole week!

Feria food is street food. Year after year the same rotisserie chicken people set up their stall.

And every year a wizened *moro*, a supposed Moroccan with a fez, sets up his little grill producing spicy *pinchitos* (little kebabs). At another stall, potato crisps are made fresh, fried in deep vats of oil. At the end of a long night of partying, it's traditional to finish with a 'breakfast' of *churros y chocolate*, deep-fried doughnuts served with thick hot chocolate.

HOT CHOCOLATE

CHOCOLATE A LA TAZA

This is more like liquid chocolate pudding than like cocoa. It's thick enough to coat a spoon. The kind made at street stalls at the *feria* is very dark, made without milk. At home, where it's served for a leisurely Sunday breakfast, it's customary to use milk as well as water.

230 g (8 oz) dark chocolate

3 tablespoons cornflour

450 ml (¾ pint) milk

4 tablespoons sugar, or to taste

½ teaspoon vanilla extract

Break the chocolate into pieces and combine it in a pan with 450 ml (¾ pint) of water over medium-high heat. Heat, stirring, until the chocolate is melted and smooth.

Stir the cornflour with 240 ml (8 fl oz) water until it is smooth. Return the chocolate to the heat. Beat in the milk, sugar, and cornflour mixture. Cook over medium heat, stirring constantly until the mixture thickens. Cook for 2 minutes longer. Remove from the heat and stir in the vanilla. Add additional sugar, if desired.

Pour into mugs and serve. The chocolate can be kept hot in a double boiler over simmering water. It can be reheated in a microwave.

SERVES 4

DOUGHNUTS
BUÑUELOS

Churros are strips or rings of dough pressed from a big tube, like a giant piping bag nozzle, braced against the *churro*-maker's shoulder. They are fried in hot oil, drained briefly on rough brown paper, and sprinkled with sugar. They are just the thing for dipping in thick hot chocolate or coffee. *Churro* stalls appear during town fairs, but are also to be found every day around bustling markets. *Churros* with chocolate make a typical *feria* breakfast, in the *madrugada* (early hours), when the carousing is done. They are also a typical market breakfast with *café con leche* (espresso coffee with milk) or, at home, a late Sunday-morning family affair, where *papá* goes out to buy *churros* at a corner shop while *mamá* makes the coffee and chocolate.

Buñuelos are similar, but the dough is yeast-raised and shaped into a ring. I find the *churro* dough difficult to work with in the home kitchen, so here I am giving the *buñuelo* recipe.

In my village, Carmela and her husband Juan are *churro*-makers at the market in the mornings and *buñuelo*-makers on Sundays and holidays. Then they set up an outdoor stall near the parish church, against the wall of the village bullring, where they fry these doughnuts in a deep cauldron of bubbling oil.

With oily hands, Carmela takes a small ball of dough, pats it, and puts a thumb through the centre to make a hole, then drops it into the hot oil. Juan uses a long-handled skimmer to flip the doughnuts and retrieve them when they are golden-brown. Dredged in sugar, they are sold to the waiting crowd.

1 teaspoon active dried yeast

155 g (5½ oz) plus 1 teaspoon sugar

450 ml (¾ pint) warm water (46°C/115°F)

1 tablespoon olive oil

1 teaspoon salt

540–680 g (19–24 oz) plain flour

Olive oil or vegetable oil, for frying

Combine the yeast, 1 teaspoon of the sugar, and all of the water in a mixing bowl. Stir. Set aside until the yeast begins to bubble, 5 minutes.

Add the tablespoon of olive oil and the salt. Begin stirring in the flour, adding 540 g (19 oz).

Turn the dough out on to a floured board and knead the dough for at least 5 minutes, adding the additional flour as needed to make a soft dough that doesn't stick to the board. Gather the dough into a ball.

Oil a bowl, put the ball of dough into it, then turn the dough so it is coated on all sides with oil. Cover with a damp cloth and put it in a warm, draught-free place to rise until doubled in bulk, about 2 hours.

Knock back the dough. With lightly oiled hands, divide the dough into balls about the size of walnuts and place them on an oiled sheet.

Pour oil into a heavy pan, deep enough to accommodate 4 cm (1½ inches) of the oil. Heat olive oil to 182°C/360°F; heat vegetable oil to 190°C/375°.

With lightly oiled hands, flatten a ball of dough into a patty, put a thumb through the centre to make a hole and add it to the hot oil. Continue shaping and frying the doughnuts, frying three or four at a time. Turn the doughnuts in the oil.

Remove them when they are puffed and golden-brown on both sides. Drain briefly on kitchen towels.

Have ready a shallow tray with the remaining sugar. While the doughnuts are still hot, dredge them in the sugar. They are best eaten when freshly made, as they do not keep well.

MAKES ABOUT 26 DOUGHNUTS

SOURCES

The foods of Spain are becoming more widely available as British supermarkets and speciality shops respond to people's demand for more varied ingredients. So you will probably have no difficulty in finding Spanish olive oil and olives, cheeses, saffron, pimentón, rice, *turrón* (almond nougat), wines and more in one supermarket or another. Other products may prove more difficult to come by. A wide range of Spanish foods and cooking equipment is available through the following shops and online-ordering companies (see websites for details of local market stalls run by online sources).

Armorica
19 Rams Walk
Petersfield
Hants GU32 3JA
Tel.: 0845 601 7262
Fax: 01730 269699
E-mail: enquires@armorica.co.uk
www.armorica.co.uk
Online ordering and shop. For paella pans.

Brindisa
32 Exmouth Market
Clerkenwell
London EC1R 4QE
Tel./Fax: 020 7713 1666
E-mail: retail@brindisa.com
Stall: Borough Market (London SE1)
For foods such as morcilla and butifarra; abada *beans; dried peppers such as* ñoras. *Also paella pans.*

Cocina Ceramics
Tel./Fax: 01752 863663
E-mail: mail@cocinaceramics.co.uk
www.cocinaceramics.fsenet.co.uk
Online ordering. Mediterranean cookware including cazuelas.

Cool Chile Co
Tel.: 0870 902 1145
Fax: 0870 162 3923
E-mail: orders@coolchile.co.uk
www.coolchile.co.uk
Stalls: Borough and Portobello Markets
(London SE1 and W11).
Online ordering. For dried peppers including choricero.

delicioso.co.uk
Tel.: 01865 340055
E-mail: info@delicioso.co.uk
www.delicioso.co.uk
Online ordering. For foods such as morcilla sausage and serrano ham, as well as paella pans.

R. Garcia & Sons
246–250 Portobello Road
London W11 1LL
Tel.: 020 7221 6119
For foods such as morcilla sausage; serrano ham; fabada *beans; special pasta (*fideos*);* Padrón *and* piquillo *peppers.*

Iberian Foods
E-mail: enquiries@iberianfoods.co.uk
www.iberianfoods.co.uk
Online company based in Spain. For most Spanish foods.

Peppers by Post
Tel.: 01308 897892
Fax.: 01308 897735
E-mail: info@peppersbypost.biz
www.peppersbypost.biz
Online ordering. For fresh peppers and tomatillos.

The Spice Shop
1 Blenheim Crescent
London W11 2EE
Tel.: 0207 221 4448
E-mail: enquires@thespiceshop.co.uk
www.thespiceshop.co.uk
Online ordering and shop. For dried peppers including ñoras.

BIBLIOGRAPHY

Davidson, Alan, and Charlotte Knox. *Seafood, A Connoisseur's Guide and Cookbook*. London: Mitchell Beazley International, 1988.

Frazier, Ronald. *The Pueblo, A Mountain Village on the Costa del Sol*. London: Allen Lane, 1973.

González Gordon, Manuel. *Sherry, The Noble Wine*. London: Quiller Press, 1990.

Grice-Hutchinson, Marjorie. *Málaga Farm*. London: Hollis & Carter, 1956.

Lujan, Nestor, and Juan Perucho. *Cocina Española – Gastronomía e Historia*. Barcelona: Ediciones Danae, 1970.

Spain Gourmetour (a food, wine and travel quarterly magazine published by ICEX, Madrid)

Varela, Gregorio. *Frying Food in Olive Oil*. International Olive Oil Council, 1994.

INDEX